Sonia Cameron Jacks
2nd November
2002.

KV-119-649

A Summer in Lochaber

John Graham of Claverhouse, Viscount Dundee, by David Paton
The Scottish National Portrait Gallery

A Summer in Lochaber

The Jacobite Rising of 1689

Catriona Fforde

Sonia Cameron Jacks

with best wishes

Catriona Fforde

For Colin

First published 2002
by House of Lochar

© Catriona Fforde 2002

The right of Catriona Fforde to be identified
as the author of this work has been asserted by her in accordance
with the Copyright, Designs and Patents Act of 1988.
All rights reserved.

A CIP catalogue record for this book
is available from the British Library.

ISBN 1 899863 84 2

Typeset in Monotye Plantin by XL Publishing Services, Tiverton
Printed in Great Britain
by Bell & Bain Ltd, Glasgow
for House of Lochar
Isle of Colonsay, Argyll PA61 7YR

Contents

Preface

It must have been in about 1986 that I first became acquainted with James Philip of Almerieclose's *Grameid* and there has hardly been a day since then when I have not thought about it. It is an epic poem in Latin describing the campaign in 1689 of Viscount Dundee in support of James VII and II. Philip was himself an eye-witness of the events he describes and his poem gives the only contemporary account of what went on in Lochaber between May and July 1689. It also gives the only account of any kind of Dundee's journey to Lochaber from Glen Ogilvie in Angus to meet his Highland army for the first time. Yet, with a few happy exceptions, scant attention has been paid to it nor does there seem to be more than a limited interest in any aspect of Dundee's campaign.

Speak to anyone about the first Jacobite Rising and they will almost always assume that you are talking about the '15; the alarms and excursions of 1689 are forgotten. It is strange that the very beginnings of Jacobitism should be so ignored and Dundee himself overlooked or confused with Montrose. Things indeed have come to such a pass that I have several times read, in works of some erudition, that Dundee's name was James and that his army was defeated at Killiecrankie, while in other works he has been excluded from descriptions of the Jacobite period and pushed back into an earlier chapter to become, as it were, a postscript to Montrose, although the Royalist, pro-Charles I exploits of Montrose had a very different basis from the Jacobite, pro-James VII struggles of Dundee and were separated from them by more than 40 years. It is as though Dundee has to be kept strictly in the 17th century along with the Civil Wars, whereas he really belongs to the 18th century with Prince Charles Edward.

For whatever reason, interest in him seems to be slight, even amongst Jacobites; yet he was the first Jacobite hero – a very charismatic one – and as such should occupy an elevated position in Jacobite hagiology. Does the distorted view of his actions against Covenanters during the Killing Time work against him? If so it is time that this view, the product of Williamite propaganda and religious bigotry, was abandoned. Napier in the early nineteenth century was the first to retrieve Dundee's reputation from the slough into which it had sunk. After Napier's revelation of Dundee's true character there still remained, and remains, an unwillingness to accept this new assessment of him. His reputation suffered in much the same way as did the reputations of Macbeth and of Richard III of England, all three being destroyed, at a change of dynasty, by the propaganda machines of the incoming wielder of power.

Recognition has of course also been withheld from the Gaels who engaged in the first Rising – Lochiel, Glengarry, Sir Donald of Sleat, Sir John MacLean of Duart and the other leaders and their clansmen who gathered in Lochaber and marched to Killiecrankie. We sometimes hear their names but hear nothing of their ages, appearance, dispositions, backgrounds, difficulties, the territories they controlled or why they supported James. This omission is all the more extraordinary if we remember that Dundee's army at Killiecrankie was an entirely Gaelic force, except for his forty horse and some of those who arrived with the Irish contingent. I hope that the account I give of them in the following pages may help to make these Gaelic captains and their men live a little for the reader and in this I am perhaps spurred on by a similar desire to that expressed by a seventeenth-century MacMhuirich – hereditary *seanachaidh* to Clanranald – who wrote in the Book of Clanranald:

> I had many stories to write on the events of the time if I undertook to do it, but what induced me to write even this much was, when I saw that those who treated of the affairs of the time have made no mention at all of the Gael, the men who did all the service.

CFf.
Glenmoriston, 2001

Note on Personal Names and Placenames

Gaelic words within the text are shown in italics, with the following exceptions:

Gaelic personal names appear in italics but only when given in full, e.g. Alasdair Dubh but *Alasdair Dubh Mac Ailean Mhic Iain*.

Gaelic placenames are not shown in italics. Apart from three exceptions they are taken from current Ordnance Survey maps. Many of them have been anglicised to a greater or lesser degree, while many are still in a pure Gaelic form. The latter group should, strictly speaking, be shown in italics, but it might be confusing to single them out for special typographical treatment, nor is it always easy to draw a line between the two groups.

Acknowledgements

Of the many helpful people who have had anything to do with the writing of this book there are some I would particularly like to mention:

Professor Duncan Poore and Mrs Judy Poore, Glenmoriston, who listened to my accounts of discoveries made and took me on several long expeditions to gather 'local colour'. Judy also read the final draft and made helpful suggestions;

Fred and Sybil Macaulay, Inverness, were a constant support. I discussed several difficult passages of Gaelic verse with Fred and they both read the final draft and made me feel optimistic about it;

Jane Anderson, the archivist for Blair and Glamis Castles, gave me additional details about these two great buildings, while E. Jarron of Hatton of Ogilvie Farm took me across his land and pointed out the site of Bonnie Dundee's castle;

Hugh Barron, formerly Secretary of the Gaelic Society of Inverness, allowed me to speak to the society about the 1689 Rising when my thoughts on the subject were only half formed;

Professor Donald Meek read part of the final draft and cheered me up – and on – in my search for a publisher;

The staff of Leominster Library, Herefordshire, produced an impressive number of obscure books for me when I first started my research fifteen years ago;

My editor, Georgina Hobhouse, kept me on the straight path through all the details that are so liable to be overlooked by the eager author;

Finally I must not forget Rosie, Martie and *Sine* (Sheena), three gallant black Labradors, who happily charged through rain, snow and swollen burns on our fact-finding walks and snoozed on the back seat during boring car drives in the Highlands and in Angus.

To all these and to my family and friends I am most grateful.

Abbreviations

Balhaldy
> John Drummond of Balhaldy: *Memoirs of Sir Ewen Cameron of Locheill, Chief of the Clan Cameron, with an introductory account of the history and antiquities of that family and of the neighbouring clans*, Edinburgh (Abbotsford Club), 1842

Grameid
> James Philip of Almerieclose: *The Grameid, an heroic poem descriptive of the Campaign of Viscount Dundee in 1689*. Edited from the Original Manuscript with Translation, Introduction, and Notes by the Rev. Alexander D. Murdoch, F.S.A. Scot., Edinburgh (Scottish History Society), 1888

Letters
> *Letters of John Graham of Claverhouse*, ed. Andrew Murray Scott in: *Miscellany of the Scottish History Society*, vol.11, Edinburgh, 1990

Orain Iain Luim
> *Orain Iain Luim. Songs of John MacDonald, Bard of Keppoch*, ed. Annie M. Mackenzie, Edinburgh (Scottish Gaelic Texts Society), 1973

Prologue

A MILE OR SO north of Spean Bridge in the Great Glen – that dramatic geological fault that, with a little help from the Caledonian Canal, splits the Highlands in two – the road ahead to the south seems to be blocked by the great mass of Ben Nevis and its satellite Aonach Mor. The hills and burns and lochs hidden behind this barrier are never seen either from the Great Glen road or from Glen Spean or from the shores of Loch Leven, where they are obscured by the Mamore peaks. Only those who take the track from Corriechoillie in Glen Spean and follow it on to the north shore of Loch Eigheach, to the west of Loch Rannoch, can enter the strange and beautiful world behind these great mountains.

The railway line coming up from Bridge of Orchy and Rannoch Station to Tulloch and Spean Bridge only approaches the foot track briefly at Corrour near Loch Ossian and only glimpses fitfully some of its beauties; the few trains that use it, rattling quietly along through the heather, are scarcely noticed in this vast, silent place. The foot track follows an old drove road by which cattle were brought from the west Highlands to Rannoch and the cattle trysts at Crieff and Falkirk. It was also used for moving "lifted" cattle, going usually in the opposite direction. At its southern end when it first leaves what is now the B846 from Tummel Bridge to Rannoch Station it is a fairly broad, flat track with wide views all round it and cattle grazing amongst the grass and heather. Huge rocks and boulders lie everywhere, covered with dark green and brown lichens. The immense, treeless spaces, with the mountains pushed away to their edges, are inviting on a clear, bright day when the birds call and swoop and the sky and grasses are reflected in the water of the lochans. But when there is snow or mist or heavy rain these spaces become limitless and menacing – the very edge of the world. This is the great Moor of Rannoch, stretching from Loch Rannoch in the east to Glencoe and beyond in the west; it was once the haunt of outlaws and of men from broken clans.

The track goes on up to the south end of Loch Ossian; the land is very low-lying and boggy here with strings of lochs and lochans, but it improves once it has left Loch Ossian behind and is heading for the south of Loch Treig. An alternative track goes via Corrour Station, reaching Loch Treig at the same point as the first.

On the map Loch Treig looks somewhat unappealing, trapped as it is between two lines of apparently undistinguished hills which squeeze it into a long narrow strip of, one feels, gloomy water, but in reality it is a wide shining flood moving away between high rounded peaks, leaving at its base a broad bay where swans float and where the loch is fed by four rivers – the Allt a' Chambhreac, the Allt Feidh Chiarain, the Abhainn Rath and the Allt na Lairige. A little island lies nearby. The water horse that inhabited the loch used to be heard here, making the hills on either side echo with its roaring.

The railway track bears right up the east side of Loch Treig, heading for Tulloch, a little to the west of Loch Laggan, but the foot track curls left round the end of the loch and takes off in a north-westerly direction, passing over the Allt a' Chambhreac and the Allt Feidh Chiarain and finally over the Abhainn Rath to Creaguaineach Lodge, now deserted. When the river is full there are lacy patterns of astonishing beauty made by the foaming water under the bridge here.

After Craiguaineach the track leaves the lochside and runs up beside the Allt na Lairige (the burn of the pass), going first through a high narrow defile of rock where flowers hang down from crevices between the stones. It goes on beside the river, through the Lairig Leacach (the pass of the flagstones), past waterfalls, huge slabs of smooth rock in the river and wide ledges of green above its eastern bank where the deer sit, gazing towards the high mountains. A mysterious and beautiful place with an open aspect, yet hemmed in by hills that obscure the great bens beyond, just as those bens hide these lesser hills and their secret landscapes from the traveller in the Great Glen. The track is faint here but not needed as a guide for one follows the river. Small burns cross the path at intervals, some quite difficult to ford in rainy weather, and to either side of the way are wide, shiny patches of quaking bog, easy to avoid when visible but lurking unseen just below the surface when there is snow on the ground. For a time the way is flat but eventually begins to rise, finally reaching the pass between Stob Choire Claurigh and Sgùrr Innse, a climb of nearly a thousand feet from Loch Treig side; here begins the slow but steady descent beside the Allt Leacach to Corriechoillie on the south bank of the river Spean.

This was the route followed in May 1689 by Viscount Dundee (Bonnie Dundee as Walter Scott called him) when on his way to Lochaber to meet the Highland chiefs who were to provide the bulk of his army in support of James VII and II against his son-in-law William of Orange. But Dundee did not find the journey as attractive as I have described it for it was an exceptionally late spring in the western Highlands that year and although the fresh grass and the early flowers were beginning to appear in Atholl it was a very different picture on Rannoch Moor and in the glens to the north-west. They were still in the grip of snow and ice, but in the boggy areas the ice was not thick enough to support the unwary traveller; it only sufficed to hide the danger beneath it.

Quite apart from the particular difficulties of the west Highlands at that time however, we find that the Jacobite era began at the end of a 200-year phase of exceptionally cold weather. In the winter of 1684 to 1685 the Thames froze so solid that stalls could be set out on it and bonfires lit. The King fell ill and in February 1685 he died, his death increasing those feelings of apprehension and doom which assail many of us during long periods of exceptional cold. In 1688 the harvest in Scotland was good but it was followed by a very long and severe winter, threatening the 1689 crop and disrupting the exchange of cattle for grain on which the Highlands relied. This was to create difficulties in feeding Dundee's army throughout his campaign and on the way into Lochaber the particular lateness of the 1689 spring in the west brought unexpected hazards to him and his companions, all or most of whom had never struggled with winter conditions in any place resembling Rannoch Moor.

John Grahame of Claverhouse, Viscount Dundee, portrait by Kneller
By kind permission of the Earl of Strathmore and Kinghorne

CHAPTER ONE

Glen Ogilvie and Dudhope

And it may be observed, that an ungoverned zeale for religion is
more fruitfull of mischief than all the other passions putt together.
John Drummond of Balhaldy

ALL HIS LIFE from the age of four, when his father died, until little
more than eight months before his death Dundee had been plain John
Graham of Claverhouse, qualified, when he came into the King's service,
by Captain and later Colonel. On the 12th November 1688 he was created
Viscount of Dundee and Lord Graham of Claverhouse and as the period
which we shall be considering in detail in the following pages covers the
months after this date we shall call him Dundee.

When his campaign in support of James began he was forty-one, married
and with an infant son, Privy Councillor, Constable of Dundee and owner
of Dudhope Castle below Dundee Law. His family, although related to
that of the Grahams of Montrose (Earls, Marquises and later Dukes), was
only a gentry family and he had to win his way to a place of influence
through his own efforts.

He was of medium height, with steadfast grey eyes and thick dark hair
which he wore, according to the fashion of the day, in long curls and
ringlets streaming over his shoulders. These characteristics are perhaps
best seen in an early head and shoulders portrait by an unknown artist –
the Melville Portrait showing the sitter wearing dark armour – and in the
beautiful pencil drawing, again by an unknown artist, after David Paton
(fl.1660–95); it is a three-quarter length miniature showing the sitter with
long, flowing hair, armour and a lace cravat, the head turned sideways
towards the observer. The famous portrait by Kneller which hangs in
Glamis Castle is a court portrait and influenced by the fashions and
conventions of the day. The sitter looks as though he is wearing a wig,
which he was not known to favour, even when his hair was beginning to
turn a little grey. According to a servant working at Duffus Castle in 1689
he kept his long hair in order, in moments of undress at any rate, by winding
it round thin strips of lead, twisted together at the ends – a seventeenth
century hair curler perhaps.[1] He appears proud and aloof, which does
certainly describe one aspect of his character, but also a little bored, even
petulant and this facial expression was not at all in line with his nature.

The Earl of Moray once called him 'of a high, proud and peremptory humour'[2] and indeed he was not hail-fellow-well-met with everyone nor was he one to carouse and sink under the table with the dead men. Patrick Walker, writing in praise of some of the Covenanters against whom Dundee was engaged as Captain and Colonel of Horse in the south-west of Scotland, says that he 'hated to spend his time with wine and women', although he hastily adds, in case this should be interpreted as a compliment, '...which made him the more active in violent unheard-of persecution'.[3] This aloofness from the more rollicking aspects of human amusement is reflected in Scott's description of him (see p.10), but is better explained and elaborated by Drummond of Balhaldy:

> ...but the vivacity of his parts, and the delicacy and justness of his understanding and judgment, joyned with a certain vigour of mind and activity of body, distinguished him in such a manner from all others of his rank, that though he lived in a superior character, yet he acquired the love and esteem of all his equalls, as well as of those who had the advantage of him in dignity and estate.[4]

Altogether he is presented to us as a complex character but perhaps the complexity lies more in his presenters than in himself. We can certainly say that he was brave, direct, reliable, loyal, determined to do his duty however difficult, with a sense of humour and an ironic turn of phrase, an inspirational leader and a charming companion. And undeniably bonnie.

He was born in 1648, the elder son of William Graham, Laird of Claverhouse and of Lady Magdalene Carnegie, daughter of the Earl of Ethie, later to become the 1st Earl of Northesk. His father owned land around Claverhouse, two or three miles north of Dundee, although by Dundee's time the house there had fallen into disrepair and there is nothing to be seen of it today. That there was a house of some sort there is suggested by the Will of Dundee's great-great-grandmother, drawn up in 1594, which is dated from the 'Barnes of Claverhouse'. William also owned land further east together with Claypotts Castle near Broughty Ferry which is now in excellent repair but in Dundee's time was in a neglected state and in any case not really suitable as a family home, being more of a fortress than a house. The third property of the Laird of Claverhouse, bought in 1640, was in Glen Ogilvie in the Sidlaw Hills between six and eight miles north of Dundee in the parish of Glamis. The glen is a short one of about four miles in length with hills, little more than a thousand feet in height at most, to either side. The Water of Ogilvie runs through it from south to north. Rich green pasture stretches right up to the top of the hills and over. In the spring curlews give their bubbling call and lapwings rise, throbbing, into the sky and plunge to earth again. Little farms, each with a few trees round it, are tucked into the hollows. To the north-east beyond

Kirriemuir lie Glen Clova and Glen Esk and the Highland hills with some patches of snow always on their sides. Nearer and to the north is Glamis Castle, the seat of the Earls of Strathmore.

An old track passing to the east of the farm of Dryburn high up the glen completes a direct link between the Grahams' castle at Hatton of Ogilvie and Claverhouse and was no doubt much used by the Grahams when moving between their two properties. The track probably coincided with the modern main road (A928) as far as Milton of Ogilvie where the modern road diverges from it to rejoin it at Hillside of Preston (see Ordnance Survey Landranger Map 54).

The castle at Hatton of Ogilvie is sometimes referred to as Claverhouse Castle, but Dundee never called it that. In his marriage contract it is described as the tower, fortalice and manor-place of Glen, with its houses, biggings, yards and orchards, which were all to be made over to Lady Jean Cochrane as her dwelling place should she outlive her husband.[5] A neighbour of Dundee, Ochterlony of Guynd, describes Glen as:

...belonging to the Laird of Claverhouse, Grahame, an ancient gentleman of good extraction and great estate in the shyre – a pleasant place, a good house, and well planted; excellent quarrie of freestone and sklait; well furnished in peat and turfe; and in the hill thereof abundance of muir-foull. The sklait is carried to Dundee on horseback, and from thence by sea to all places within the river of Forth.[6]

Not a stone of this very substantial tower house now remains but its position in a field near the farm of Hatton of Ogilvie is still known and the road which approached it, though now only a farm track, is sufficiently well established to be shown, with its duck pond, on the Ordnance Map. No doubt many of the farmhouses and steadings around incorporate stones from the building that once housed Bonnie Dundee. It was here that he spent most of his childhood.

The years prior to his birth had been a time of great uproar. There was civil war in England and in Scotland continuing argument and dissension which had originated in King Charles I's attempt to force the Scottish prayerbook of 1637 upon the Scots. The Earl (later Marquis) of Montrose, after first siding with the Covenanters (those who signed the National Covenant protesting against the King's interference in the Scots' religious affairs), came to hate their increasing bigotry and gave his allegiance to the King. In 1644 to 1645 he carried out a brilliant campaign in the Highlands with the help of the Highland clans and a Scots-Irish army under Alasdair MacColla, a kinsman of the Earl of Antrim. Having won all his battles he was at length defeated at Philiphaugh and later disbanded on instructions from the King, seeking refuge in Holland. In England the situation worsened for the King and in 1649 he was executed and the reign of Cromwell began. Dundee was about one year old at this time. Scotland was then to see the return of Montrose in 1650, his further attempt to restore the Stuarts, his capture and his execution. This was followed by the arrival of Charles II in Scotland, his coronation at Scone in 1651 and the disastrous invasion of England, ending in complete defeat for the King at Worcester. Destruction and misery followed in Scotland, Cromwell being determined to subdue that country. In 1651 the town of Dundee was besieged and many of the townspeople slaughtered. General Monck, the Cromwellian officer commanding the besieging army and the man who, nine years later, triggered the movement towards the Restoration of Charles II, granted an order of protection to Lady Carnegie of the Glen (Dundee's mother), who was staying quietly in Glen Ogilvie hoping to escape the raids and plundering of Monck's army. Where Dundee's father was at this time is not clear. He had not played an active part in Montrose's campaign although he sympathised with him. He may have been in poor health as he died in the following year when Dundee was only four years old.

Dundee will have learnt of these events by hearsay rather than experience and will have cherished more particularly the better elaborated tales of Montrose's victories at Inverlochy or Auldearn and of how he was betrayed and taken captive in Assynt and brought in slow stages, his feet tied together under the belly of a sheltie pony, to Edinburgh, feverish from an uncared-for wound. The journey planned by the Covenanters to humiliate him became more like a triumphal procession and is described in James Fraser's Chronicle of the Frasers as:

> ... the fatall preludium and parrad of one of the noblest and gallantest generals this age saw in Brittain, whose unexampled atchievements might frame a history; were its volume farr biggar than mine, it would yet be disproportionat to the due praise of this matchless heroe.[7]

These tales, which the young Dundee will have heard from his own family and perhaps from Highland servants within his household – for Glen Ogilvie is so near the Highland line – must have been greatly enhanced by the reflection that the 'matchless heroe' was a member of his own family, if not a very near one. Perhaps he also heard of the night Montrose spent at Skibo Castle where Lady Gray, furious because the officer commanding his captors, Major General Holbourn, had taken the seat next to her instead of leaving it to Montrose, seized the leg of mutton lying before her on its dish and hit the miscreant on the head with it, thus seriously injuring both his uniform and his pride. When he had retreated from the place of honour and Montrose was established in it the lady retrieved the mutton from the floor and calmly proceeded to carve it.[8] The humour and the sadness of this tale will not have been lost on Dundee.

But he will have been much closer to one event which took place when he was thirteen. In 1661 his cousins Graham of Fintry and Graham of Duntrune played a part in a ceremony ordered by Charles II; the remains of Montrose, then still adorning the gates of the principal towns in Scotland (for he had been hanged and quartered), were gathered together and given a state burial in St Giles Cathedral. The young boy must have worried his older cousins until he had squeezed the last detail out of them. Fate was to give him a career that resembled that of his celebrated kinsman in many ways.

After leaving St Andrew's University where, like Montrose, he had interested himself not only in military studies and in mathematics but also in the classics and general literature, Dundee spent some years abroad, at first possibly in France and afterwards in the Low Countries to which many Scots went at that time to study military strategy and tactics as this area was the victim of French expansionist policy. Here, ironically, he was fighting in support of William of Orange and on one occasion actually saved his life. After returning to Scotland be became, at the age of twenty-nine, a Captain of Horse and helped to police those parts of south-western Scotland which were disturbed by 'fundamentalists' opposed to the religious policy of Charles II.

Charles was determined not to restore the Assembly of the Kirk, which had been dissolved by Cromwell, because he believed it was impossible to impose peace in a country torn apart by the sort of dissensions fomented by that body. Charles was also determined, however, that the Scots should have the form of worship they wanted. There were therefore no prayer-books, no surplices, no confirmation and no altars. There were, however, bishops; it was thought the clergy needed to have someone to control and direct them. Patronage also survived. The clergy of the south-west refused to worship under these arrangements and took their congregations with them out into the open to worship there. These meetings were known as conventicles but were seldom the pious gatherings of the faithful which earlier historians have described. Rather they were opportunities for preachers to rage against their loss of power and to indulge in invective and sedition. Their services were regarded by the authorities as taking on more the aspect of recruiting drives with the aim of destroying the hated Charles Stuart and his minions. Fanatics amongst the Covenanting clergy seem to have been strangers to Christian ideas of love and forgiveness, as Montrose himself had already discovered, and intent only on leading a Holy War that aimed at forcing everyone to worship exactly as they prescribed. They had already tried, as part of a bargain, to force Presbyterianism on England.

As a person trying to control these elements and to prevent actual civil war Dundee was bound to be thought of as a persecutor. He was, after all, trying to prevent them from indulging in their favourite occupation, that is, persecuting others. It is not the object of these pages to present a full biography of Dundee, indeed we shall be dealing in detail only with the last year, particularly the last three months of his life, but it is necessary to say something to counter the accusations generally levelled at him and most succinctly expressed in the soubriquet he acquired at this time – Bluidy Clavers. Aid to the civil power is not a duty generally sought after by military men and Dundee, though he thought his work necessary, would yet often have found it distasteful.

The legends that attached themselves to him show him as the servant of the devil, who could appear in several different places at the same time, who rode always on a black horse (although he actually favoured a roan) and who could only be killed with a silver bullet. Sir Walter Scott was fascinated by him; he had a portrait of him hanging above his desk at Abbotsford. But he still believed those old stories and presented him as a demonic figure whilst at the same time setting him apart from other demons, giving him a romantic gloss and none of the horrid attributes of evil. In Redgauntlet he is introduced into Wandering Willie's Tale where he is one of a gathering of dead souls carousing in a room in Redgauntlet Castle:

> There was the fierce Middleton, and the dissolute Rothes, and the crafty Lauderdale; and Dalyell, with his bald head and a beard to his girdle; …And there was Claverhouse, as beautiful as when he lived, with his long, dark, curled locks, streaming down over his laced buff-coat, and his left hand always on his right spule-blade, to hide the wound that the silver bullet had made. He sat apart from them all, and looked at them with a melancholy, haughty countenance; while the rest hallooed, and sung, and laughed that the room rang.[9]

It is difficult to kill stories that have taken root and remained in the popular imagination for centuries. Of those associated with Dundee's name during his time as Captain and Colonel of Horse in the south-west almost all can either be attributed to someone else in some other place or happened when he was not in the area at all. For much of the time he had no justiciary powers. He often recommended mercy for prisoners he handed over; but he could demand none. In some cases people who are now still thought of as martyrs were never actually killed at all. When Dundee did arrest people it was because they were guilty of sedition, that is, they had refused to take an oath promising not to rebel against the law and/or were found in possession of arms. During the whole of his time in the south-west (eight years) – a time of great national emergency – he was directly responsible for precisely one death – that of John Brown the so-called Christian Carrier. He was arrested by Dundee's troop near his home and given a chance to repudiate the declaration which Renwick (a young fanatic) had affixed to market crosses throughout the south-west. This declaration maintained the right of all those acting 'in defence of our covenanted reformation' to kill the King's officers and their servants and denied 'the authority of Charles Stuart, and all authority depending on him'. This declaration Brown refused to repudiate. He was shot on the spot and afterwards found to have been in possession of arms.

On many other occasions when sending prisoners off for trial Dundee sent messages with them detailing extenuating circumstances and suggesting leniency; or he would point out some physical difficulty or disability which deserved some consideration. Andrew Hislop, for instance, had been arrested by Dundee and when he was subsequently brought into court was sentenced to be executed by firing squad, the squad to be provided by Dundee. Dundee had no justiciary powers at this time but he did his best for Hislop by protesting against the sentence, as he thought the prisoner might be reclaimed if reprieved. As this clemency was refused by the justices he had no alternative but to carry out their sentence. 'The man's blood is on your head Westerhall. I am free of it' he said to the presiding judge. One can hear the bitterness in his voice as he turned to the task of shooting a man whom he had wished to save.

Dundee's way of settling the south-west was to take a tolerant view and be willing to compromise and persuade people to be law-abiding. He believed in treating the small man gently and punishing the ringleaders. In this he must have been much in advance of his contemporaries for how often do we not find that the commander of a dissident army is let go and subsequently regains his titles and power while his poor soldiers are killed, imprisoned or transported. He did his best to secure justice for those he was obliged, as a soldier, to arrest and to turn the wrath of the establishment from little people. His approach had great success in course of time but unfortunately he was taken away from the work before this success could be consolidated and those who followed him adopted different methods.

It was during his work in the south-west that he met his future wife. Before this time he had been negotiating to marry Helen Graham who was likely to become heir to the title and lands of her cousin the Earl of Menteith. The negotiations began with all the aspects of a dynastic marriage, although at the end, when things were going badly, Dundee declared himself willing to take Helen 'in her smock'. In 1684 this failed attempt was more than two years behind him. His marriage in that year to Jean Cochrane was certainly not a dynastic one, in fact it was likely to be very damaging to his career. Jean's grandfather, the Earl of Dundonald, had served the Stuarts faithfully and got his earldom in return. But the next generation had very different ideas. William Cochrane, Jean's father, had married a daughter of the Earl of Cassilis who was a firm Covenanter. William died in 1679 but before as well as after his death his house was run on strictly covenanting lines and his brother, John Cochrane of Ochiltree, had gone so far as to be implicated in the Rye House Plot to kill King Charles and his brother James. The murder was planned to take place near Newmarket but failed because the royal party left the race meeting earlier than expected.

Dundee found it necessary to excuse his choice of a wife, writing to James, Duke of York, and to the Marquis of Queensberry and other political leaders to assure them that it would make no difference to his loyalty. In one letter to Queensbury dated the 19th May 1684 he writes with reference to his political enemies: '...but or long I will in dispyt of them lait the world see that it is not in the pouer of love, nor any other folly, to alter my loyalty'.[10] The King and the Duke of York supported his marriage plans as did Jean's grandfather, the Earl of Dundonald, but her mother did not and was not present at the wedding. What with the family difficulties that had to be overcome and the possible serious setback to his career that Dundee himself had to risk we cannot doubt that they married for love.

Between 1678 and 1686 Dundee spent less of his time soldiering and more of it as a courtier and politician. He came to know and like Charles II and his brother James. There were often Scottish affairs to discuss with the King and they would stride along together at Newmarket or in London. Charles with his long legs and active habits could tire out most members of his court, thus managing to avoid their importunities, but he could not tire Dundee. The King's wit and Dundee's sense of humour and irony must have mixed well together.

James became even better known to him than Charles when the former was in Edinburgh where he was sent for a time by his brother to take the heat out of the succession dispute. James had just declared himself a Catholic and there was a movement to cut him out of the succession, which Charles would not countenance at any price.

In 1683 Dundee was made a Privy Councillor and on the 23rd April 1684, with the help of the King, acquired Dudhope Castle near the town of Dundee. He explained to Queensberry in a letter dated the 20th March 1683 that he would like to have Dudhope because 'I have no house and it lays within half a myl of my land...', adding that it would also suit him because 'I cannot have the patiance to build and plant'.[11] He evidently regarded his home in Glen Ogilvie merely as a future dower house.

Dudhope had belonged to the Scrymgeours who feature in the family tree of the Grahams of Claverhouse. When the last Scrymgeour in the direct line died it became the property of the Crown and was given to Lord Hatton who was Master of the Mint in Scotland. As a result of skullduggery while in this post he lost the castle and Dundee was able to acquire it although against some opposition. With it he acquired the Constableship of Dundee and his first act as Constable was to visit the Tolbooth, where, finding several prisoners who had been sentenced to death for petty thieving, he asked the Privy Council that they might be given some lesser punishment; his request was granted.[12] Not the sort of thing one would expect of Bluidy Clavers but typical of the character of Bonnie Dundee as revealed in any impartial account of his career.

Dudhope is a seventeenth-century courtyard castle which once had a sixteenth-century tower house attached to it, but this has been demolished. It lies just below and slightly to the east of Dundee Law. Its main entrance is to the east, incorporating twin towers and there are round towers with conical roofs at each corner. The walls are harled and painted white but each window is framed in sandstone blocks, the glazing bars cutting up the glass into small rectangles. It is not certain whether the harling was in place in Dundee's time or whether the whole building showed the soft pink stone still visible as a frame to the windows. The building is very simple and beautiful and has a distinctly French appearance. Perhaps 20 yards from its south wall the ground sweeps down in the direction of the town. In Dundee's time few buildings of any kind would have interrupted the green vista to the Firth of Tay. Behind the castle the ground rises to give beyond a gently sloping area of grass with trees and shrubs and there are further areas of trees and flowers to the west. Although the amount of space round the castle has been greatly reduced by the expansion of the town of Dundee during the past 300 years it is still possible to feel what it was like at the end of the seventeenth century, standing on its airy ledge with trees and fields and orchards round it and a view of the blue Tay and of the county of Fife beyond it. Ochterlony of Guynd, who also left us the description of Glen (see above), tells us that Dudhope was:

...ane extraordinare pleasant and sweet place, a good house, excellent yards, much planting, and fyne parks. It lyes pleasantly on the syde of the hill of Dundie, overlooks the town, and as of purpose built there to command the place. Dundie Law is at the back thereof, ane exceeding high mott hill.[13]

Notes
1. Constance Gordon Cuming: *Memories*, Edinburgh (Blackwood), 1904.
2. Letter from the Earl of Moray to Queensberry, the 4th April 1685, in: *Historical Manuscripts Commission, Buccleuch and Queensberry MSS*, vol.ii, p.47.
3. Patrick Walker: *Six Saints of the Covenant*, ed. D. Hay Fleming, 2 vols., London, 1901, vol.2, p.64.
4. Balhaldy, p.274.
5. Mark Napier: *Memorials and Letters illustrative of the Life and Times of John Graham of Claverhouse, Viscount Dundee*, 3 vols., Edinburgh (Thomas G. Stevenson), 1859, vol.II, p.393.
6. ibid.: vol.III, p.727n.
7. James Fraser: *Chronicles of the Frasers. The Wardlaw Manuscript entitled 'Polichronicon seu policrata temporum, or, the true genealogy of the Frasers, 916–1674*,

   ed. William Mackay, Edinburgh (Scottish History Society), 1905, p.353.
8. Dunrobin MS, quoted in Ronald Williams: *Montrose: Cavalier in Mourning*, Glasgow, 1975, pp.359–60.
9. Sir Walter Scott: *Redgauntlet*, London and Glasgow (Collins Clear-Type Press), undated, p.156.
10. *Letters*, p.219.
11. ibid., p.189.
12. Privy Council Register, Edinburgh, 10.9.1684.
13. Napier: *Memorials...* op cit., vol.III, p.727n.

Dudhope Castle
Photograph by Duncan Poore

CHAPTER TWO

The Convention

When willt thou go and leave me here,
O do not so my dearest dear,
The sun's depairting clouds the sky
But thy depairting mak's me die.

Thou cannst not go, my dearest hairt
But I must quit my chiefest pairt,
For with twa hairts thou must be gone
And I sall stay at home with none.
                    Seventeenth-century song

IN 1685 CHARLES died and James succeeded him. James was a very honest straightforward man. If he believed something was the right thing to do he did it and if he had made a promise he kept it, however inconvenient to himself. For instance, he seduced Anne Hyde, daughter of Chancellor Hyde, Earl of Clarendon, under promise of marriage and when she became pregnant he stuck to his promise, although everyone from his brother down tried to persuade him from it and although his passion for her had subsided considerably. But these qualities are not always, alas, the best ones to ensure good government. James was not a diplomat, nor did he have the charm of his brother Charles. When he came to the throne he wished to make changes to the laws which disadvantaged Catholics but he was incapable of going about this either slowly or in anything other than a direct manner. He wished to give toleration to everyone, Catholics and Protestants, including even Quakers. A very good friend of his with whom he regularly corresponded was William Penn. It tells us a lot about his lack of diplomacy and the power of Orange propaganda that he is still regarded by many as a tyrant and a Catholic bigot. Raymond Campbell Paterson has assessed him in the following words:

The new King was in every sense a 'man of principle', very much in the same mould as his father, King Charles I. He had a clear sense of duty, and a desire to do what his conscience dictated, regardless of the political cost. As a man, he had many admirable qualities; but intelligence and good sense were not among them. As the principle target of Shaftesbury and the Whigs during the Popish Plot, he had felt the distant lash of persecution, under which his Catholic subjects had suffered for many years. There is absolutely no evidence that he planned to re-establish Catholicism as the state religion, but he was determined to lift the legal restrictions which prevented the Catholic minority from enjoying full liberty of conscience, even if this meant clashing with established interests.[1]

By 1688 England was becoming very restive; many people who had hoped for important jobs at court or in the wider country had found them going to Catholics, and many were irritated by the priests flocking round the King's private chapel. But they were prepared to put up with things as they were for James's lifetime as they could look forward to a Protestant monarch in the shape of Mary or Anne, the daughters of James's first marriage to Anne Hyde. When however James's second wife, Mary of Modena, produced a son who would, of course, be brought up a Catholic, many felt it was more than they could stomach and an invitation was sent to William of Orange to come to England and set matters right which he promptly did by becoming King himself.

A Scottish army with Dundee in charge of its cavalry was sent into England to help James, for the Scots were naturally angry that England should dethrone a King of the Scottish royal house without any reference to them. But James was in no mood for resistance; he seems to have been in a state of acute depression brought on by poor physical health – he had recently suffered several extremely severe nose bleeds – and by the anguish of seeing those he believed to be his friends, including his two daughters, turn against him. He did however envisage some sort of campaign in the future and is thought to have asked Dundee to take charge of military affairs in Scotland. After the King had left for France Dundee therefore returned home with the general idea of keeping the flag flying there, but with no precise instructions as to how to do this or even anything to show that James had appointed him as military leader. He had been raised to the peerage on the 12th November, seven days after the Prince of Orange landed.

For the time being he remained quietly at Dudhope. Everyone was waiting for the Convention (of Estates of the Realm – less formal than a parliament) due to meet in Edinburgh in March 1689 to determine who should wear the Crown of Scotland and the country was in a state of general uncertainty. The Earl of Annandale, for instance, changed sides five times in as many months.[2] But Dundee never wavered in his support for James. When he first met James the latter was Lord High Admiral of England, generally admired for his bravery and leadership. It was only his conversion to Catholicism that brought a decline in his popularity and Dundee was not the man to be diverted from his loyalty by a turn in public opinion, nor did he ever have any doubts about James's desire for toleration in religious matters. He always asserted that the Episcopal Church, of which he was a devout member, would be safe under James's kingship. In the meantime he and his friend Colin Lindsay, Earl of Balcarres, had begun a correspondence with James and had sent him a draft letter which, it was suggested, should be sent to the Convention under his (James's) signature. It was a tactful letter and there was some hope of its being regarded favourably.

March came and the Convention met. Edinburgh was packed, not only with its members and their attendants, but with hard-line Covenanters from the south-west, brought in by the Duke of Hamilton, the President of the Convention. They were a potential threat to anyone supporting James and, in view of where these hard-liners had come from, to Dundee in particular. The King's letter was read out to the Convention but it bore no resemblance to the draft Dundee had sent to James; it was hard and unyielding whereas a letter from William was flattering and conciliatory.

In his poem about Bonnie Dundee Walter Scott wrote:

To the Lords of Convention 'twas Claver'se who spoke,
'Ere the King's crown shall fall there are crowns to be broke;
So let each Cavalier who loves honour and me
Come follow the bonnet of Bonny Dundee.

Dundee, however, did not say any such thing to the Convention. It would have been most unwise of him to do so, bearing in mind the composition of the mob outside and the political leanings of the President and the bulk of the other members. He was bitterly disappointed by James's letter. It may very well be that his draft had never reached the King but had been discarded by Melfort, his chief Secretary of State, who was thought by many of James's supporters to be, at best, an extremely poor interpreter of James's intentions.

Once it became clear that opinion in the Convention was going against James Dundee made an excuse to leave, saying, perhaps with truth, that there was evidence of a plot to murder him. He decided to leave not only the Convention but Edinburgh as well and Balcarres and the Marquis of Atholl agreed to leave with him. But when the time came Atholl asked for one more day before he committed himself and Balcarres waited with him (to his own detriment as it turned out, as he was arrested and spent some time in prison). Dundee however refused to wait and left Edinburgh quietly with a small band of followers in a manner very different from that detailed in Scott's poem:

Dundee he is mounted, he rides up the street,
The bells are rung backward, the drums they are beat,
...

Come open the West Port, and let me gang free,
And it's room for the bonnets of Bonny Dundee.[3]

The West Port however opened towards the Castle where the Duke of
Gordon was holding out for James. There was a great deal of coming and
going there of soldiers besieging the Castle and Dundee might well have
been arrested on the Convention's orders had he tried to make his exit
there. He himself was uncertain how to act or what resources, if any, were
available to him. His life and therefore the cause in which he believed
himself to be engaged were in danger from the hostile forces within the
city. He therefore left quietly by the Netherbow on the east side of the
city. This gate was pulled down in 1764. It was the gate through which
Lochiel and his Camerons gained entry to Edinburgh in 1745. Once
through the Netherbow Dundee and his followers rode towards Calton
Hill and turned west along the ridge where Princes Street now runs, which
put them on the road to Stirling. They stopped at the west end of the
castle rock beyond the Nor' Loch which at that time filled the space now
taken up by Princes Street Gardens. Dundee rode down to the foot of the
castle rock and climbed up to the postern gate to talk to the Duke of
Gordon over the wall – not an easy feat, especially when booted and
spurred. It involved a climb up an almost vertical rocky face and is said
to have been witnessed by crowds of the citizens of Edinburgh who had
come out to see what was going on.[4] The Duke's situation was by no
means enviable, shut off as he was from any communication with those
of like mind and even uncertain of what James wanted him to do. His
morale needed bolstering. Dundee had already visited him to discuss the
situation and it was important to let him know that some idea of a rising
was developing in his (Dundee's) head as there would have been no point
in the Duke's holding out in the castle if there was no movement in support
of James in the country.

Having descended to earth again Dundee rode on to Linlithgow, Stirling
and Dunblane. His Highland adventure had begun, although he did not
know it at the time. When the Duke asked him where he was going he is
said to have replied: 'Wherever the spirit of Montrose shall direct me'. His
condition was beginning to parallel that of his illustrious kinsman, one
difference being that Montrose carried a Commission from his King
appointing him Lieutenant-General of his forces in Scotland, whereas
Dundee had no instructions whatever from James.

In Dunblane his party was met by Alexander Drummond of Balhaldy
who had been sent by his father-in-law, Sir Ewen Cameron of Lochiel.
Lochiel had been consulting with other Highland chiefs, amongst them
Glengarry, Clanranald and MacLean of Duart, and it had been suggested
that there should be a rendezvous in Lochaber on the 13th May. Dundee's
path now began to be clear to him, if he might only receive a commission

from James enabling him to act. While waiting for this to come and for the disastrously long winter in the Highlands to give way to spring it seemed politic to go home and keep quiet until the date of the Lochaber rendezvous came nearer. Accordingly he rode on to Dudhope Castle where his wife was awaiting both him and the birth of their first child. While at Dudhope he received a summons from the Convention demanding that he lay down his arms and attend the next session, to which he returned the following reply, addressed to the Duke of Hamilton:

Dudhope March 17th, 1689
May it please your Grace, The coming of an herauld and trumpeter to summon a man to lay down arms, that is living in peace at home, seems to me a very extraordinary thing, and, I suppose, will do so to all that hears of it. While I attended the Convention at Edinburgh, I complained often of many people's being in arms without authority, which was notoriously known to be true, even the wild hill men; and, no summons to lay down arms under the pain of treason being given them, I thought it unsafe for me to remain longer among them ... Besides, tho' it were necessary for me to go and attend the Meeting, I cannot come with freedom and safety, because I am informed there are men of war, and foreign troops in the passage; and, till I know what they are, and what are their orders, the Meeting cannot blame me for not coming. Then, my Lord, seeing the summons has proceeded on a groundless story, I hope the Meeting of States will think it unreasonable, I should leave my wife in the condition she is in.

If there be any body that, notwithstanding of all that is said, think I ought to appear, I beg the favour of a delay till my wife is brought to bed; and, in the meantime, I will either give security or paroll not to disturb the peace. Seeing this pursuit is so groundless, and so reasonable things offered, and the Meeting composed of prudent men and men of honour, and your Grace presiding in it, I have no reason to fear farther trouble. I am, may it please your Grace, your most humble servant.[5]

He was not burning his boats entirely, but must have had his tongue well in his cheek when he wrote this letter, particularly the last paragraph. He still did not know what James wanted him to do, if anything. As a reply to his letter the Herald on the 30th March denounced him as a fugitive and rebel at the Market Cross of Edinburgh.

Soon after this his son was born and given Montrose's name and the King's name – James. He was baptised on the 9th April. On the 11th William and Mary were declared King and Queen of Scots in Edinburgh. It was at about this time too that Dundee's commission from James at last arrived in Scotland but it did not reach him then as it had fallen into the hands of his opponents.

On the 16th April Dudhope Castle, so recently the scene of celebrations for the birth of James Graham, was in the midst of preparations for war. Servants ran in and out, grooms brought horses from the stables, riders mounted them in the courtyard and arms were distributed. In the castle Dundee was saying farewell to his two-week-old son and to his wife, for whose love he had risked his whole career. Dundee's standard bearer, James Philip, portrays her full of pride in him yet fearful for his fate, helping to prepare his arms, uttering the words so many women have uttered or tried to utter on seeing their men go off to war:

Go now, my dearest one, under happy auspices... Go fortunate, whither the Fates call you, where your valour and devotion, and the ardour of your noble heart, carry you. Go where the honour of your King commands. Thus speaking, she sadly took, unconsciously, her last farewell of her husband; and with her prayers she followed him as he went, ardent for the war, straining her bright eyes after him as long as he was in sight.[6]

But, as we shall see, they may have met once more in Glen Ogilvie.

Not much more than a quarter of a mile nor-nor-west of Dudhope lies Dundee Law, the site of an Iron Age fort, where in April 1645 Montrose had set up his headquarters when besieging the town below, as it commands an excellent view of it. It is easy to observe from Dudhope Castle what is happening on the Law and Lady Dundee and her bodyguard and servants would have been able to see the stream of horsemen riding up to its summit; Dundee himself in a scarlet coat, his brother David behind him, his kinsman James Philip carrying the standard and men from his own troop of horse, their arms and armour glittering in the sun. The town of Dundee below them stayed quiet as the Royal Standard was unfurled and there was no rush of citizens eager to support their Constable. He stayed only a while on his eminence, hoping that the rest of his old troop of horse, shut up in their barracks in Dundee, would find some means of joining him, but there was no movement from below and eventually he rode off through the Sidlaw Hills to Glen Ogilvie where he remained for three days. Then, having been warned by his scouts, he left just a day before Sir Thomas Livingstone's dragoons arrived to seize him.

Up to this moment his life had been that of a conscientious officer, a good public servant, the confidant of kings, but there had been little of that glory associated with the name of his kinsman, Montrose, the 'matchless heroe'. Now, with his declaration of war against William he had thrown away all his accrued advantages, all his successes in the world and had embarked on a dangerous and uncharted course which duty enjoined upon him and to which honour beckoned him.

There followed a fortnight of riding up and down in north-east Scotland, as weather conditions were so bad that they were obliged to confine their movements to the east. They spent their time recruiting but had to avoid General Mackay since they were too few to give him battle then. Hugh Mackay of Scourie was William of Orange's general in Scotland. He was then forty-nine and although a Highlander by birth, coming from Sutherland in the far north-west, he had spent almost his entire life in Holland and had forgotten Highland ways.

As far as recruiting went Dundee found, like Montrose, that he was unable to attract any of the great magnates to his cause. He picked up Lord Dunkeld and Halyburton of Pitcur en route and also the Earl of Dunfermline, brother-in-law to the Duke of Gordon. James Seton was the 4th Earl of Dunfermline. The 1st Earl, Alexander, had bought Fyvie Castle in Banff and Buchan in 1596. He became in turn Lord Fyvie, Chancellor of Scotland and Earl of Dunfermline. In 1603, just before he left for England, James VI appointed him guardian of his second son, the future Charles I, who, being only three years old, was left behind in Scotland when the rest of the family went south. He remained in the care of the 1st Earl until July 1604 when he joined the rest of the family. The 2nd Earl supported Charles I enthusiastically against the Covenanters and it is therefore not surprising to find the 4th Earl remaining loyal to James VII and raising as many of his brother-in-law's tenants as he could. He was only joined by fifty gentlemen, the bulk of the Duke's tenants being unwilling to go, perhaps because the Duke himself was absent – still holding out in Edinburgh Castle.

By the end of the fortnight Dundee had gathered about 100 men. He had no ammunition or supplies and no money, apart from his own resources, which would not have been great.[7] Nor did he have the King's Commission, although he knew that it had been sent. His followers were drawn to him by their own beliefs and traditions of loyalty and above all by the force of his personality. Mackay at this time complained of the disaffected attitude of 'Persons of Quality' in the north of Scotland and attributed this to Dundee having 'played his personage' amongst them.[8] Yet although they may have been sympathetic he did not manage to persuade more than a handful of them to join him.

In the first week in May he left Strathbogie where he had picked up Dunfermline and the Gordons and rode to Inverness. The account generally given of his arrival there is that he had been told that the chiefs had sent MacDonald of Keppoch to meet him there and conduct him into Lochaber; that he was angry to find Keppoch holding the town to ransom, with the town councillors shut up in his tent until they paid up; that he publicly castigated Keppoch for his behaviour, so deleterious to the King's service (surely a dangerous thing to do to a Highland Chief surrounded by his clansmen all armed to the teeth); that Keppoch apologised but refused to join him in an attack on Mackay, who had by this time brought up a large force of men to Elgin and that Keppoch had then departed with his clansmen and their loot.

This account is largely drawn from the *Memoirs of Sir Ewen Cameron of Locheill* written nearly fifty years later by John Drummond of Balhaldy.[9] An eye-witness account however says merely that Dundee heard there were Highlanders assembling at Inverness and decided to join them.[10] No specific reference is made to a request from Dundee that Keppoch join him against Mackay but Keppoch's refusal is implied in that Dundee was disappointed at losing a chance of attacking the enemy.[11]

We also have an account of this meeting in a dispatch sent to the King:

The Lord Viscount...marched...from thence [Castle Gordon] to Inverness where he found the Laird of Keppoch at the head of seven hundred men, the most part volunteers. They plundered Macintosh's lands, and the neighbourhood; *which Macintosh in a manner deserved, because the Viscount had written twice to him, to declare for the King, and had got no return...* The magistrates of Inverness came and informed him that Keppoch had forced them to promise him four thousand merks. My Lord Dundee told them that Keppoch had no warrant from him to be in arms; much less to plunder; *but that necessity had forced him out*; and said he would give his bond that at the King's return (since they had not yet declared the Prince of Orange king) they should have their money repaid them. After which he desired Keppoch to march his men with him, and he would go and engage Mackay. But the men, partly the Camerons, said they could not without consent of their master. But the truth was, they were loaded with spoil, and neither they nor their leaders had anything else in head. So they went home plundering on the way.[12] [My italics]

A further account is to be found in *Memoirs of the Lord Viscount Dundee*:

The town of Inverness gave Keappoch 2,000 dollars to be gone: Dundee mildly composed all their disputes, and showed himself so generous a peace-maker, that he gave his bond for the money. Afterwards Dundee sent friendly for Mackintosh, to reconcile him and Keappoch together, who denied coming to his lordship though that [they] were relations [Macintosh was Dundee's cousin]. Upon which, Dundee ordered Keappoch to drive away Mackintosh's cattle, some of which were kept for the service of the army, and the rest were sent to Keappoch's tenants.[13]

This suggests even more strongly Dundee's sympathy with Keppoch; but it is an unreliable source although, at the least, it is a third account disagreeing with Balhaldy.

Only Balhaldy says anything about Dundee's castigating Keppoch or about Keppoch apologising or, indeed, about Keppoch having been sent there to bring Dundee into Lochaber. He makes no reference to any attempts to accommodate Macintosh or to Dundee's opinion that he had deserved the treatment he received from Keppoch. Dundee evidently realised and regretted the Keppoch MacDonalds' eagerness for plunder but was prepared to admit that they had need of it. Was it felt politic, at the time Balhaldy's account was written, to present Macintosh in a good light and Keppoch in a bad one? Specialists on the period immediately prior to the '45 might throw more light on this.

The most reliable of these four accounts must presumably be the despatch to the King, written by Dundee himself, using the then normal convention of the third person. We can therefore assume that Dundee heard Highlanders were assembled near Inverness and rode there in the hope of adding them to his still very small force. When the true situation became known to him he may have protested in some diplomatic way to Keppoch, who then left with his loot, mostly from Macintosh's lands (the reasons behind the feud between Macintosh and Keppoch are discussed later). There was no question, and had never been any question of Dundee's accompanying him, as there were several things he still wished to do – make a further attempt to gather up the members of his old troop shut up in Dundee (he had heard from his wife that they were still eager to join him) and carry out a raid or two to collect money (the King's taxes) which must have been running very short by that time – and there was time enough to deal with these before the rendezvous, the date of which had in any case not yet finally been fixed. He stayed a few days longer at Inverness. Did he stay to calm the town down in the hope of winning its support for James? Or did he go recruiting amongst the neighbouring clans?

Chambers regards the Inverness episode as a diplomatic triumph for Dundee in that it secured if not the support then at least the indulgence of Inverness and the military support of Keppoch who might not otherwise have been willing to give it (see pp.76–78). Chambers thus echoes the words of an eyewitness: 'Not however without praise does he [Dundee] leave the blue waters of the Ness.'[14]

Dundee eventually left in the only direction possible to him, i.e. the direction Keppoch had taken, as Mackay's army blocked any passage to the east, and rode down Stratherrick, roughly along the route later used by General Wade for his military road south from Inverness and also used in 1773 by Boswell and Dr. Johnson during their Highland jaunt. This route took him through Fraser country to Cill Chuimein (Fort Augustus) where Montrose had paused on his way north after his raid into Campbell territory and where Keppoch's bard, *Iain Lom*, still alive in Dundee's time, had brought him a message that there was a Campbell army behind him at Inverlochy. He had turned aside and, in the cold of winter, had gone over the mountains and down Glen Roy, reaching Inverlochy before any of the Campbell scouts could give warning of his coming. Dundee must have thought much about this as he approached Cill Chuimein. Tradition still remembers where Montrose drew up his army and paused for a time; a stretch of flat ground south of the village and roughly following the route of what is now the A82 is still known locally as Montrose's Mile. From Cill Chuimein Dundee aimed to go eastwards but he first rode down to Invergarry, a distance of about seven miles, perhaps in the hope of encountering the chief of the Glengarry MacDonnells. It seems, however, that there was nobody at the castle so he turned about and rode back the way he had come, halting at the kirk of Cill Chuimein where he stayed the night. In the morning he went up on the high bank above the river Tarff and over the Corrieyairack Pass (Ordnance Survey spelling for the Gaelic *Coire Ghearraig*), later to become General Wade's military road to Laggan. He spent a night at Presmukerach and from there issued a letter in the King's name finally setting the date of the rendezvous for the 18th May. He then rode through Blair and Killiecrankie to Dunkeld where he took over the taxes that had been collected for William's government, went on to Perth and took charge of the public purse but was careful not to seize any private money or to damage the town in any way. He also took prisoners from the garrison. By the 13th May he was at the Earl of Strathmore's castle at Glamis where they all rested 'on the green grass' before going on to Dundee. It was on his way to the town of Dundee that he was joined by Halyburton of Pitcur and Fullarton of Fullarton, both neighbours.[15]

At Dundee he rode down to the very walls, causing great alarm and confusion within the town, to give his old troop a chance to slip out and join him but once again he had no luck; they were all shut up in their barracks by their new commander, nor could he provoke the garrison to a fight. He appeared once again on Dundee Law, wearing a scarlet coat with breastplate and back piece and a helmet covered with black fur. There was still no response from the town, apart from skirmishers who felt safe to show their valour once Dundee began to withdraw. It would have been dangerous to visit Dudhope which he could see lying below him with its towers and fields and orchards open to the May sunshine. In any case it was empty. He turned his horse and left it all behind him, seeking his older home in Glen Ogilvie.[16]

Notes

1. Raymond Campbell Paterson: *A Land Afflicted. Scotland in the Covenanter Wars 1638–1690*, Edinburgh (John Donald), 1998, p.279.
2. Paul Hopkins: *Glencoe and the End of the Highland War*, Edinburgh (John Donald), 1986, p.122.
3. *The Poetical Works of Sir Walter Scott*, ed. J. Logan Robertson, London (Henry Frowde, OUP), 1909, in: The Doom of Devorgoil, p.903.

4. Sir John Dalrymple of Crastoun: *Memoirs of Great Britain and Ireland from the Dissolution of the last Parliament of Charles II*, 2nd ed., 3 vols., London, 1970, vol.1, p.221.
5. *Letters*, pp.234–5.
6. *Grameid*, Book II, lines 202–10.
7. *Letters*, p.242.
8. Hugh Mackay of Scourie: *Memoirs of the War Carried on in Scotland and Ireland, 1689–91*, Edinburgh, 1833, p.17.
9. Balhaldy, p.237.
10. *Grameid*, Book II, lines 292–4.
11. ibid., Book II, line 329.
12. *Secretary Nairne's Papers*, published by James MacPherson, vol. iii, p.352. Docketted "News from Scotland with Mr. Gay. Received 7th July 1689".
13. *Memoirs of the Lord Viscount Dundee, The Highland Clans and the Massacre of Glenco. etc. by an Officer in the Army*, ed. Henry Jenner, London (F.E.Robinson & Co.), 1903, pp.17–18.
14. *Grameid*, Book II, lines 330–3. Robert Chambers: *History of the Rebellion in Scotland under the Viscount of Dundee and the Earl of Mar in 1689 and 1715*, Edinburgh (Constable), 1829, pp.48–49.
15. *Grameid*, Book II, lines 454–466.
16. ibid., Book II, lines 469–625.

CHAPTER THREE

To Lochaber

Nunc et victor ovans gressum tendebat ad altos
Ingentis Grampi trans ninguida culmina montes
Abria qua vastis boream petit ardua silvis.

The Grameid

(Now as a victor he advances to the Highlands, over
the snow-clad Grampians, to where rugged Lochaber
courts the cold winds with her vast forests.)

IT WAS WITH these words that Dundee's kinsman, James Philip of
Almerieclose by Arbroath, began his account of the journey from Glen
Ogilvie to Lochaber. They are part of a long epic poem in Latin in which
Philip describes Dundee's Highland campaign in florid dactylic hexameters, resembling the style of Lucan, who was both Dundee's and
Montrose's favourite Latin poet. Philip called it, with a glance at Vergil,
The Grameid. It is written in a heroic, bombastic style with lengthy flour-
ishes and descriptive passages, full of classical allusions, which the
historian might well be glad to exchange for more practical details. It would
be churlish however to complain of its often wearisome rhetoric and hyper-
bole without acknowledging its immense value to the historian and its
poetic qualities, as, for instance, when Philip speaks of Lochaber 'parting
the north wind with its frozen ridges'.[1]

The poem covers the campaign from its very inception and stops a few
days short of Killiecrankie. It is here at least that the extant version ends,
although as it is obviously a fair copy the rest of the text may exist in a
rough form to be discovered one day perhaps between the leaves of a dusty
volume in some forgotten library. Its main interest from the point of view
of the present study is that it is an invaluable source of information about
the first Jacobite Rising, being written by an eye-witness who served, as
he tells us, as Dundee's standard bearer; as regards the journey to Lochaber
and the gathering of the clans it is indeed our only source of reference.
Some of it also appears to have been written very close to the time of the
actions described, before the passage of time could confuse the memory,
for the poet tells us that he wrote '*Arma inter media et squalorem carceris
atri*'.[2] (Amidst arms and in the squalor of a dark prison). The dark prison
was in Arbroath where he was confined for a time for having told the

magistrates what he thought of them. What a help it would be to know which are the parts he wrote '*arma inter media*'. We should then know those passages on which we could place most reliance. Or perhaps he just made notes as he went along and converted them, in more peaceful surroundings, including the dark prison, into Latin hexameters. If the latter we can be reasonably certain of the correctness of the facts he gives which would mean that we may have an even more reliable account here than that in Wishart's account of Montrose's wars which are based chiefly on conversations in Holland with Montrose after he had disbanded and gone abroad.

Several copies were made of the manuscript of *The Grameid* which is dated 1691, the original being in the author's handwriting, as he declares at the beginning. It was first published by the Scottish History Society in 1888, appearing with a preface, translation and notes by the Rev. Alexander D. Murdoch. Murdoch apologises for any deficiencies in his work but explains that he had not originally intended a full translation, only a summary of the contents, and he seems to have had less than a year to complete the extra work, which includes long notes on many of the protagonists and venues, whilst still carrying out his own work.[3] He was the incumbent of All Saints', Edinburgh. Given these circumstances it is not surprising that there are mistranslations and omissions and in pointing some of these out to the reader I do not intend in any way to suggest that his work is not greatly to be appreciated and admired.

James Philip was born in 1656, so he was thirty-three when he joined Dundee. He certainly survived the death of William of Orange in 1703, probably living until 1713. His father, James Philip (or Philp), the son of Dr. Henry Philp, a baillie of Arbroath, married Margaret Graham, Dundee's second cousin, who was a daughter of Walter Graham of Duntrune, the grandson of Sir William Graham of Claverhouse. Sir William was the curator and friend of his cousin, Montrose. The house in which our James Philip was born was the former Almeshouse Chapel, standing to one side of the Abbey. Ochterlony of Guynd, whom we have already met describing Glen Ogilvie and Dudhope, gives the following description of the Chapel in 1684:

The Almeshouse Chapple, as now possesst by James Philp of Almryclose. His house is built of the stones thereof, and has all the apartments belonging thereto. The fabrick was great and excellent, having many fyne gardines and orchards now converted to arable ground, about which is a high stone wall, and now by the King's gift belongs to the Bishop of Brechine [i.e. the superiority belongs to the bishop].[4]

Like Dundee and Montrose before him Philip attended the University of St Andrews, taking his degree in 1675 when he was nineteen or twenty. He became laird in 1695 or 1696 when his father died. He had two sons, James and John; we can guess for whom the second one was named.

The learning displayed throughout *The Grameid* and the absence of any further information about his life before Dundee's Rising would suggest that the years up to that time were mainly filled up with study, although he cannot have been chained too closely to his desk or he would not have been physically capable of undertaking the rigours of Dundee's campaign. It is normally supposed that seventeenth century Lowlanders knew little of the Highlands, yet Philip seems to have a reasonably good grasp of Highland topography, particularly if we remember that he was not able to pore over Ordnance maps as we are. Of Highland chiefs he also seems to have a fairly good understanding, whether gained before, during or after the campaign. It is by a happy coincidence that Philip's manuscript eventually found a resting place in the Advocates' Library in Edinburgh which had been opened on the 1st March 1689 by Sir George Mackenzie of Rosehaugh, a close friend of the Viscount Dundee.

The other main contemporary source for the Lochaber period, apart from Dundee's own letters, is the *Memoirs of Sir Ewen Cameron of Locheill* by John Drummond of Balhaldy which we have already referred to above. These memoirs were probably finished by about 1737 and must have been written under rather difficult circumstances as, in a letter from the author to Donald Cameron of Lochiel (the Gentle Lochiel) we hear that: 'The injury Sir Alexander Murray of Stanhope did in carrying away the first book, and other three MSS was an action very unbecoming a gentleman'. (It certainly was!) 'But though I can never make up the loss of my MSS, yet I have fully repaired that of Sir Ewen's life, from the memoirs and vouchers I had by me'.[5] This explanation might cause a certain disquiet as to whether the 'memoirs and vouchers' were really as sufficient as the writer suggests, but as the first book only goes up to the Restoration the books material to the period we are considering here may not have been affected, although that depends, of course, on what was in the 'other three MSS'.

The Drummonds of Balhaldy belonged to the Clan Gregor; it had lost all its lands, and its clansmen had become outlaws, forbidden even to use their own name. Drummond was one of the names particularly favoured as a pseudonym. There is some confusion as to who exactly this particular Drummond of Balhaldy was. Biographers of Dundee seem very undecided on the matter, not surprisingly perhaps as the editor of this volume of memoirs, as published for the Abbotsford Club, is rather uncertain himself, but seems to be most in favour of the theory that John was the grandson of Lochiel.[6] Confusion has been increased by the prominence in Jacobite affairs of two other members of the family – John's father Alexander, Lochiel's son-in-law, who has already featured in these pages

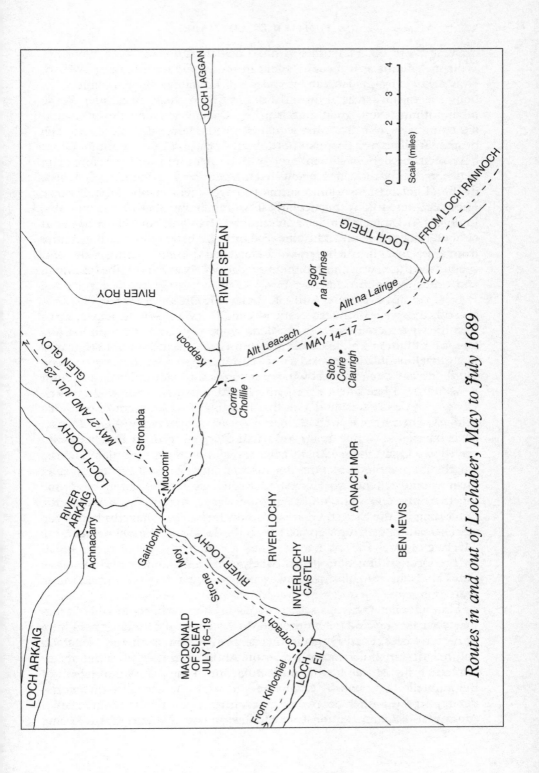

Routes in and out of Lochaber, May to July 1689

carrying messages to Dundee from Lochiel, and John's elder brother William, famous as a Jacobite agent in the period surrounding 1745–6. One writer calls our John the grandson of Lochiel at the beinning of his book and son-in-law later on and also gives his name as Alexander. Some other authors favour great-grandson. We do at least know, however, that his name was John from the signature to the letter quoted above. His brother William was born possibly about 1688 and John might therefore have seen the light of day in, say, 1689 to 1694 and was therefore aged between twenty-three and twenty-eight when his grandfather, Sir Ewen, died and between forty-three and forty-eight in 1737 when the *Memoirs* were completed. It is therefore reasonable to suppose that the writer of Lochiel's Memoirs was indeed his grandson John; he would have been old enough to obtain some of his material from his grandfather and certainly from his father, but he seems to have relied a great deal on Balcarres' account of the Rising and on Philip's *Grameid*[7] as well as on the 'memoirs and vouchers' he mentions.

But to return to Dundee himself. On leaving Dundee Law he rode north towards the 'walls of the tall castle of Glen Ogilvie'.[8] Was he expecting to find his wife there? As we have seen, Philip says that she took her last farewell of him at Dudhope on the 16th April but it does not seem very likely that he would have failed to make arrangements for her greater safety. Dudhope had been visited by the dragoons shortly after Dundee left and it would have been better for Lady Dundee to make her way to Glen Ogilvie where her husband's mother had found refuge from Cromwell's soldiery when he was a child. The *Memoirs of the Lord Viscount Dundee* (that unreliable source again) says that Dundee went to Dudhope and stayed two nights there with his wife[9] and although both the place and the length of stay are incorrect this does at least suggest that there was another meeting between the two. Even so they will have had only a very brief time together, just one night, and then she must let him go again and watch him riding up the road to Glamis. By now he had probably discarded the scarlet coat in which he appeared on the Law and the helmet with its covering of black fur and had assumed a buff coat and a chapeau which let his long curling hair stream freely over his shoulders. How many times she had seen him ride away before, but never on so perilous a journey.

They left Glen Ogilvie on the 14th May. There were about 100 of them – Dundee himself and his brother David, his more distant kinsman Philip of Almerieclose, Lord Dunkeld, David Halyburton of Pitcur, a kinsman and neighbour, Fullarton of Fullarton, another neighbour, Kinnaird of Culbin on the Moray Firth, Graham of Duntrune, a cousin, Graham of Balquhapple, who had been a witness at young James Graham's christening, Sir Alexander Innes of Coxton from Coxton Tower three miles south-east of Elgin, Edmonstone of Newton from Newton Castle beside

Doune Castle (the Edmonstones were hereditary keepers of Doune), John Gordon, the famous Glenbuchat, aged only sixteen or seventeen at the time, the Farquharsons of Inverey and Balmoral and Lord Dunfermline and his Gordons along with John Grant of Ballindalloch who had defied the Laird of Grant and joined with Dunfermline. Friends and tenants made up the number and there were also probably the prisoners they had taken at Perth including William Blair of Blair. But there were none of the great ones for whom Dundee had hoped. Perhaps Kinnaird of Culbin best epitomises the weakness of Lowland support since he was, as Bruce Lenman has rather cruelly said, chiefly distinguished by the fact that his land had been almost entirely engulfed in drifting sand.[10] The sand became unsettled because the local lairds had allowed bents, broom and junipers to be pulled up (a situation very familiar to conservationists today). This was prohibited in 1695.[11]

A journey of more than 100 miles lay before them, partly on fairly well-used highways, for there were roads in the Highlands before General Wade but they were only passable in good weather. The last forty miles or so, however, would be along very rough tracks and heath-clad slopes and often over boulder-strewn or boggy ground. Philip gives their itinerary, after Glamis, as Coupar Angus, Dunkeld, valley of the Tay, dark Appin, Weem, Comrie and Garth Castles, Loch Rannoch.[12]

From Glen Ogilvie they rode to Glamis Castle where local tradition has it that the Earl of Strathmore came out to meet them and wish them well. He was a personal friend of Dundee but was not to join him at this juncture. In a letter to Melfort, the King's Secretary, dated the 27th June Dundee writes:

> Panmure [James Maule 4th Earl of Panmure] keeps right and at home; so does Strathmore... All these will break out and many more when the King lands... But they suffer mightily in the meantime; and will be forced to submit, if there be not relief sent very soon.[13]

Patrick, the 3rd Earl of Strathmore, had inherited debts of £40,000, an astronomical sum in modern terms. His father, the 2nd Earl, had been a friend of Montrose, but only during the latter's Covenanting days. Later, when Montrose became an enthusiastic supporter of Charles I, the 2nd Earl could not find it in his conscience to continue the friendship and indeed went so far as to reduce himself to penury by helping to finance the Covenanting army. When he died in 1646 and Patrick was only three the estates were thought to be irrecoverable, but by 1686 Patrick had not only restored them to their previous condition but had undertaken an ambitious programme of building and improvement. Philip describes Glamis 'with its lofty porticos and halls reared aloft in superb turrets, all testifying to the genius of its magnificent master'.[14] With all this now completed and with the hope, no doubt, that he could spend the rest of his life enjoying the results of his work, it must have been bitter for him to contemplate the fact that by supporting his King he might have everything snatched away from him. He was forty-six at the time of Dundee's Rising and died six years later. His grandson John, the 5th Earl, was killed in 1715 fighting on the Jacobite side at the battle of Sheriffmuir.[15]

The ties between Glamis Castle and the Tower of Glen Ogilvie were close and are reflected in local tradition which not only reports that Lord Strathmore wished Dundee well on this occasion but also that he rode with him on his second visit to the town of Dundee.[16] There are also stories of an underground passage between the two castles. At Glamis a passage was certainly found under the Dutch Garden on the east side of the castle but was covered over again without being further investigated. At Hatton of Ogilvie farm a very large stone was recently uncovered which, it is believed, could be something to do with a tunnel. It does not look like a naturally placed stone but it would require heavy lifting gear to raise it.[17] If such a connecting tunnel does exist however it would have to be at least two miles long. Glamis Castle has not forgotten its connections with Bonnie Dundee; it has on display a bullet-proof leather jerkin of his, his black thigh boots with the toes cut off square and his black cartridge case. In the drawingroom, in a place of honour near the fireplace between Charles I and Charles II, is the Kneller portrait.

Patrick Strathmore was only one of the people throughout the Lowlands and eastern Highlands who were ready to rise when the King came but could not follow Dundee immediately for a variety of reasons, some due to caution, some economic, some geographical as they were surrounded by people in the opposite camp. Dundee worried about them and felt himself responsible for them. He said later in a letter to Melfort that he would like to take his army to the south to help them but could not as his men, being unpaid, would have to live off the country and that might make enemies for the King.[18]

Leaving Glamis they rode on towards Coupar Angus, passing on the way the lands of Fullarton of Fullarton who was in Dundee's train and had joined him shortly before his second descent on Dundee. His land was in the Strath of Isla – very flat and very green between low hills. Once past it Coupar Angus was soon reached and here they were about three miles from Pitcur Castle, the home of Halyburton of Pitcur who also rode with them, a great mountain of a man and one of Dundee's closest allies. His castle sits to the south of Coupar in the Sidlaw Hills, a sixteenth-century tower house, originally of four storeys and still reaching nearly to three. It is built of dark stone and looks rather melancholy now, closely hedged in as it is by farm buildings.

By crossing the River Isla just beyond Coupar Angus, probably at Couttie, they would have been well placed to follow the north bank of the

Tay and could so go on via Meikleour, Spittalfield and Caputh to the little town of Dunkeld and its cathedral, the broad river of Tay rushing past between wooded banks. Across the river is Birnam Wood where Macbeth's enemies plucked branches from the trees to use as camouflage, or so Shakespeare tells us.

The Grameid says in the words of its translator that they hastened past Dunkeld, but the Latin is actually rather more urgent than that: '*Atque Caledoniam raptim praetervolat urbem*' (They flew hurriedly past the Caledonian town – Caledonian because the Gaelic name from which Dunkeld derives is Dùn Chaillean (the Fort of the Caledonians).[19] This suggests that they did not ride through the streets of the town, which reach down close to the river, but went as fast as they could behind it and its cathedral and away from the river, possibly passing through the land now surrounding Dunkeld House. They could not have passed on the river side without being noticed, which may have been what Dundee wished to avoid.

After Dunkeld the route they followed becomes less obvious; they had left Angus and its castles and villages and relatively well-trodden paths long behind them and were about to venture into unknown territory, into that part of Britain of which, it has been said, the average person knew less than he did about darkest Africa. Unless one of their number was closely acquainted with the next stages of the journey, which is doubtful as they were all Lowlanders, although some may have had Highland servants, it is likely that somewhere after Dunkeld they picked up guides to take them across Rannoch Moor.

Philip does not mention anywhere between Dunkeld and Weem, apart from telling us that they travelled up 'the beautiful valley of the finny Tay',[20] that is northwards up the river to Ballinluig where, to go further up-river, one has to turn to the west.

Dundee could have taken the east or the west bank up this lovely strath with its high forested hills to either side, pushed back behind bright green fields, as flat as though some gigantic roller had been propelled to and fro over them. The west bank would have been more out of the way of any of Mackay's forces coming down from the north, but if, as I believe, Dundee had cut off a corner by going behind Dunkeld he would already have been a little way up the road on the east bank and with this road he was in any case familiar, from the days he had spent recruiting in the eastern Highlands. It now forms a section of the modern A9. Having stuck to the east bank he could then have forded the Tummel a little to the north of Ballinluig. This ford was used by drovers coming from Aviemore and other places in Strathspey and going to Amulree on the road to Crieff. The drovers first crossed the Tummel and then went over the Tay at a ford called 'Stair Cham' (crooked stepping stones) near Logierait. They then went south-west over the hills by Loch Skiach to Amulree.[21] There is an inn beside each of these fords and these inns, or the buildings they replaced, must have served the drovers before and after negotiating the rivers. It seems unlikely that Dundee would have used this second ford and ridden along the south bank of the Tay here – which takes the heaviest traffic today – because that would have involved a further crossing of the Tay to get to Weem. The rivers may have been full with spring rains and melting snow and there was no bridge at Aberfeldy. The village of Aberfeldy grew up round the bridge built by Wade about thirty years later. Before then drovers coming up from Amulree and heading north or west went into the Birks of Aberfeldy, over the Urlar Burn and crossed further west near the village of Dull (this route coincides almost exactly with a line of electricity pylons; Ordnance Survey Landranger Map 52).[22] Dundee, of course, did not do this as it would have by-passed Weem Castle (Castle Menzies), the next point in Philip's itinerary; this means that he must have followed the north bank of the Tay after crossing at Ballinluig and gone straight on to Weem and beyond, passing on his right the lands of Patrick Stewart of Ballechin who was later to be of such help to him. Later on, across the river and to his left, he may have seen the tower of Grandtully Castle, a sixteenth-century tower house. In the past he had been acquainted with its owner, Sir Thomas Stewart, from whom he had bought a horse in 1676 and who later on, because there had been some quibble about the price, sent him the present of a setting bitch.[23] Mackay made use of Grandtully Castle during Dundee's campaign and this might have been an additional reason, if one were needed, for avoiding the south bank of the Tay here.

Castle Menzies lies to the west of the village of Weem; it is a castle built to a Z-plan which makes it possible to defend both front and back entrances from the side and is of similar date and style to Dundee's own castle of Claypotts. The bartizans at each corner, the gun ports on the ground floor and the shot holes in every room in the upper storeys point to its unsettled past. The Menzies of Weem had had a difficult time in the fifteenth and sixteenth centuries, being harried by their Campbell neighbours in Glenlyon, by the landless MacGregors holding on to life as best they could in the wilds of Rannoch, by the MacDonalds of Keppoch, who marauded into their territory and most of all by the fierce Stewarts of Garth, descendants of the dreaded Wolf of Badenoch, the son of King Robert II, who, by burning down their earlier home in 1487, caused them to build a new fortress called Place of Weem, near the present castle. When this too was burnt down in 1502 they built the castle as we see it today. There they were attacked as late as the reign of Charles II by the MacDonalds of Glencoe. Their disinclination to join Dundee – indeed they never seem to have been in his sights as far as recruits were concerned – reflects their experiences at the hands of the Stewarts, the MacGregors and the MacDonalds of Keppoch, all clans that were to flock to Dundee's banner.

In 1644 Alexander Menzies of Weem was an adherent of Argyll and his clansmen attacked the rear of Montrose's army as it passed on its way to Tippermuir. In 1689 Robert Menzies the Younger raised a party of his father's clansmen to serve as an outpost for Mackay and on his retreat after his defeat at Killiecrankie it was in Castle Menzies that Mackay first sought shelter. The castle eventually declined into a ruin and is now being lovingly restored by the Clan Menzies. It lies at the eastern end of the Appin of Dull. Appin means abbey lands and the Abbey of Dull, destroyed at the Reformation, was a Celtic foundation and once a seat of great learning. Comrie and Garth Castles also lie within this area which Philip refers to as 'the field of dark Appin'.[24] Why does he call Appin dark? Could it be a pun on 'Dull'? The Latin word he uses is *niger* which sounds rather too black to represent 'dull'; however *niger* does mean dark-coloured as well as black while the Latin equivalents for 'dull' only concern such aspects of the word as blunt, sluggish, etc. and do not relate to colour.

Leaving Castle Menzies behind him Dundee rode on through Coshieville and Keltneyburn, passing Comrie Castle (the former home of the Menzies) and Garth Castle; its Gaelic name is *Caisteal a' Chuilein Churta* (the castle of the bad whelp, the Wolf of Badenoch). The Stewarts of Garth were represented in the late eighteenth/early nineteenth centuries by a surprisingly gentle and scholarly descendant – Major General David Stewart of Garth. He was also a successful soldier. In 1822 he published his famous *Sketches of the Character, Manners, and Present State of the Highlanders of Scotland, with Details of the Military Service of the Highland Regiments*. Two of its four sections deal with Highland regiments and the other two describe old Highland ways and people and the melancholy decline in Highland life in the age of the Clearances which he bitterly attacks.[25]

Once past these two castles there are two possibilities. One can either continue north to Tummel Bridge or branch off a little before Tomaphobuill and go over the Braes of Foss. This latter route seems more likely, for Philip tells us that after Garth Castle they went through wild country and came to Rannoch by rugged paths.[26] Boggy Rannoch is what the poet actually says but Murdoch (his translator), rushing to get his work done in a year, is prone to leave out a word here or there. As we shall see later, Philip had good reason to remember that Rannoch was boggy! The Braes of Foss route was and still is a much less frequented route than the road to Tummel Bridge which subsequently became a Wade road. It is signposted 'The Schiehallion Road' and runs round the foot of that mountain and through Strath Fionan, twisting and turning on its way down to Lochan an Daimh, to Crossmount and so to the south-east corner of Loch Rannoch. Most writers believe that Dundee took the north bank of Loch Rannoch but I cannot agree. From Crossmount he would have been able, by following the south bank of the Loch and turning north at its west end, to perform the 'circuit of the long reaches of the loch'[27] and to pass woods which exactly fall in with Philip's description of woods 'made sad by the blasts of the north wind'.[28] This is my translation, as Murdoch's is a little at fault; he renders '*et tristes boreali turbine silvos*' as 'thickets stunted by the cold blasts', thus losing the force of '*boreali*' (of the north wind) which is very important here as it is the southern woods, including the Black Wood of Rannoch, which would have felt the north wind most, those on the north side of the loch being protected from winds from that direction by the slope of the land behind them.

Having come to the western end of Loch Rannoch by the south shore he turned north round the end of it, and crossed the River Gaur where he 'emerges upon the road to Inverness' (*Ingrediturque viam Nessi quae ducit ad urbem*).[29] Had they taken the north side of the loch they would already have been on that road. The 'road to Inverness' seems to be a rather far-fetched description of the road from Rannoch Station to Tummel Bridge, the present B846. Along this road and to the east of Loch Rannoch and of Drumglass there is a road going north to Trinafour (the present B847) and thence to Dalnacardoch on the present A9, these roads representing two sections of the old drove road from Dalnacardoch to Amulree and the south. Mackay and his army could well have been marching down from Inverness at that very moment. His advance southwards from Inverness and his subordinate's (Ramsay's) advance northwards from Edinburgh had been expected for some days, although in fact Mackay did not leave Inverness until the 26th May and Ramsay did not reach Perth until the 22nd. Had one or other of them been earlier, however, and had he received news of any movement of men in the area, he might well have sent a party of scouts along the road westwards from Drumglass. It was essential to keep away from Mackay while making the journey to the west and to keep him in the dark about the actions and whereabouts of Dundee's small force. That the Lochaber expedition was kept quiet is evidenced by the fact that many people thought Dundee was dead or in hiding and his following melted away. As soon, therefore, as he was obliged to emerge onto the potentially dangerous 'road to Inverness' he stopped, raised his standard and sent out scouts.[30]

The 'road to Inverness' has caused a lot of confusion in the minds of those writers who have spent little, if any time looking at maps. Napier, for instance, sends Dundee to Loch Rannoch and from there *to Loch Treig via Inverness*, while a modern biographer tells us that having traversed the wide reaches of Loch Rannoch he headed back to Tummel Bridge and so to Dalnacardoch on the '*Great North Road to Inverness which crossed desolate Rannoch Moor*'.[31]

While they waited for the scouts to return they rested beside the Gaur which runs between Loch Rannoch and Loch Eigheach. Here was the wildest country they had yet seen. The river flowed over rocky slabs and huge mounds of black boulders lay on its banks. The vast moor of Rannoch swept away to the west and north, the hills were obscured by cloud or, where visible at all, showed snow-covered tops and wet mists rolling down their sides.

The scouts came back having nothing to report. When they were rested they set off westwards along the bank of the Gaur with Meall Chomraidh guarding the south and the endless vistas of Rannoch Moor before them. Beside them the shallow river struggled sluggishly between the larger rocky outcrops, for it was beginning to ice over. It tumbled down small water-falls or coated the stones with a glassy white when the cold hindered its flow. Past the junction of loch and river and half way along Loch Eigheach they turned up a wild track leading to Loch Ossian or, as Philip puts it: '...(Dundee) led his troops through the mountains, forcing his way by plain and rock and cliff, by sweltering bog and gully'.[32]

In his *Grameid* Philip is not very helpful as to how far they travelled each day. He only mentions resting at Bridge of Gaur and camping by Loch Treig. Other writers have kept closely to what he says and have treated the rest at Bridge of Gaur as the first stop on the first day, the 14th, thus concluding that they reached Loch Treig on the second day and Glen Spean on the third, the 16th. But this condemns them to a journey of eighty miles in one day, which would be impossible, even if they could have changed horses, which in any case they would not wish to do. There were some spare horses running with them but these would not have been fresh mounts as a horse from a change house would be. In England, in the reign of Elizabeth I, Queen's Messengers were expected to travel at seven miles per hour in summer and five in winter. When travelling from London to Berwick on the Great North Road they were supposed to cover the 350-mile journey in forty hours (9 miles per hour) in summer and in sixty hours (6 miles per hour) in winter, the greater speed probably being attributable to the better condition of this very well established highway. In actual fact the journey often took as much as eight days. There were twenty change houses on this route, that is, one on average every twenty miles. Hired horses were ridden hard, as is evident from the frequent claims for damaged horses or horses that had to be destroyed.[33] The standard of roads was not much improved until the days of Macadam. Fifty years after Elizabeth, when Charles II was making his escape from England after the battle of Worcester, forty miles seemed quite far enough to travel in a day. At one point in his adventures when there was a question as to whether they should spend the night at Hinton Daubnay, only two miles distant, or whether, as Lord Wilmot suggested, they should go to a neigh-bour of Lord Southampton who lived ten miles or more away, Charles, 'who had ridden forty miles already, saw no reason to extend his journey unnecessarily'.[34] We also need to remember that a Queen's Messenger had only himself to bother about and Charles only two or three companions, whereas the hundred men and horses accompanying Dundee could be delayed by any small misfortune affecting even one of them, nor were the prisoners they were bringing with them an asset in this respect.

If we take the winter figure of five miles per hour as being appropriate to the terrain Dundee had to cover, the journey to Bridge of Gaur would take twenty-two hours – quite impossible in one day without rest and without change of horse. But a better indication of the difficulties than can be obtained on the basis of English conditions is provided by a journey undertaken by Dundee himself in April 1689 in the eastern Highlands. After raising the standard on the 16th he rode to Glen Ogilvie where he stayed for three days.[35] He then rode north, reaching Keith on the 21st.[36] He thus had three days, or nearly three, to cover roughly eighty-five miles which works out at about twenty-eight miles a day; and he was in a hurry.

On the Lochaber journey they had left Glen Ogilvie on the 14th May and as Dundee would have hoped to reach Glen Spean on the 17th in time for the rendezvous on the 18th they had four days in which to cover the 100–110 miles. As will be seen later they only travelled between ten and fifteen miles on the last day and on the last day but one, the 16th, assuming that they only had a short rest at Bridge of Gaur, they ended the day with a ferociously tough sixteen miles from Bridge of Gaur to Loch Treig.

A possible timetable might therefore be:

14th May: 45 miles; this would get them past Ballinluig (better roads on this stretch)
15th May: 30 miles to a point south of Kinloch Rannoch
16th May: 9 miles to Bridge of Gaur plus 16 miles from there to Loch Treig, a total of 25 miles
17th May: 12 miles to Glen Spean

Even this was pushing it a little.

It is about fourteen miles from the River Gaur to Loch Ossian and a further two to three miles to Loch Treig, where they eventually camped for the night. Their difficulties may not at first have been very great along the initially broad, flat track and it was probably when they were getting near Loch Ossian, amongst the strings of little lochs, that they found it hard to follow the track and sometimes wandered into the quaking bog hidden below the thin ice. Many of the horses, who were to form the core of any cavalry regiment they might be able to deploy in the future, sank in the treacherous ground and though their riders all managed to escape and though some of the terrified animals could be brought to firm land again by exhausting and time-consuming labour, most of those who fell were lost.[37] Highland garrons would remain still until helped out but not these highly bred creatures from the south; their kicks and struggles only pulled them further into the black pools.[38] Philip himself lost his horse and had to do the rest of the journey on foot, carrying his saddle on his shoulders. They must have been in sad case when they reached Loch Treig and set up their camp for the night in a landscape devoid of human habitation, as it still is today, surrounded by high snowy mountains and gripped by the cold of a late spring which sometimes seems worse than the cold of winter. They were exhausted, perhaps hungry. Had they yet learnt the Highlander's way of keeping body and soul together on the march; a handful of oatmeal, carried in the sporran, mixed with a little cold water? They had lost many of their horses, some of them no doubt loved companions, were uncertain of what awaited them beyond the pass in Lochaber, or what success or failure might await beyond that. The frost gripped them, the freezing damps soaked them as they lay down to rest under a sky sometimes obscured with sleety cloud, sometimes revealing a cold moon and colder stars.

They had great need of that firm bond that exists between fighting men and they needed too Dundee's supporting personality, as described by Sir John Dalrymple of Cranstoun, a Whig and therefore not likely to be biased in Dundee's favour. He wrote:

> If anything good was brought to him to eat, he sent it to a faint or sick soldier. If a soldier was weary, he offered to carry his arms. He kept those who were with him from sinking under their fatigue, not so much by exhortation as by preventing them from attending to their sufferings.[39]

When the dawn broke they found the frost not one whit abated, their hair and beards were stiff with ice and they had to drag themselves from the frozen ground. The sun came out – cheerful no doubt, but promising another Arctic day.[40].

Many writers believe that Dundee then went up the east side of Loch Treig to Glen Spean and so down the glen as far as Glen Roy. Perhaps they are mesmerised by the railway which goes that way, having come from the south-west and cut across our track above Corrour. Glen Spean itself would also delude them as today it is a main route from the western to the eastern Highlands, but in 1689 the tracks there were little used except for local traffic and the great highways to the east were the Corrieyairack and the route from Glen Fintaig, beside Loch Lochy, to Glen Gloy and so over to Melgarve and Garva. The east side of Loch Treig is also quite steep and not easy terrain for manoeuvring large numbers of men and horses. The trains that go along there appear to be seeking their way carefully along a carefully engineered ledge.

Instead of taking this route they skirted the end of Loch Treig and followed the west bank of the Allt na Lairige and so up the Lairig Leacach to the top of the pass overlooking Corriechoillie, as described in the Prologue, or, as Philip has it:

> *Jamque viam carpit, scopulosaeque ardua rupis*
> *Excelsosque apices scandit, praeruptaque saxa.*
> *Perpetuo damnata gelu, loca nullius ante*
> *Trita pede, et nullis equitum calcata catervis…*[41]

(We pursue our way through regions condemned to perpetual frost and never before trodden by the foot of man or horse.)

A strange way one might think of describing an ancient highway and old drove road; it points up the peculiar awfulness of the conditions, raising the expedition almost to the level of Montrose's march through the mountains to meet the Campbells at Inverlochy in February 1645. Dundee went:

> By mountains, rising above the airy flight of birds, and cliffs towering to the sky, by devious paths among the time-worn rocks, our march unlocks the iron bolts of Nature.[42]

This is Philip's view of the second leg of their journey from Loch Rannoch. There is no mention of lacy patterns in the water of the Abhainn Rath for they were stilled and sharpened by ice and few would have had the heart to admire their glittering beauty. In the rocky defile none of the flowers of May hung down as they passed, only icicles and frozen moss. The waterfalls of the Allt na Lairige hung suspended in the air or, if they still moved, had a band of frozen spume around them like a tie holding back a curtain. The deer had left their green ledges above the stream and their hours in the sun and were all away in the ceaseless search for mosses and lichens to bring them through the rest of the cold season.

The patches of quaking bog they were careful to avoid and in any case there were far fewer of them than during the previous day's march. They came up the rise to the top of the pass between Stob Coire Claurigh and Sgùrr Innse, their horses' hooves slipping on the glassy stones. At the top they paused to see what lay ahead and were rewarded by the sight of the comparatively smooth way down into Glen Spean.

> *Hannibal haud tanto contrivit saxa labore… aereas… rumperet Alpes.*[43]

(Hannibal with less labour, clave his way… across the lofty Alps.)

said Philip as he went gratefully down to Corriechoillie.

Even allowing for poetic licence the journey had been a bad one. They went on over the hard rocky ground until the path levelled out and they found themselves on the gentle slopes of heather that lead to the River Spean.

Abria jam gremio Gramum accipit ardua laeto.[44]

(Gladly Lochaber receives the Graham into her bosom.)

Notes

1. *Grameid*, Book III, lines 23–24.
2. ibid., Book I, line 793.
3. ibid., Preface, p.xlvii.
4 ibid., Preface, p.xvii.
5. Balhaldy, p.xliii.
6. ibid., p.xli.
7. ibid., pp.235–6.
8. *Grameid*, Book II, lines 624–5.
9. *Memoirs of the Lord Viscount Dundee…*, op. cit., p.18.
10. Bruce Lenman: *The Jacobite Risings in Britain 1689–1746*, London (Methuen), 1984, p.47.
11. Acts of Parliament Scots, p.452.
12. *Grameid*, Book II, lines 636–642.
13. *Letters*, p.244.
14. *Grameid*, Book II, lines 451–3.
15. Robert Innes-Smith: *Glamis Castle Guidebook*, Derby (Pilgrim Press), 1997, p.27.
16. *Grameid*, p.64, note 3.
17. Personal communication from Mr. E. Jarron of Hatton of Ogilvie Farm.
18. *Letters*, p.247.
19. William J Watson: *The History of the Celtic Place-Names of Scotland*, Dublin (Irish Academic Press), 1986, p.21.
20. *Grameid*, Book II, line 638.
21. A.R.B.Haldane: *The Drove Roads of Scotland*, Newton Abbot (David & Charles), 1973, p.130.
22. Michael Pollard and Tom Ang: *Walking the Scottish Highlands: General Wade's Military Roads*, London (André Deutsch), 1984, p.66.
23. *Letters*, p.142.
24. *Grameid*, Book II, line 639.
25. Colonel David Stewart: *Sketches of the Highlands of Scotland*, 2 vols., Edinburgh (John Donald), 1977. See also James Irvine Robertson: *The First Highlander*, East Linton (Tuckwell Press), 1998, pp.124–133.
26. *Grameid*, Book II, line 642.
27. ibid., Book II, 643–4.
28. ibid., Book II, line 644.
29. ibid., Book II, line 645.
30. ibid., Book II, lines 647–51.
31. Napier: *Memorials…*, op. cit., III, Index p.764, first 3 lines. Andrew Murray Scott: *Bonnie Dundee*, Edinburgh (John Donald), 1989, p.116.
32. *Grameid*, Book II, lines 672–673.
33. A.R.B. Haldane: *Three Centuries of Scottish Posts. An Historical Survey to 1836.* Edinburgh (University Press), 1971, pp.3–9.
34. Richard Ollard: *The Escape of Charles II after the Battle of Worcester*, London

(Constable), 1998, p.121.
35. *Grameid*, Book II, lines 219–220.
36. *Letters*, p.236.
37. *Grameid*, Book II, lines 677–691.
38. *Burt's Letters from the North of Scotland*, Edinburgh (Birlinn), 1998, pp.165–6.
39. Dalrymple: *Memoirs of Great Britain and Ireland...* vol.ii, Pt.II, Book II, p.74.
40. *Grameid*, Book II, lines 691–701.
41. ibid., Book II, lines 703–6.
42. ibid., Book II, lines 706–11.
43. ibid., Book II, lines 713–14.
44. ibid., Book II, line 729.

Glamis Castle
By kind permission of the Earl of Strathmore and Kinghorne

CHAPTER FOUR

Lochiel

Stigh an cridhe do dhùthcha,
Togail bhallachan dùbailt,
Chan faca dithis no aon duine,
Taigh no sabhul 'na smùidrich,
Bean no leanabh 'gan rùsgadh,
Mart 'ga gearradh fo 'lùithean.
Dòmhnall Bàn Bàrd

(In the heart of your country double walls were erected. Nobody ever saw a house or barn smoking, a woman or child stripped naked or a cow being houghed.)

THE RIVER SPEAN used to flow out of Loch Laggan in a lackadaisical manner, as if it had no mind to leave that long, blue, sand-bordered haven, and then wandered in serpentine coils through the flat land until, just west of Roughburn, it gathered itself together for a straight flow of two miles or so. Today the pattern is different; the flat land in which the river once meandered has been flooded and the loch extended by building a dam to the west, just where the straight stretch of the river begins. Now any reluctance it has in leaving the loch is in vain, for it is thrust through the dam, as required, whether it will or no. It then completes its two-mile straight course as before, flowing between steep sides until their grip on it relaxes a few miles before Tulloch and it can wander a little, but not too much, as hard rocks have to be negotiated and by the time it reaches Tulloch it has carved out a deep stony trough for itself in which it boils and rushes for several miles to the delight of people travelling alongside it in the train from Tulloch Station. After this it widens out and seems about to become fat and sleepy, but never does, seizing every chance to leap over rocks and pebbles, charge down miniature waterfalls and deceive the traveller by its shallows on one side or the other, for always, beyond the shallows, there is a yard or two of deep water, effectively keeping people on one bank from those on the other.

After it has passed the modern Spean Bridge the river begins its final downward course, cutting deeper and deeper into the earth between its closely wooded banks and roaring, when it is in spate, like a convocation of water horses as it pushes on towards the River Lochy. Here again there has been a change; the engineers working on the Caledonian Canal, faced with the problem of getting river and canal together through a narrow space, diverted the Lochy and brought it to join the Spean a little higher up than their original confluence, thus allowing the new canal to flow for a short while in the river bed.

How to cross the Spean had always been a problem, and our assessment of the problem is now made more difficult by the Loch Laggan dam which has altered the amount of water coming down. In the early part of the eighteenth century General Wade, bringing a new road up from Fort William to Fort Augustus as part of a plan for military control of the Highlands, solved the problem of the Spean by building a bridge at High Bridge, between Auchnahanate and Brackletter. It was here that the first skirmish of the 1745 Rising took place, when a handful of Highlanders, rushing to and fro through the bushes and shouting to each other, convinced two companies of Guise's regiment that they were facing the entire Jacobite army; they laid down their arms and were the first prisoners to be taken in that campaign. But before Wade's time there were points at which cattle and people could splash across, or wade across if the river was full and so make their way to or from Corriechoillie and the Lairig Leacach; one of these was at Dalnabea, a little upstream of the present Spean Bridge. Montrose is believed to have crossed here when he came down Glen Roy heading for Inverlochy and it would be reasonable to suppose that Dundee too, having come up the Lairig Leacach from the south, would have turned west at Corriechoillie and crossed at Dalnabea, since his first aim must have been to meet Lochiel who lived further west still, beyond the Lochy river. So it is a surprise to read, at the end of the second book of *The Grameid*, the words:

Calce premit foetas et molli gramine ripas;
Transmittensque altam Glen Roae fluminis undam. [1]

(At last our march is ended, and Dundee plants his foot on level ground, and presses with his heel the verdant bank, as he crosses the deep waters of Glenroy.)

Glen Roy is well to the east of Dalnabea and of Corriechoillie. It was also the country of MacDonald of Keppoch, whom Dundee had already encountered outside Inverness. Keppoch's people had retreated into the hills to avoid the attentions of Macintosh (see p.77) and he himself was at Armadale in Skye on the 18th May, accepting the Lieutenant-Colonelcy of a regiment to be raised by his kinsman Sir Donald MacDonald of Sleat. [2] Even if Dundee had wanted to meet him then he would still not have needed to cross the Roy to do so, as Keppoch House was, and its successor still is on the west bank. We are therefore left with the problem of why

Dundee crossed the Roy at all and why no crossing of the Spean is mentioned. We come across the same problem later on in *The Grameid* where Dundee is discovered setting out his camp by the banks of the 'sounding Roy',[3] although there is little room there for a camp of the size he was envisaging and we know anyway from *Iain Lom*, the Keppoch bard, that the camp lay in the Great Glen between the Lochy and the Spean.[4] A further point is that Dundee wrote his letters while in Lochaber from Moy or Strone, both these places being on the north bank of the River Lochy. He would hardly have set up his headquarters there if his men had been encamped in Glen Roy which is at least twenty miles away, whereas the camp *Iain Lom* talks of is more like five miles distant.

Surely Philip must have made a mistake and confused the two rivers. Or could it be that the river formed by the mingling of the Spean and the Roy was at that time known as the Roy whereas today it is called the Spean? Murdoch (Philip's translator) himself suggests this possibility but does not elaborate upon it.[5]

The theory gains some further slight support if we consider the relative importance, as highways, of the three glens, Gloy, Roy and Spean. Glen Gloy was the most important of these, being an ancient highway leading to Garvamore and the east and strategically placed to take traffic from further west beyond the Great Glen. Of the other two Glen Roy was more important than Glen Spean as it took traffic from the south up to Glen Gloy whereas Glen Spean was only of local importance. The insignificance of Glen Spean in terms of traffic might have coloured the way the two rivers, Spean and Roy, were looked at.

Philip only once refers to the Spean and then he is speaking of it as it comes out of Loch Laggan, long before it encounters the Roy.

Having made all these points I am bound to admit that there seems to be no local recollection of any such reversal of names now. But Philip's repeated use of the River Roy where we would expect the River Spean no doubt explains the insistence of many writers, particularly the earlier ones, that the camp was in Glen Roy.

After Dundee had crossed the river, whatever its name then was, he probably continued westwards for a while but not perhaps for long, as the journey up from Loch Treig could well have taken him most of the day for many of his companions were now reduced to travelling on foot. We can only guess at where he stopped for the night. Wherever it was the impression given in *The Grameid* is that they met nobody and after another freezing night spent the next morning running up and down the hills to see where they were and finding everything unrelentingly cold and awful. Balhaldy attempts a verse translation of the relevant passage:

Arrived on Abria's skirts we nothing spy,
But mountains frowning in the clouded sky,

And rugged rocks which round in fragments lye;
Impetuous torrents rage in vales below,
And pools and lakes, their lazy waters show.
Thin cotages the unequall fields adorn,
O'erspread with briars, and rough with prickly thorn;
With warring winds and storms the air is toss'd.
And the ground hardened with perpetual frost!
A desart wild, impatient of the plough,
Where nought but thistles, shrubs, and bushes grow,
And barren heath: And on the mountains high
Deep snow in frozen beds afflicts the eye;
While streams benumb'd with cold forgett to flow,
Stiffen in ice, and into solid grow![6]

Not as close to the Latin, of course, as Murdoch's prose translation but it gives a vivid picture of the weather and the wild scenery they had, so unexpectedly, to face. Little wonder that Dundee's followers lamented their situation:

'Alas' they cry, 'to what unknown land has our fate carried us, to what ungenial clime? 'Mid wood and rock and desert we wander, in regions of eternal snow, where Russian winter holds all things in its icy grasp. Lochaber, surely, is the extremity of that earth which Amphitrite, nurse of the stars, holds in her watery bosom.[7]

Whether on their first morning they really ran up the hillsides to look around them, as Philip tells us, seems unlikely. The description of what they saw: Ben Nevis, Corpach, Keppoch, the Gloy, the Roy and Loch Laggan, may be just Philip's way of explaining their geographical position. I cannot in any case believe that all these places can be seen from a point near Roy Bridge as the translator suggests.[8]

They will have found their situation little improved when they emerged from Glen Spean into the wider landscapes of the Great Glen. Some softer winds from the sea may have reached them there but they were also faced with the great bulk of Ben Nevis and its attendant bens. On a winter's day of snow the great mass of whitened rock, even though it may shine in the cold sunlight, seems to send out freezing blasts borne to the traveller by some means other than the wind; they settle into his bones more and more surely as the day declines.

But spirits began to rise once the news of their arrival got abroad. According to Balhaldy Lochiel appeared to welcome them and offered Dundee the use of a house which Balhaldy says was a mile from Lochiel's own.[9] But Lochiel had two houses; his original home at Tor Castle and his new one at Achnacarry. The ruins of Tor Castle can still be seen today on the west bank of the Lochy about three miles north-east of Banavie, It is hidden away amidst mossy woods and stands high above a deep, still pool in which the river, rock-filled and turbulent a little higher up, lingers for a time before making a further turn in its course. This old castle, or its predecessor upon much the same site, is believed to have been the castle of the Thanes of Lochaber and thus of Shakespeare's Banquo, if indeed he ever existed at all. In the beautiful woods beside the river about a mile higher up is a secluded avenue known as Banquo's Walk; it is about twenty feet wide and a quarter of a mile long. It begins and ends abruptly, the trees closing in at either end and the way becoming uneven. It may once have been part of an approach road to the castle; there are certainly stretches between it and the castle which suggest a highway but the planting of trees round about has made it difficult to see exactly how the castle was originally approached. Soft moss and grass and wild flowers grow over this avenue and on its banks to either side, barely a foot higher than the walk itself, are beech and oak, sycamore and birch, letting the sunlight in shafts into the damp, green silence. Here, according to traditions going back at least 200 years, for Banquo's Walk is mentioned in the Statistical Account of Scotland prepared at the end of the eighteenth century,[10] Banquo used to walk, turning over the problems of his time and hearing at the back of his thoughts the River Lochy swirling and bubbling amongst great stones as it fought its way between winding rocky banks to Loch Linnhe and the sea.

At Tor Castle however Lochiel had felt himself overlooked by the Fort at Inverlochy about five miles away to the south as the crow flies. The fort had been built by Cromwell as part of his system of surveillance of the Highlands and, although Tor Castle could not be seen from it, parties of men could walk out along the opposite bank and keep an eye on what Lochiel was doing which, given the situation prevailing in the 1650s, was not a good idea. Lochiel had therefore moved during that decade to a new house at Achnacarry, very close to where the present Achnacarry House stands. It was 'all built of Fir-planks, the handsomest of that kind in Britain',[11] but the gable wall was of stone and is still standing – the only part of the house which survived burning by Hanoverian troops in 1746. Lochiel's fir planks will have burnt well. By Dundee's time there was no fort at Inverlochy; it had been 'slighted' at the Restoration – but having once moved to Achnacarry Lochiel would not have wished to return to Tor Castle, although it was occupied by family members until well into the eighteenth century.

Of the two places, Strone and Moy, from which Dundee wrote his letters and which he probably used as headquarters Strone is four or five miles from Tor Castle and more than ten from Achnacarry whilst Moy is six to seven miles from Tor Castle and eight from Achnacarry, so we have to stretch Balhaldy's 'mile' a little whichever house he means. Whether

Dundee used Strone and Moy much except as somewhere quiet to write his letters or for occasional meetings of his officers is unclear. He certainly sometimes slept at the camp with his men for when he sent for MacSwyne to take a letter to James in Ireland it was night and MacSwyne found him at the camp.[12]

Earlier writers were for a time under the misapprehension that Strone stood for 'Struan', which caused them to presume that Dundee spent the weeks from May to July in Badenoch. It has also been suggested, with a great deal more reason, that Strone was actually Stronaba[13] – an area of land bordering on the present A82 north of the Commando Memorial. It almost overlooks the fields where the clans gathered and would thus have been eminently suitable as a dwelling for Dundee. Stronaba, however, was in the territory of the MacMartin Camerons and so would not strictly speaking have been in Lochiel's gift. Also, Strone and Moy must have been near one another as they were used interchangeably and they must also have been on the west bank of the Lochy as *Dòmhnall Gorm Og* of Sleat (the younger Sir Donald) passed them on his way to the camp from Kinlocheil (see below p.131).

Lochiel comes to us out of the pages of Balhaldy's Memoirs as the first mover and organiser of the Jacobite clans and the greatest of Highland chiefs. Balhaldy however was his grandson and therefore not an entirely impartial observer. It would also appear that the Memoirs were written largely at the instigation of the Gentle Lochiel to counteract criticisms of the Camerons, stemming probably from the behaviour of Ewen's grandfather during Montrose's wars, from Ewen's own behaviour during the last few years of the Protectorate, when he had collaborated with Cromwell's officers and made quite a good thing out of it, but mainly and more recently from the collapse of the Cameron contingent at Sheriffmuir; the left wing, where they were placed, broke and ran away, whereas the right wing, which included the MacDonalds, was victorious. This gave rise to some ribald remarks by the Camerons' MacDonald neighbours, including scathing verse from the Keppoch poetess, *Sìlis na Ceapaich*.[14] David Bruce, writing in 1750, describes the cloud hanging over the reputation of the Camerons:

> Their neighbours the McLeans, McDonalds and Stuarts used to upbraid them with being good Plunderers but bad Soldiers, 'till about 100 years ago that Sir Evan Cameron their Chief, a Bold Resolute man, brought them to perform Considerable Feats against Cromwell and afterwards against King William at Killicrankey, but in his Son's Time they behaved so shamefully at Sheriff Muir and were so often upbraided with their Cowardice and bad behaviour that the Scandal of this did not a little Contribute to make them Exert themselves in the Late Rebellion, that they might (as they calle'd it) recover their Character.[15]

Most of us, seeing what fine supporters of the House of Stuart the Cameron chiefs were in 1689 and in 1745–6 assume that they were so always. But if we look closely into the records of the mid-seventeenth century a rather different picture emerges, paricularly in relation to Montrose's great victory at the battle of Inverlochy. The recorded details on which we have to draw for a picture of the Clan Cameron's position at that time are as follows:

1. Wishart, Montrose's Chaplain, does not mention the Camerons at any time in his *Deeds of Montrose*.
2. Most historians mention a Cameron presence at Inverlochy but give no clear picture of what they were doing there or exactly who they were.
3. John Stewart of Ardvorlich in his history of Clan Cameron glosses over Inverlochy, a name so often invoked by the seanachies (historians) of Clan Donald that it seems incredible that any exploits of Clan Cameron at that battle should not have been described by the Cameron seanachies and made much of.[16]
4. Balhaldy says that Ewen's grandfather, *Ailean Dubh Mac Dhòmhnuill Dhuibh*, brought in 300 Camerons to Montrose's army after the latter's return from the raid into Argyll. He also says that it was Ailean who sent a warning to Montrose at Cill Chuimein to the effect that Argyll was at Inverlochy; Ailean watched the battle and waited on Montrose afterwards.[17]
5. Camerons from the west of the Lochy river were brought in after Inverlochy by Ailean, according to Father MacBreck, who got his information from a priest who accompanied Montrose's Irish soldiers,[18] while Mackenzie confirms that they went over to Montrose after the battle, having been regarded as allies by the Campbells.[19]
6. According to the *Book of Clanranald* only Camerons from the east of the Lochy joined Alasdair MacColla when on his way back from recruiting for Montrose in the west; this was before the raid into Argyll.[20]
7. Cowan says that Ailean hesitated about joining Montrose but did send some Camerons to Inverlochy,[21] whereas Calum I. MacLean has a story, but he does not give his source, that Ailean's son John, with a party of Camerons, was sent to the battle but that John stayed at a copse called Bad Abraich between Corpach and Banavie and merely watched.[22] Apart from the fact that John had been dead for ten years and someone else must have been in charge, this seems a plausible tale as some of its details fit in with the statement made by Archibald Colquhoun of Port Appin that the Cameron clansmen were on the Braes of Corpach and were encouraged to come over to Montrose by *Iain Lom*. The rest of this traditional story, as recounted

by Archibald Colquhoun and recorded by J.F. Campbell, describes how Ailean, hearing that Argyll was going off in his galley and leaving the direction of the battle to the gentlemen of his clan, went to him at Corpach and said: '*Theid mi fein leat, ach cha gheall mi gun theid mo dhaoine leat*' (I will go with you but I cannot promise that my men will go with you). He then went into the galley with Argyll and they sailed to Camus nan Gall on the Ardgour side of Loch Linnhe from where they could watch the battle, leaving Ailean's clansmen still on the Braes of Corpach.[23]

From these diverse but to some extent corroborative accounts the following scenario might be deduced:

Ailean went down to Inverlochy with a party of his clansmen under the command of some of the gentlemen of the clan. His intention was that they would support Argyll but he was doubtful of their response, hence his remark to Argyll '... *ach cha gheall mi gun theid mo dhaoine leat*'. After he had gone into Argyll's galley his clansmen stayed in the Braes of Corpach, uncertain what to do. *Iain Lom* may have tried to persuade them to go over to Montrose but they did not do so until after the battle. Their defection from Argyll is corroborated by John Willcock,[24] who accuses them of turning traitor and abandoning Argyll.

Ailean's behaviour becomes understandable if we remember that his son John had married a daughter of Robert Campbell of Glenfalloch (later, on the death of a brother, of Glenorchy) and that Argyll was the guardian of his eldest grandson; also, Ailean himself, after struggling all his life against claims on his lands and attempts by Huntly to seize part of them, had accepted Argyll as his superior for his northern territories. He would appear, at the same time, to have accepted Argyll's political and religious outlook.[25] We know that he, together with others including Duncan Cameron (presumably MacMartin) of Letterfinlay, petitioned the Presbyterian Synod in 1642 to send a minister to Lochaber.[26]

The Synod Records list only a few Camerons who were excommunicated for following Montrose, these being Alexander of Glen Nevis, Angus of Inverlochy and Cameron of Blarmachfoldach.[27] They are all Camerons from the east of the Lochy and it is probably they who feature in accounts of Montrose's Inverlochy battle line – too few in number to excite much comment. Alexander of Glen Nevis had been in arms against Ailean in the past.[28]

It would therefore appear that Ewen took over from his grandfather with a distinctly non-royalist tradition behind him, although it seems extremely likely that the other gentlemen of the clan had not seen eye to eye with Ailean and might be glad if their new chief were to take a different view.

When Dundee first met Sir Ewen Cameron or, to give him his Gaelic patronymic, *Eoghan Dubh Mac Ailean Mhic Dhòmhnuill Dhuibh*, the latter was sixty years old. (I am only assuming here that they had not met before; it is not impossible that they may have met if they both happened to be in London or Edinburgh at the same time, but there is nothing in the literature to suggest this.) Ewen's mother, it will be remembered, was a daughter of Robert Campbell of Glenfalloch (later of Glenorchy) and although her family was a branch of the Campbells of Breadalbane it was by no means entirely outwith the influence of Argyll.

It was usual for the sons of chiefs to be fostered during their early years by other members of the clan or even closely associated clans – a custom which strengthened the bonds between chief and clansmen or between chief and neighbouring gentlemen. Indeed the bonds between a foster child and his foster parents and brothers seem to have been particularly strong and there are many cases where a foster brother saved his chief's life thinking himself honoured to be able to give his own life for a man who was both brother and chief; Ewen himself was to be saved in this way. His foster father was MacMartin of Letterfinlay, the MacMartins being a sept of Clan Cameron, absorbed into the larger unit because of proximity and a need for mutual protection.

Until Ewen was twelve years old, his father having died when he was six and his grandfather being a very old man, his upbringing was shared between MacMartin and Cameron of Fassfern, his uncle, but at this point the Earl of Argyll (8th Earl and later 1st and only Marquis) felt it advisable to take his education in hand and Ewen therefore went to live at Inveraray Castle, the chief stronghold of Clan Campbell, where he became a favourite of his guardian. Argyll had difficulty persuading Ewen's friends to allow this. Here we have what seems today to be a quite piquant situation, that is, a close tie between a future Cameron chief and the head of the hated Clan Campbell, but the dividing line between the two was not as sharp as we tend to believe today and there were lots of arrangements, intermarriages and kindly acts which blurred the line between the two camps. During the 1650s, for instance, Ewen several times asked for advice and help from his former guardian, although he was engaged in military activities quite opposed to the government of the time of which Argyll was a pillar.

Whatever reservations we may have about the 8th Earl, he certainly did his duty as guardian well, but we can be equally certain that he did not burden his charge with the opinions of his own political opponents or even tell him much of what was happening in the greater world. This left Ewen quite in the dark about Montrose, his political beliefs and his exploits on behalf of the King, so that if he heard anything about his grandfather's stance during that period he will not have been surprised by it.

In 1645 Montrose's first campaign ended in his defeat at the battle of Philiphaugh. His supporters were being rounded up, amongst them Sir Robert Spottiswoode and William Murray, the brother of the Earl of Tullibardine, a young man of about the same age as Ewen. Hearing of the fate awaiting them Ewen visited them while in St Andrews with his guardian. He was profoundly impressed by all they told him and greatly moved by their courage and resolution. The next day he was obliged to watch their execution and subsequently revealed to his guardian his unease with the political views he had up to then taken for granted.

Balhaldy expresses surprise that Argyll, in spite of the fact that he was entirely dedicated to supporting the Covenant, whereas the Camerons, as Balhaldy saw it, or as he wishes us to see it, were determined to restore the King, should yet have continued his care for the education of the young man who had now, in 1647, at the age of eighteen, become Chief of the clan on the death of his grandfather. His relationship with Ailean and his fondness for Ewen must have had something to do with it, but he must also have had it in mind that it would be no bad thing to have the leader of the Camerons in his pocket. It is interesting that in expressing his surprise Balhaldy points out that

> ...the Camerons and their Chief sided openly with that hero [Montrose], and that old Locheill, though unable to serve in these wars on account of his age and other infirmitys, was, however, the true instrument that drew on the battle of Inverlochay, which coast Argyle the lives of so many of his friends...[29]

This suggests that a veil had been drawn over Ailean's behaviour by Ewen or that a veil was being drawn by Balhaldy himself to preserve the good impression that his Memoirs were supposed to create.

Ewen, whom we must now call Lochiel as his grandfather was dead, had his eighteenth birthday in 1647 and was determined to leave his guardian and take his place as Chief of Clan Cameron. The gentlemen of the clan were equally determined to get him back and were finally able to persuade Argyll to let his favourite go. On his return to Lochaber he found that he had to face the same difficulties over claims to his lands that had faced earlier chiefs, indeed the chiefs of any clans which held their lands *còir a' chlaidheimh* (by the sword) and not 'by sheepskin', the parchment on which a grant of land would be written. These difficulties arose essentially because a feudal system which applied in the lowlands and the royal court was impinging on the patriarchal system which applied in the Highlands. In the patriarchal system the chief did not own the land, it belonged to the whole clan; in Scotland the title of the monarch, reflecting the attitudes of this system, which had originally applied all over Scotland, was not King of Scotland but King of Scots. This belief in the common ownership of land persisted in the minds of many Highlanders until well into the nineteenth century when, at the time of the Clearances, the idea that they could be removed from lands on which their families had lived for centuries was quite incomprehensible to the dispossessed.

Much of the unrest and feuding between clans, particularly after the disintegration of the Lordship of the Isles in 1492, was the result of subinfeudation, the introduction of a 'middleman' between the King and owners or inhabitants of an area of land. The middleman was usually some great noble to whom the King wished to show favour. He could override the chief of the clan occupying that land and demand duties from those who lived upon it, duties which they were used to giving to their chief. This could not be done of course where the chief involved possessed a charter confirming his ownership of the land, but many chiefs did not have this. They had held the land over the centuries by right of the sword or, in some cases, by charters from the Lords of the Isles which the King of Scots felt at liberty to ignore once the Lordship had been abolished. In fact all the charters of the Lords of the Isles were declared null and void by James IV. The Cameron lands had always been held by the sword and clan affairs had been bedevilled for many years by claims made against them by the Earls of Huntly and by Macintosh of Macintosh. It would take too long and be too tedious to relate all the ins and outs of Lochiel's skirmishes with these magnates, but they remained a constant thorn in his side for many years.

When Charles I was executed in 1649 the Scots, few of whom had done anything to help him, were nevertheless incensed that a King of the House of Stuart should be deposed without any reference to them. They therefore invited his son to come over from Holland and crowned him at Scone in 1651. The very uneasy accommodation that was arrived at between Charles II on the one hand and Argyll and the Covenanters on the other soon came to an end and in 1652 Lochiel who, mercifully for his clan, had missed the disastrous Battle of Worcester because of some delay or other, found himself taking 700 Camerons to join the Earl of Glencairn's Rising in support of the King in the north of Scotland.[30] During his time with this army Lochiel distinguished himself in both set battles and guerilla attacks and received the congratulations of the King. It was while he was away on these exploits that Cromwell decided to build a fort at Inverlochy to control the disaffected clans. All the materials for the fort were brought in by sea and Lochiel got back to Tor Castle too late to do anything about it. The soldiers at this fort were a constant annoyance to him, not only keeping an eye on him, as already described, but also cutting down his timber without so much as a word to him, not to mention taking game and wild fowl. In a series of raids and attacks in which Lochiel always had far fewer men than his opponents, he chased them off his territory and killed large numbers of them. Although all his attacks on the soldiers of the fort were doubtless indirectly of use to the King's supporters we are obliged to admit that they were made more in the spirit of an enraged landlord than as aid to the House of Stuart.

Lochiel was eventually persuaded that a truce with the Fort and with Cromwellian structures in general would be in his interest; other chiefs had already come to an accommodation with Cromwell but Lochiel was determined to obtain good terms in any agreement he made. He had the bright idea of bagging three English colonels along with Lieutenant-Colonel Duncan Campbell who, he had heard, were staying together at an inn near Inveraray. He led an expedition there, seized the four men and brought them back to Lochaber, where he installed them on the island in Loch Arkaig. Their quarters cannot have been exactly luxurious but in other ways Lochiel was the perfect host. He visited his captives every day, arranged feasts for them and took them ashore so that they could hunt the many deer in his forests. This was done by the gruesome method of driving the deer into a confined area and then rushing in amongst them with broadswords which, Balhaldy tells, the captives greatly enjoyed as they had never done it before.[31] In his conversations with his captives Lochiel assured them of his intention to continue his war against Cromwell and they in their turn tried to persuade him to make peace, but he was clever enough only to dissemble his desire for war and to give the appearance of being gradually persuaded to their way of thinking, provided that the terms would be as far as possible of his own choosing. Argyll, '...who still honoured him with his friendship as much as ever',[32] helped with the negotiations.

It was agreed that the Camerons should keep their arms, provided that they kept the peace, and should not be obliged to take an oath to the Protector, whose name was not even to be mentioned in the agreement. Also, which must have been an enormous relief to Lochiel, any bygone duties which Macintosh had demanded of him should be cancelled, any future duties being decided by Monck (Cromwell's General in Scotland).

On a bright day in May in 1655 Lochiel prepared to lay down his arms. He persuaded his ex-prisoners to accompany him to the Fort and set out from Achnacarry, superbly accoutred and accompanied by his 'tail'. A chief's 'tail' at that time could consist of some or all of the following:

piobair	piper
bàrd	poet
seanachaidh	historian, seanachie
fear sporain	treasurer
teachdaire	herald
fear brataich	bannerman
gille airm	armour bearer
gille mòr	sword bearer

gille cas fliuch	attendant who carried the chief over streams, etc.
gille comh-sreathainn	attendant who took care of the chief's horse
gille cium	body servant
gille cupa	cup bearer
gille phiobar	piper's attendant. The piper was a gentleman and could not be expected to carry his own pipes
gille truis-airnis	baggage carrier
gille coise	henchman
luchd taighe	fighting men

No doubt Lochiel brought as many of these as he could! The gentlemen of the clan and the clansmen followed. All were fully armed and looking their best as they marched down beside the Lochy and drew up, pipes playing and banners flying, in front of the Fort. The Governor brought out his men and drew them up in lines and the Camerons laid down their arms in the name of the King and took them up again in the name of the State (as arranged there was no mention of the hated Protector). A feast followed but Lochiel and the Governor were careful to keep the two groups separate in case any brawling or memory of past animosities, not to mention deaths, should upset the tranquil scene. Friendship with the Fort increased in the following years and Lochiel found, with his enemies Huntly and Macintosh held at bay by the presence of Cromwell's standing army, that he was really doing well out of the arrangements. In 1657 he even had time to marry a girl on whom his heart had long been set, the sister of Sir Allan MacLean of Duart.

In 1660 came the Restoration which we might reasonably expect to be even more acceptable to Lochiel, but he was soon to discover that the opposite was the case, for there was no longer a standing army in Scotland or a Fort at Inverlochy to keep the peace. The King had ordered all the forts to be 'slighted' and had to return to the old method of controlling affairs by means of local magnates; in short, there was no protection against Macintosh should he start his machinations against Lochiel again. And indeed he was not very long in doing so and managed to get on far enough to obtain a Commission of Fire and Sword against Lochiel. His only difficulty was that all the people who were supposed to help him in this suddenly became very busy with something else or expressed grave doubts as to their suitability for the work.

Agreements were made and unmade and compromises suggested, but Macintosh remained unappeased. In 1662 he was granted a decree permitting him to remove Lochiel's clansmen from the disputed lands but this came to nothing and he arrived eventually near Achnacarry with 1,500 men and faced Lochiel across the River Arkaig. The future Earl of

Breadalbane (*Iain Glas* – Sallow John – a kinsman of Lochiel on his mother's side) arrived with 300 men, determined to stop any bloodshed and declared that he would come in on the side of whoever was attacked first. Macintosh was already in some strategic difficulty due to Lochiel's manoeuvring of his forces around Loch Arkaig and this final blow forced him to come to an agreement which at the time appeared to end the dispute forever. Unfortunately other disputes arose with Argyll (the son of Lochiel's guardian) and with Atholl, relating to Lochiel's problems in obtaining the money he had to pay to Macintosh as part of the agreement reached. Finally Lochiel found himself involved with Macintosh again because that chief was disputing the ownership of the land of his neighbour, MacDonald of Keppoch.

Throughout these difficulties the King was on Lochiel's side, as was the Duke of York, but they could not intervene on any point of law. Lochiel was knighted by York in Edinburgh in 1682 in recognition of his services to the King during the 1650s, services diluted, some would say, by his fraternisation with the Fort in the last years of the Protectorate – hence perhaps the lateness of the honour.

Ewen was a larger-than-life character. His grandson and memorialist says of him:

> He was of the largest size, his countenance fresh and smooth, and he had a certain air of greatness about him which struck the beholders with awe and respect.[33]

In *The Grameid* he appears:

> ...mounted on a grey horse, he shines in a tricoloured tunic trimmed all round with gold lace...His savage glance, and the swarthy hue of his Spanish countenance, his flashing eyes, his beard and moustache curled as the moon's horn...[34]

In the oil painting of him at Achnacarry his moustache has not yet reached this excessively curly stage, as the portrait is of a younger man, but we see his thick, dark hair, his bright eyes and dark complexion and, above all, his intense vitality as though he were ready to jump out of the canvas at us. He put up a tremendous fight for the King and for his clansmen who, under a weaker chief, might well have been expelled from their lands and blown about the Highlands like chaff – broken, landless men, like the MacGregors, seeking a place to stay wherever they might, some with friendly clans, others perhaps in the wilds of Rannoch, that refuge of caterans and thieves.

A splendid reminder of Sir Ewen can still be seen in the Clan Cameron Museum at Achnacarry – his very large brown boots. They are displayed more or less at eye level with a little notice begging us not to touch them, an injunction which I have so far managed to obey. How splendid it would be to place just one finger on that smooth, shiny leather surface. The boots are in very good condition, I suspect because they were little worn. On the way to Killiecrankie it is said that he dropped behind for a few moments to remove his footwear so that he could run on more easily and fight more comfortably on foot.

This was the man who came to meet Dundee somewhere to the west of Dalnabea. He offered him the use of his houses at Strone and Moy and promised him food until they had eaten the last cow in Lochaber, a time which might have arrived rather quickly in that hard season, had it not been for the skill of his neighbour, MacDonald of Keppoch, who could always find cattle for the taking and who had already, as we have seen, taken quite a few from Macintosh.

A camp was established. The weather continued very cold and the men who had arrived with Dundee continued to find their conditions far from enviable. They were obliged to drink water instead of wine and to eat black bread, bannocks made with oats blackened from being fired to dry them and burn off the husks.[35,36] According to Murdoch's translation of *The Grameid* they sheltered from the weather in 'rude huts', but the Latin words used are *'sub pellibus tonsis'*[37] – under clipped skins – so it seems more likely that they wrapped animal skins round their shoulders to make up for their perhaps rather light clothing. They had, after all, been expecting a summer campaign.

But in the face of all these miseries Dundee himself remained indomitable; they were the least of his worries:

> Under the miserable hardships of this barren land secret complaints arise among the companions of the Graham, but he himself neither hunger nor cold nor tempest affect, strong in his devotion to his King. Unmoved by the bitterness of his fate, in the midst of difficulties and hardships he maintains his martial bearing, his fiery vigour, his steady constancy of mind, his unswerving fidelity. He frets only against the delays of war.[38]

But the delays of war were not to be long. Dundee had arrived, as arranged, by the 17th May and had met Lochiel on the 18th. The fiery cross was sent round to the loyal clans; they were to meet on the 25th, a week after Dundee's arrival:

> When the seventh morn, arising in Eastern light, had now shone forth and poured its rays over the waves...[39]

Notes

1. *Grameid*, Book II, lines 727–8.
2. Lord MacDonald's Papers. See Norman H. MacDonald: *The Clan Ranald of Lochaber*, published by the author, undated, p.26.
3. *Grameid*, Book III, line 224.
4. *Orain Iain Luim*, p.184, line 2362.
5. *Grameid*, p.94, note 2.
6. Balhaldy, p.239.
7. *Grameid*, Book III, lines 37–45.
8. ibid., p.80, note 1.
9. Balhaldy, p.239.
10. *The Statistical Account of Scotland 1791–1799, Inverness-shire, Ross and Cromarty*, Wakefield (EP Publishing Ltd.), 1481, pp.144–5.
11. *An Enquiry into the Genealogy and Present State of Ancient Scottish Surnames, etc.* by William Buchanan of Auchmar, p.129.
12. *Grameid*, Book III, line 527.
13. Michael Barrington: *Grahame of Claverhouse, Viscount Dundee*, London (Martin Secker), 1911. See map opposite p.400 on which Stronaba, near Mucomir, is marked as Strone.
14. *Bàrdachd Shìlis na Ceapaich*, ed. Colm Ó Baoill. Edinburgh (Scottish Gaelic Texts Society), p.40, verse 5. See also John Sibbald Gibson: Lochiel of the '45, Edinburgh (University Press), 1994, pp.41–43.
15. *The Highlands of Scotland*, ed. Andrew Lang, Edinburgh, 1898. Quoted in Gibson, op. cit., p.42–3.
16. *The Memoirs of James Marquis of Montrose 1639–1650*, ed. Rev. George Wishart, D.D., London (Longmans, Green & Co.), 1895. John Stewart of Ardvorlich. *A History of Clan Cameron*, published by the Clan Cameron Association, 1974.
17. Balhaldy, p.71.
18. William Forbes Leith: *Memoirs of Scottish Catholics during the Seventeenth and Eighteenth Centuries*, 2 vols., 1909, vol.I, p.323.
19. A. MacKenzie: *History of the Camerons*, 1884, p.92.
20. *The Book of Clanranald* in: Rev. Alexander Cameron: *Reliquiae Celticae. Text, Papers, and Studies in Gaelic Literature and Philology*, ed. Alexander Macbain and Rev. John Kennedy, Inverness, 1894, vol.II. Poetry, History, and Philology, p.181.
21. Edward J. Cowan: *Montrose. For Covenant and King*, Edinburgh (Canongate), 1995, p.179.
22. Calum I. MacLean: *The Highlands*, Edinburgh (Mainstream), 1990, p.97–8.
23. Quoted in Kevin Byrne: *Colkitto*, Colonsay (House of Lochar), 1997, p.145.
24. John Willcock: *The Great Marquess. Life and Times of Archibald, 8th Earl and 1st (and only) Marquis of Argyll (1607–1661)*, Edinburgh and London (Oliphant Anderson and Ferrier), 1903. p.174.
25. Walter Cameron: *Clan Cameron and Their Chiefs, Presbyterian and Jacobite*, in: *Transactions of the Gaelic Society of Inverness*, vol.XLVII, 1971–72, p.404.
26. ibid., p.404.
27. Synod Records, vol.1, p.25.
28. Walter Cameron: *Clan Cameron and Their Chiefs*, op. cit., p.405.
29. Balhaldy, p.71.
30. ibid., p.98.
31. ibid., p.143.
32. ibid., p.146.
33. ibid., (Editor's Introduction) p.24.
34. *Grameid*, Book IV, lines 149 - 163.
35. ibid., Book III, lines 225–6.

36. *Burt's Letters from the North of Scotland*, op.cit., pp.270–1.
37. *Grameid*, Book III, line 229.
38. ibid., Book III, lines 243–253.
39. ibid., Book IV, lines 42–3.

Sir Ewen Cameron of Lochiel (1625–1719),
from the oil painting at Achnacarry

CHAPTER FIVE

Dalcomera

Montrosio novus exoritur de pulvere phoenix,
Gramus...

The Grameid

(The Graham as a new phoenix rises from the ashes of Montrose...)

PERHAPS TO ACHIEVE a fine dramatic effect Philip waits until
the beginning of the fourth book of *The Grameid* and the very morning of
the gathering to tell us the name of the place where Dundee's Highland
army paraded before him:

Est locus Abriacis fama celebratus in oris
Ardua qua latos pandit Dalcomera campos
At vero aequoreae qua littora spectat Iernae.[1]

(In the coasts of Lochaber is a place of great fame where high Dalcomera
spreads out her wide fields and looks towards the shores of sea-girt
Ireland.) [Author's translation]

It is so vast a place he tells us that it could not be filled by the hosts of
Xerxes or by the bands of Agamemnon. Is it a place of great fame because
of Dundee's gathering there? Or was it already famous from earlier gatherings or battles? If the latter these have all vanished from the folk memory
and only a vague feeling that battles and gatherings did take place there
now remains.

Dalcomera is not a name you will find on any map, being a latinised
version of a Gaelic placename. General opinion and local tradition have
it that it was the land lying (before the canal was built) between the Lochy
and the Spean and stretching up towards Stronaba beside the present A82.

In a document dated 1466 granting lands in Lochaber to Macintosh
this area is named Nucomer and on Pont's map (surveyed 1590 to 1610)
it is Mackomer. Nucomer could be a mishearing of *Magh comair* (the plain
of the confluence) or it could be a version of *Dail na comair* (the field of
the confluence) with *dail* left out. Mackomer resembles *Magh comair* and
is actually a good representation of the way these words might be

pronounced by someone with English as mother tongue.

According to Somerled Macmillan the place came to be called Dalmacommer after 1689 because of Dundee's gathering there, the earlier form being Mucomir (*Magh comair*), as it is today.[2] If he is right *dail* must have been dropped later on as memory of the gathering receded. His theory is supported by the fact that it is unusual to find *magh* and *dail* in the same placename, as the two words have similar meanings. On the other hand if the name was Mucomir at the time of the gathering why did Philip call it Dalcomera, inserting *dail* and omitting *magh*? He must have regarded *magh* as an element that could justifiably be dispensed with and this gives rise to the question: Was it *magh* that then stood before *comair* or was it a more insignificant word, i.e. *na*, the genitive of the article?

It is perhaps worth pointing out here that the 'mu' of Mucomir possibly derives from *muigh* the dative of *magh*; the dative form gained ground because place-names occur more often in the dative than in the nominative, e.g. The house is at Mucomir. I am going to Mucomir, etc.

Young Clanranald, in a letter written after the '45, says that the Prince marched (from Loch Eil) to Moy (which is north of Glen Loy). He then crossed the Lochy (place unspecified but presumably at the Dalcomera ford) and encamped at the foot of Glen Loy (he must have meant Glen Gloy) on the high road between Fort Augustus and Fort William at a place called Dalnacomar.[3] So *dail*, whenever it was introduced, was still in use until at least the middle of the eighteenth century and usage at that time had come down on the side of *na* as the intermediate word and not *magh*. Or perhaps it was just a question all the time of mishearing the very similar consonants 'n' and 'm'.

But whichever of these versions may be the correct one, the stress certainly falls on the syllable 'com' in all of them, including the Latin form – Dalcomera – as we can see if we scan Philip's lines. Given all these conflicting possibilities it is perhaps simplest to stick to Philip's Latin version. It embraces all opinions and all times.

Dalcomera is flat or at most on a gentle slope, as its name would suggest; it provides an open area of more than a square mile, a rare phenomenon amidst these mountains. In Dundee's time, of course, it was not cut in two by the re-routing of the Lochy river and Philip tells us that it was covered with heather,[4] whereas today it is a series of quiet fields, grazed by sheep and cattle and, from May onwards, full of daisies. It rises gradually towards Stronaba and Blairour which form part of a rounded ridge above which rises a line of high mountains culminating to the south in Ben Nevis. This ridge obscures the lower portions of these great hills, making them seem smaller than they are, whilst at the same time giving to the flat area a feeling of height, although it is actually only 70–100 metres above sea level. This perhaps explains why Philip called it 'Dalcomera ardua'.[5]

To an army Dalcomera has the great advantage that all points of the compass are accessible to it – Inverness and Fort Augustus further north up the Great Glen, Inverlochy to the south, Laggan and Blair Atholl to the east through the deep cleft of Glen Gloy, Rannoch via the Lairig Leacach and Glencoe by branching off the Lairig through the mountains above Kinlochleven. To the west lie two routes to the coast and the islands, one taking the traveller beside Loch Arkaig and through Glen Dessary or Glen Pean and the other going towards Loch Eil and so to Ardgour, Morvern, Ardnamurchan and Arisaig. It is also hidden away in the wilds of Lochaber and had available to it a ford over the River Lochy which eased the movement of men and animals. This is not the case today of course as the canal with a swing bridge over it has taken the place of the river and its ford.

For us with our complicated system of roads and bridges it is hard to imagine the difficulties faced in earlier centuries when confronted by a full and turbulent river. Burt, an Englishman who travelled in the Highlands in the 1720s, probably as an agent of General Wade, describes a party of Highlanders he saw negotiating a river which he had just ridden through himself:

Having passed the hill, I entered the river, my horse being almost at once up to his mid-sides; the guide led him by the bridle, as he was sometimes climbing over the loose stones which lay in all positions, and many of them two or three feet diameter; at other times with his nose in the water and mounted up behind. Thus he proceeded with the utmost caution, never removing one foot till he found the others firm and all the while seeming impatient of the pressure of the torrent, as if he was sensible that, once losing his footing, he should be driven away and dashed against the rocks below... The instant I had recovered the further side of the river, there appeared, near the water, six Highland men and women; these, I suppose had coasted the stream over rocks, and along the sides of steep hills, for I had not seen them before. Seeing they were preparing to wade, I stayed to observe them: first the men and the woman tucked up their petticoats, then they cast themselves into a rank, with the female in the middle, and laid their arms over one another's shoulders; and I saw they had placed the strongest towards the stream, as best able to resist the force of the torrent. In their passage, the large slippery stones, made some of them now and then lose their footing: and on these occasions, the whole rank changed colour and countenance.

I believe no painter ever remarked such strong impressions of fear and hope on a human face, with so many and sudden successions of those two opposite passions, as I observed among those poor people, but in the Highlands this is no uncommon thing.[6]

The ford by Dalcomera, always important, became still more so when Cromwell built the fort at Inverlochy. Making a crossing near Inverlochy under the eyes of the garrison, was not always very desirable and it was better, for instance when coming from the west along the north shore of Loch Eil, to continue up the west bank of the Lochy river to a point a little above where the Lochy was joined by the turbulent waters of the Spean. Another still more prudent alternative incorporating this ford and made use of by Prince Charles Edward on his march from Glenfinnan to the Corrieyairack, was to make a detour from the north shore of Loch Eil up Glen Suileag and down Glen Loy. This avoided the whole corner of land under the surveillance of the Fort and brought one out onto the road beside the Lochy about four miles south-west of Dalcomera. (The route via Corpach and Glen Laragain, which some believe was the one the Prince actually took, made similar use of the Dalcomera ford.)

The Prince used the ford again, in the opposite direction, on his final journey from Cluny's Cage to Loch nan Uamh to join the ship which took him back to France. The weather was wet and the river very full, but they managed to get hold of a leaky boat:

As they were approaching Lochiel's seat, Achnicarry, they came to the river Lochy at night, being fine moonshine. The difficulty was how to get over. Upon this Cluns Cameron met them on the water side at whom Lochiel asked how they would get over the river. He said, 'Very well, for I have an old boat carried from Lockharkaig that the enemy left unburnt of all the boats you had, Lochiel.' Lochiel asked to see the boat. Upon seeing it he said, 'I am afraid we will not be safe with it.' Quoth Cluns, 'I will cross first and show you the way.' The matter was agreed upon. Cluns upon reflection said, 'I have six bottles of brandy, and I believe all of you will be the better of a dram.' This brandy was brought from Fort Augustus, where the enemy lay in garrison, about nine miles from that part of Lochy where they were about to cross... Upon this three of the bottles were drunk. Then they passed the river Lochy by three crossings, Cluns Cameron in the first with so many, then the Prince in the second with so many, and in the last Lochiel with so many. In the third and last ferrying the crazy boat laked so much that there would be four or five pints of water in the bottom of the boat, and in hurrying over the three remaining bottles of brandy were all broke. When the Prince called for a dram it was told that the bottles were broke, and that the common fellows had drunk all that was in the bottom of the boat as being good punch, which had made the fellows so merry that they made great diversion to the company as they marched along.[7]

Others who used this ford may have included Calum Chille (St Columba), on his way to visit Brude, King of the Picts, at his fort at Creag Phàdraig by Inverness, and Macbeth, in his coffin, going to wait at Corpach (the field of bodies) for the ship that would take him for burial in Iona. Now Dundee was to use it often, going between his headquarters at Strone and the camp, as also would many of the clans arriving to join him from the west.

The chiefs and their clansmen arrived at Dalcomera at different times during the following two months. Many were there on the appointed day but some came in later, depending on how far away they were and whether or not they first had to deal with some local disturbance related to the current unrest in the country.

Philip, again perhaps for dramatic effect, or perhaps to get the whole question of who joined Dundee out of the way to save interruptions to his narrative later, describes everyone as being on the field on the 25th May and perhaps we should do the same. They make a most brilliant, not to say overwhelming picture and, luckily for their finery and panache, the weather had suddenly changed, as so often happens when softer weather has been long delayed.

The chiefs and the clan gentry wore dress of a most exalted nature, a scarlet coat perhaps, smothered in gold lace, or a 'golden' (presumably brass) helmet, but whatever they wore it generally incorporated a tartan plaid or some article of tartan clothing. The tartans we wear today, all with their clan names attached to them, are actually of Victorian origin; the original patterns were lost after the '45 when the wearing of tartan was forbidden, and the patterns had to be reinvented. In earlier times tartans were not attached to any particular clan but rather to a district and were woven to suit the taste of the local weaver or perhaps the wearer's wife. Thus a man's clan was not identified from his tartan but from the sprig of bog myrtle (Campbell) or pine (Grant) or oak (Cameron) he wore in his bonnet. Portraits of chiefs of this period often show them wearing two or three different tartans at once, none of them being the tartan we would associate with their clans today.

William Sacheverell, the Governor of the Isle of Man, who visited the West Highlands in 1688 with a view to recovering the Spanish treasure thought to have been sunk in Tobermory Bay, described the dress of that time as follows:

The usual outward habit of both sexes is the pladd; the women's much finer, the colours more lively, and the squares larger than the men's and put me in mind of the ancient Picts. This serves them for a veil, and covers both head and body. The men wear theirs after another manner, especially when designed for ornament; it is loose and flowing, like the mantles our painters give their heroes. Their thighs are bare, with brawney muscles...a thin brogue on the foot, a short buskin of various colours on the legg, tied about the calf with a striped pair of garters. What should be concealed is hid with a large shot pouch, on each side of which hangs a dagger and a pistol, as if they found it necessary to keep those parts well guarded. A round target on their backs, a blew bonnet on their heads, in one hand a broadsword and a musquet in the other. Perhaps no nation goes better armed; and I assure you they will handle them with bravery and dexterity, especially the sword and target.[8]

Perhaps amongst the most appealing pictures Philip paints of the assembled chiefs is of the young Sir John MacLean and his cousin Alexander (Philip calls him a brother), each mounted on a pure white horse and wearing scarlet tunics 'scaly with gold' (presumably gold lace), while over the shoulders of each floats a 'flowing plaid with yellow stripe'.[9] MacNeill of Barra has 'as many colours woven into his plaid as the rainbow in the clouds shows in the sunlight'.[10] Some chiefs and gentlemen may have worn *triubhas* (trews), trousers and hose in one piece of woven cloth, others the *fèileadh mòr*, the great belted plaid, superceded in the eighteenth century by our present 'short' kilt. Lochiel must have worn his tri-coloured tunic trimmed with gold lace over the *fèileadh mòr* as his tartan hose were visible.[11] The *fèileadh mòr* was an immense piece of cloth, two yards wide and six or more yards long, pleated at the back and tied round the waist by a belt. This left the top half hanging down over the belt; it could then be draped gracefully from one shoulder and held in place by a pin. When properly arranged it is the most beautiful of garments. It is also the most useful for in bad weather the top half can be used as a cape to cover shoulders and head and at night the whole can serve as a blanket.

The clansmen all wore the *fèileadh mòr*. Some had tartan hose, woven not knitted and held up with a garter. They also wore a saffron shirt reaching to the knee. William Camden in *Britannia*, written in 1586, says of a Highland army, 'They shine with yellow'. Saffron seems to have been a favourite colour of the Celts and the substance itself was a favoured specific against illness of all kinds. Philip tells us that when Keppoch assembled his men outside Inverness they were clad in a saffron colour and when speaking of those about to assemble at Dalcomera he describes them as 'stained with the crocus dye'.[12] The original *leine chròich* (saffron shirt) had consisted of 24 ells of linen (which works out at a staggering thirty yards) tied round the middle with a belt and reaching to the knee.[13] It was tightly pleated from top to bottom making it a sort of sculpted suit of armour known as an aketon and frequently to be seen depicted on ancient grave slabs; a coat of mail was often worn over or under it.[14]

The Keppoch MacDonalds assembled outside Inverness may have given a largely saffron impression because they had cast their plaids ready for battle. There are frequent references to clansmen casting their plaids before taking on the enemy and when they did so they would knot their shirts between their legs. There is a good illustration of this as part of the personal arms of Sir William Macpherson of Cluny, showing two fierce, bearded warriors with helmet and targe and tartan jacket over a shirt with its ends neatly tied in a bow over their private parts.[15] However, I do not personally believe that plaids were always cast, otherwise the great early eighteenth-century Jacobite poet, *Alasdair Mac Mhaighstir Alasdair*, would not have written in his poem *Am Breacan Uallach*, in praise of the plaid:

> 'S ciatach 'san adbhàns *thù*,
> Fo shrannaich nam pìob 's nam bratach.
> Cha mhios' anns an dol sìos thù,
> 'N uair sgriobar a duille claisich;
> Fior-earradh na ruaige,
> Gu luas a chur anns na casaibh![16]

(Graceful in the advance thou art,
When bagpipes sound and banners flutter.
Thou'rt splendid too, when comes the charge,
And swords are drawn from scabbards.
The finest garb to set the rout,
And in the feet put swiftness!)

A plaid cannot be splendid in the charge or graceful in the advance if it is lying in a heap on the ground.

It is not clear on what principle, if any, Philip arranged the order in which he presents the clans on the field of Dalcomera. Was it the actual order? This is hardly likely, except perhaps in part, as some of them did not appear until later. Or was it an order that suited him for some reason or other, e.g. indicating the chiefs he felt to be more important? It is even possible that there was no formal review at all. Balhaldy says nothing about it and it could just be a device for presenting the various dramatis personae. It is interesting however that the first person he introduces is not Lochiel but Glengarry.

Alasdair Dubh Mac Raonuill Mhic Dhòmhnuill was acting chief of the Glengarry MacDonnells as his father was an old man; he did not become 11th Chief until 1705. He was a youngish, tall man with dark hair and at Dalcomera appeared on a foaming steed '... towering in glittering arms...claymore in hand, his cloak shining with gold'.[17] A lament for his death in 1721, written by the poetess *Sìlis na Ceapaich*, who was the sister of Coll MacDonald of Keppoch (see below), praises him because:

> Bu tu ceann air céill 's air comhairl
> Anns gach gnothach am biodh cúram,
> Aghaidh shoilleir sholta thlachdmhor,

Cridhe fial farsaing mu 'n chùinneadh;
Bu tu roghainn nan sàr-ghaisgeach,
Ar guala thaice 's tu b' fhiùghail;
Leómhann smiorail fearail feumail,
Ceann feachda chaill Seumas Stiùbhart.

Bu tu 'n t-iubhar thar gach coillidh,
Bu tu 'n darach daingean làidir,
Bu tu 'n cuileann 's bu tu 'n draigheann,
Bu tu 'n t-abhall molach blàthmhor;
Cha robh do dhàimh ris a' chritheann
Na do dhligheadh ris an fheàrna;
Cha robh bheag ionnad de 'n leamhan;
Bu tu leannan nam ban àlainn.[18]

(You were the leader in wisdom and counsel in every activity where responsibility was concerned; bright, pleasant and handsome face, heart generous and liberal with money. You were the choice of excellent warriors, a shoulder to support us, as you were worthy to be; a courageous, manly and effective lion, a leader whom James Stuart has lost.

You were the yew above every forest, you were the strong steadfast oak, you were the holly and the blackthorn, you were the apple-tree, rough-barked and many-flowered. You had no kinship with the aspen, owed no bonds to the alder; there was none of the lime-tree in you; you were the darling of beautiful women.)

Philip seems to regard him as the most important of the chiefs, calling him 'the great glory of the Grampians, the heroic Glengarry'.[19] He may have been looking at him in the reflected glory of his predecessor, Lord MacDonnell and Aros, or perhaps Alasdair's record at Killiecrankie caused him to introduce or add these phrases after that battle. Philip tells us that he had 'borne the brunt of battle in his early years',[20] but as he was probably born in the 1650s he could not have fought in Charles II's battles or Glencairn's Rising and could therefore not have been involved in anything more than local skirmishes. Balhaldy gives us a more perceptive account of him which also throws some light on how a chief often needed to behave to keep a hold on his lands and to support his people. He was, Balhaldy tells us:

...a person of great penetration and good natural parts, but affected more to act in the manner of a politician than in that of ane open, frank, and sincear neighbour. Most of his actions might well admit of a double construction; and what he appeared generaly to be was seldome what he really was. Meer trifles seemed to be of the greatest consequence under his management; and he loved to meddle with no affair but what bore some distant view of honour or profite; such of his neighbours as were inferior to him in estate or command he cajolled and flattered, so that they became, in a manner, dependant on him, while he had use for their service; but that over, he seldome gave himself the trouble of returning their favours by suitable expressions of gratitude; yet, still he had that address and dexterity in his conduct, as to reingage them as often as he had occasion, and still the blame of any ill-useage they mett with was artfully charged upon themselves. By this means he ordinarly made as good a figure in the field as some of his neighbours that had double his command and following. With his supperiors and equalls he lived in constant emulation and jealousey, and governed his Clan with the authority and state of ane independent Prince. The leaders and captains of tribes he suppressed and keept doun, and seldome allowed any of them the honour of being admitted into his councill but with his commons he affected great popularity; and, what was odd, he was not only negligent of his person, but even of the economy of his house and family and the reason he gave for it was, that he loved not to deviate from the customes of his predecessors. Though he was ingaged in every attempt that was made for the restoration of King James and his family, yet he managed matters so that he lossed nothing in the event. The concerts and ingagements he entered into with his neighbours, in the issue of any undertaking for the common good, he observed onely in so far as suited with his oun particular interest, but still he had the address to make them bear the blame while he carried the profite and honour. To conclude, he was brave, loyall, and wounderfully sagacious and long-sighted; and was possessed of a great many shineing qualitys, blended with a few vices, which, like patches on a beautifull face, seemed to give a greater éclat to his character.[21]

After the damning indictment contained in most of the above quotation one wonders what the 'shineing qualitys' were. The charge that he acted more '... in the manner of a politician...' was certainly confirmed a few weeks later in connection with a cattle raid into Glen Urquhart by a party of Camerons. During this raid a MacDonald living in the Glen was killed and Glengarry fell into a great rage over the fate of one of his own clan, making a feud between himself and Lochiel seem very likely. Lochiel himself kept calm and Dundee was able to smooth things over, pointing out that life would be impossible if every chance killing were to be regarded as intentional and taken as a reason for a quarrel. Having expressed his wrath against the Camerons well within the hearing of his own clansmen, Glengarry then sat down to dinner with Lochiel and the other chiefs, as usual, quite amicably, and nothing more was heard of the matter for, as Balhaldy says:

...the truth is, Glengary, who was a person of profound judgement and great courage, acted merely out of policy, and meant nothing more by the great noise he made, but to ingratiate himself with his people, by humouring their vanity and shewing them that the least injury offered to the very meanest of them was equally his own quarrell; by which means he gained so upon his commons, that they assisted him to suppress and humble such of the better sort as pretended either to rivall or contradict him.[22]

Glengarry's lands lay about his castle of Invergarry on the west bank of Loch Oich and down Glen Garry itself to the sea. From the castle, now a ruin, there are long vistas up and down this narrow loch, thickly wooded on both sides. Behind the castle and to the west lies beautiful Glen Garry with its string of lochs; first Loch Garry itself with Ben Tee (possibly Beinn an t'Sith, the Fairy Hill) presiding over it, then Glen Quoich with Gleouraich and Sgurr a' Mhaoraich to the north and the hills hiding Glen Kingie to the south. Finally the sea loch, Loch Hourn, fed by the Allt Coire Sgoireadail, which plunges over rocky slabs and twists and turns to reach Kinlochhourn with rowans planting their feet in its bed and the sharp tops of the Glenshiel Forest peaks above it. Lovely Loch Hourn, narrow and steep at its head but gradually opening out its arms to Skye across the Sound of Sleat; slipping past Barrisdale, past Corran and Arnisdale below Beinn Sgritheall with the Cuillin peaks afloat in the western sky. Further off but still within the bounds of Alasdair Dubh's territory are Loch Nevis and the land of Knoydart, the Rough Bounds, still only accessible from the sea or on foot from Kinlochhourn to Barrisdale and so through Gleann an Dubh Lochan to Inverie.

Alasdair had a very different background from Lochiel. Whereas Lochiel's grandfather had been pro-Covenant to neutral during Montrose's wars, Glengarry's father, Ranald of Scotus, had taken over from his childless cousin german *Aonghas Mac Alasdair Dheirg*, the 9th Chief, created Lord MacDonnell and Aros in 1660. Aonghas had joined Montrose at Cill Chuimein, fighting in the centre of the front line at Inverlochy with the rest of Clan Donald. He also fought at Auldearn, Alford and Kilsyth. After Kilsyth he seems to have gone to the west with Alasdair MacColla who was trying to settle the affairs of his family in the face of Campbell aggression.

As Alasdair MacColla will be mentioned several times in the following pages it might be appropriate to say a few words about him here. His Gaelic name was *Alasdair Mac Cholla Chiotaich* (Alasdair son of Coll the Left-handed). Coll the Left-handed (*Colla Ciotach*) played an important part in the affairs of the MacDonalds of Dunyveg (in Islay) and the Glens (of Antrim) – *Clann Iain Mhoir* – but he has been rather overshadowed by his son Alasdair, who went to Scotland in 1644 at the behest of his kinsman

Randal, 1st Marquis of Antrim, to support Charles I's fortunes there. Alasdair took 1,100 hand-picked men with him from amongst the MacDonalds (or MacDonnells) of Co. Antrim and from neighbouring Irish clans, notably the O'Cahans. They formed the core of Montrose's army and without them it is doubtful whether he would have won such a series of brilliant victories. Amongst English speakers Alasdair is still sometimes known as Major-General Sir Alexander MacDonald and by earlier historians, confusingly, as Colkitto, an anglicisation of his father's name – Colla Ciotach. Recent writers, notably David Stevenson, have established the use of Alasdair MacColla as a suitable name for him.

But to return to our quarry Aonghas, 9th Chief of Glengarry. Early in 1647 he was obliged, along with Alasdair MacColla and the Marquis of Antrim to withdraw from Kintyre to Ireland. Aonghas was for some time imprisoned there, along with Clanranald, after being captured in a battle. They were released not long afterwards, largely by the intervention of the Marquis of Antrim's wife, 'my dear old Duchess' as Antrim called her, for when she married Antrim she was the widow of the celebrated Duke of Buckingham, one of James VI's favourites.[23]

When Charles II came to Scotland in 1650 Aonghas joined him and later fought at Worcester, a battle with huge casualties which he managed to survive. Subsequently he kept the Highlands in a perpetual ferment on behalf of the King. Aonghas was the last to make peace;[24] Monck reported in May 1655 that 'none [were] out but Glengarry', although Balhaldy declares that Lochiel was the last to come to terms with Cromwell. Aonghas did not obtain such good terms as Lochiel as his arms had to be handed in and the agreement mentioned the hated name of the Protector, which Lochiel, it will be remembered, was determined to avoid at all costs. After the Restoration, when Aonghas was created Lord MacDonnell and Aros (it is from this time that the use of the form 'MacDonnell' dates), there are constant references to quarrels and duels, sometimes with other chiefs, and to the misbehaviour and lawlessness of his clansmen. He was not a quiet man.

His successor, after Ranald of Scotus, Alasdair Dubh, was probably in his late twenties or early thirties at Dalcomera and had been the Captain of the clan for nearly nine years.

Glengarry was followed by the other Clan Donald chiefs – Glencoe, Sleat, Clanranald and Keppoch.

Alasdair Mac Alasdair Mhic Iain, 12th of Glencoe, was chief of a clan that was notorious for its cattle raids and general depredations. Glencoe runs roughly from south-east to north-west, beginning in the desolate moor of Rannoch, itself the haunt of outlaws and the dispossessed, and ending at Loch Leven where the River Coe has its mouth. The only flat areas of land of any size are around the river mouth and in the middle of the glen and these were and still are used for the grazing of cattle. The bright green grass lying around Loch Achtriochtan forms one of these flattish areas. Above it to the south tower the Three Sisters, round hills of similar size and shape, formed of dark rock covered with moss and lichen. These again lead up to Bidean nam Bian and Stob Coire nan Lochan, both over 3,000 feet and the highest mountains in the glen. Two corries separate these three hills, one going very steeply up to the base of Stob Coire nan Lochan and the other flattening out half way up into a wide, smooth meadow with gravel at its edge. This second one, Coire Gabhail (the Booty Corrie), was used by the Glencoe men to hide their stolen cattle. A little stream, the Allt Coire Gabhail, begins high up on the slopes of Bidean nam Bian, disappears underground where the meadow begins and reappears where it ends, to flow on down the corrie to join the Coe at the bottom. It was a fine place to hide stolen beasts with the jagged walls of the higher hills around them on three sides and their presence hidden from anyone down below in the glen by the rowan trees and small birches growing out of rocks beside the bed of the stream. I cannot quite visualize how cattle could be urged over the many large boulders which now litter the track up to the plateau. I can only suppose many of them to have fallen since the corrie was last used as a hiding place. Back at the bottom of the glen again one is confronted by its north wall, the jagged line of Aonach Eagach, the Notched Ridge. It is here by the River Coe, running clear over smooth pinky-grey rock, that one can best appreciate the spirit of the place. The bastions of the glen on either side seem infinitely high against the blue sky or, in wet weather, pass in and out of the mist like forlorn sentinels guarding the rim of the world. The modern road through the glen is at a much higher level than the river or the old road and deprives those remaining in their cars of the full effect of the high peaks here.

A grand place for walkers and climbers but not the best place in which to get a living unaided, hence the many raids far and near.

Alasdair MacAlasdair was married to a daughter of the 15th Chief of Keppoch, a clan which often joined the Glencoe men in their raids, having similar difficulties. Alasdair had been about twelve at the time of Montrose's campaign in which his father had taken part, fighting along with Alasdair MacColla at Mingary in Ardnamurchan and with the rest of Clan Donald at Inverlochy. In 1689 when Dundee called upon the help of the clans the Glencoe Chief turned down the handsome bribe offered him by Mackay and joined Dundee. He must have been fifty-six at the time and 6 feet 7 inches tall. Philip saw him:

> ...covered as to his breast with raw hide, and towering far above his whole line by head and shoulders...turning his shield in his hand, flourishing terribly his sword, fierce in aspect, rolling his wild eyes, the horns

of his twisted beard curled backwards, [he] seems to breathe forth wrath wherever he moves.[25]

They seem to have been fond of this magnificently twirly facial topiary, for it will be remembered that Lochiel's moustache was 'curled like the moon's horn'.

We should not be too much carried away by Philip's descriptions; he had his eye on antiquity and the verses of Vergil and Lucan. These wild chiefs, rolling their eyes and shaking their broadswords were cultured gentlemen, many educated in the University of St Andrews, or, in the case of Catholic families, often in France. Lochiel had been destined by his guardian for Oxford, but because of the unrest at the time had had private tutors at Inveraray. Alasdair of Glencoe himself could probably read Latin, Greek and French. They were not like Xerxes or Agamemnon although their lives may have touched them at some points.

Alasdair was destined to be the chief victim of the Massacre of Glencoe in 1692 and Balhaldy wrote of him:

He was a person of great integrity, honour, good nature, and courage; and his loyalty to his old master, King James, was such, that he continued in arms from Dundee's first appearing in the Highlands, till the fatal treaty that brought on his ruine. He was strong, active, and of the biggest size; much loved by his neighbours, and blameless in his conduct.[26]

So much for his reputation as a cateran!

The lands of the MacDonalds of Sleat were in Skye, in the peninsula of Sleat itself and in the eastern 'wing' of the island, called Trotternish; they also had lands in North Uist.

Sleat is the more southerly part of Skye, its south-eastern shore looking across to the mainland of Knoydart and Morar, to the great peaks of Beinn a' Chapuill and Beinn Sgritheall and the lochs of Hourn and Nevis in Glengarry's lands. Sleat always seems to be warmer and sunnier than the rest of Skye; its mineral-rich soil gives it fine trees and rich grass beside the sea and in spring the verges of its roads are crammed with bluebells and wild garlic. Its north-western shore is more open to the weather, its trees shorter, often stunted, and the great cirque of the Cuillin hills towards which it is turned is at once threatening and inspiring.

Trotternish faces the hills of Wester Ross, from Applecross up to Gairloch. It has a bare rocky coast enclosing the mysterious green oasis of the Quirang; the coastline itself has unexpected outbursts of vegetation, as at Flodigarry where one comes suddenly upon rich meadows near the shore and fine trees growing tightly together with moss and wild flowers at their feet.

The most westerly lands of MacDonald of Sleat were those in North

Uist, a treeless but beautiful part of the Outer Hebrides, where the machair in spring is full of flowers and the clear water of the sandy bays changes through every shade of green and blue. It is a place of fierce, invigorating winds, hence the absence of trees, and even on a quiet day one feels a continuous, even flow of air.

Sir Donald MacDonald of Sleat – *Dòmhnall Mac Sheumais Mhic Dhòmhnuill Ghuirm Oig* – was descended from a younger son of Alexander, 9th Lord of the Isles. He was the 3rd baronet and the 10th Chief. His father, Sir James, the 2nd baronet – *Seumas Mòr Mac Dhòmhnuill Ghuirm Oig* – had been a prudent man, very anxious for his clan's welfare and he had been doubtful about joining Montrose. When Alasdair MacColla first tried to recruit him he made the excuse that Alasdair's Irish contingent was too small to have any chance of success. Later on, however, he was impressed by Montrose's early victories and when Alasdair came on a recruiting drive a second time he sent 400 of his men with him. They stayed with Montrose until he disbanded and then joined the Engagers, whose aim was to free Charles I from the clutches of Cromwell. Although they were heavily defeated at Preston they went on to join Charles II when he came to Scotland and later to fight at the battle of Worcester. Only a remnant of the original force returned; so many were slain in the battle or transported afterwards and so many died on the way home. After these lowering experiences Sir James seems to have thought it best to co-operate with the Cromwellian government, as Lochiel did, although at a rather later date. Sir James did a lot to ensure the stability of the Highlands, one of his main concerns being to keep quiet Glengarry (Lord MacDonnell and Aros) who, it will be remembered, did his best to keep the Highlands on the boil during the 1650s. Sir James died in 1678 and his son, the elder Sir Donald in Dundee's campaign. *Dòmhnall Gorm* (Blue-eyed Donald) inherited vast debts incurred largely as a result of helping other branches of the Clan Donald, particularly Clanranald. Sir Donald was an implacable enemy of William of Orange and for a long time after the collapse of Dundee's Rising resisted all attempts of the Williamite government to squash him. These included the sending of two frigates which fired on his house at Armadale but which he overcame, killing all their crews. In *The Book of Clanranald* Sir Donald is referred to as 'a great courtier with King Charles'[27] and *Iain Lom* repeats this idea in his *Cumha do Shir Dòmhnall Shleite*' (Lament for Sir Donald of Sleat):

> *Dòmhnall Gorm bu ghlan gnùis,*
> *Fear bu mhine de'n triùir,*
> *Cha bu chorrcheann thu 'n cùirt Righ Seurlas.*[28]

(Domhnall Gorm, fair of face, mildest of the three, you were not out of place in the court of King Charles.)

Balhaldy calls him:

> ...a person of great honour and integrity, and conducted all his actions by the strictest rules of religion and morality. Unalterable in his attachment to the Royall Family, he lett slip no opportunity of expressing his zeall in that service, and that without any other view than of fulfilling his duty. He looked upon his Clan as his children, and upon the King as the father of his country; and as he was possessed of a very opulent fortune, handed down to him from a long race of very noble ancestours, so he lived in the greatest affluence, but with a wise economy.[29]

The last sentence does not seem to square with his financial situation as inherited from his father.

It was this Sir Donald's son, another Sir Donald – the 4th baronet, *Dòmhnall Gorm Og* (Young Blue-eyed Donald) – who commanded the clan at Killiecrankie, his father having fallen ill and having had to return to Skye. His age at the time is not known but according to Philip he was 'illustrious in war beyond his youthful years'.[30] *Iain Lom* wrote of *Dòmhnall Gorm Og* at Killiecrankie:

> *Mo ghaol an Dòmhnall Gorm Og*
> *O'n Tùr Shlèiteach 's o'n Ord;*
> *Fhuair thu deuchainn 's bu mhór an sgeula e.*
>
> *Mo ghaol an Tàinistear ùr*
> *'S a gheur Spàineach 'na smùid:*
> *Cha b'e'n t-ùmaidh air chùl na sgéithe e.*[31]

(Beloved by me is the renowned Domhnall Gorm Og from the Tower of Sleat and from Ord; you were put to the test and it was a great tale to tell.
Beloved by me is the young heir-apparent with his sharp Spanish blade smoking in his hand; he was no poltroon behind a shield.)

Another youthful commander was MacDonald of Clanranald – *Ailean Mac Dhòmhnuill 'ic Iain* – who was only sixteen; his father had died three years previously. His clan lands lay in Benbecula and South Uist and on the mainland covered most of Arisaig and Moidart, marching with the lands of Glengarry to the north and of Lochiel to the east and south. Their main stronghold was Castle Tioram in Loch Moidart, the dry castle, so called because, although it is built on an island in the loch, there is a causeway to it negotiable except at very high tides. It is one of the most beautifully placed of castles, sitting on its rocky height with soft grass and sand around it and behind it to the north the wooded slopes of the linked islands of Shona and Shona Beag. A high rocky ridge thick with trees faces it on the western shore, with a boulder on it known as Clanranald's Seat, on which the Chiefs were said to sit to observe their kingdom; it is particularly associated with Ailean's last departure from the castle in 1715 to join the Jacobite Rising when, having ordered that the castle be burnt so that none of his enemies could make use of it, he watched it burn from this seat. He was killed in the same year at Sheriffmuir. The ruins, however, show no signs of having been damaged by fire.

Ailean's father, Donald, was only chief for the last sixteen years of his life. With his father, John, he had been in Montrose's raid on Inveraray and they afterwards fought in the centre of the front line at Inverlochy. They remained with Montrose until after Kilsyth and Donald subsequently went to Ireland with Alasdair MacColla, Glengarry (later Lord MacDonnell and Aros) and the Marquis of Antrim, as we have already seen. By the time Ailean was born Charles II had been restored and had reigned for thirteen years, which meant that the Highlands were relatively quiet. Ailean was educated in Inverness and under private tutors. He was an exceptionally cultivated and charming young man, as he was to show when he eventually returned from exile in France and lived with his wife at his house at Ormiclete in South Uist, a house which became famous for the hospitality it offered and the musicians and poets who frequented it. Philip saw him at Dalcomera 'in the first flower of his age, glowing from his youthful studies' – he had left his desk in Inverness scarcely more than a week before – 'showing the preludes of a mind great beyond his years'.[32]

The MacDonalds of Keppoch under their 12th Chief, *Dòmhnall Glas*, had joined Montrose in 1644 and remained with him until after his last victory at Kilsyth. Coll MacDonald the 16th Chief – *Colla Mac 'ic Raonuill* – was already known to Dundee from their meeting outside Inverness. It is also possible that Dundee had met his father, *Gilleasbuig Mac Alasdair*, the 15th Chief, as he had joined government troops in the south-west of Scotland and was present at Bothwell Brig. Coll was about twenty-five in 1689, having been chief since 1683. His lands lay around Glen Spean and Glen Roy including the area known as Brae Lochaber. They marched with the lands of Lochiel and Glengarry and were very close to those of the MacDonalds of Glencoe, whom Keppoch often joined in raids and forays.

Glen Spean is relatively flat, lying under the influence of Ben Nevis and Aonach Mòr and their eastern satellites, but not sufficiently close to be oppressed by them. Glen Roy is steep-sided, rising sharply from the north bank of the Spean. It is home to the mysterious parallel roads – markings along the sides of the glen thought to have been produced by the differing levels of an ancient glacier. Its river has its origins in Loch Roy between the Brae Roy and the Glen Shirra forests. There is good grazing by the Spean and in Glen Roy, especially on the slopes of Maol Ruadh (Mulroy).

The Keppoch chiefs lived in a castle on Tom Beag on the west bank of the Roy, near where it joins the Spean, but in 1663, following the murder of the 13th Chief, Alexander – *Alasdair Mac Dhòmhnuill Ghlais* – and his brother Ranald, it was pulled down and there is little to be seen of it today. The house in which Coll lived was near the old castle but was burnt by Cumberland's soldiers in 1746 and replaced in the early 1760s by the 18th Chief. The two murder victims had finished their education in Rome and when they returned to Scotland and Alexander assumed the position of Chief, the clan having been managed since his father's death by his tutor *Alasdair Buidhe*, he and his brother made themselves very unpopular. Alexander was determined to introduce 'improvements' of which his clansmen did not approve and he persisted with these new ideas in the face of their opposition; he even raided the lands of one of his tacksmen, *Alasdair Ruadh* of Inverlair, destroying houses and driving away cattle, sheep and horses, merely because Inverlair had obtained a lease of his land direct from the Marquis of Huntly without reference to him. He had perhaps imbibed autocratic and feudal ideas while abroad and could not settle down to government by consultation with the clan gentry; alternatively his clansmen may have suspected that he was preparing to come to terms with Macintosh, who held a charter to the Keppoch lands, – terms unfavourable to the honour and wellbeing of the clan.[33] Eventually things came to such a pass that two sons of *Alasdair Buidhe* – *Ailean Dearg* and *Dòmhnall Gorm* – along with *Alasdair Ruadh* of Inverlair and four of his kinsmen entered Keppoch castle early in the morning and killed the chief and his brother. The clan took no action, as though perfectly satisfied with the murders. Only *Iain Lom*, the Keppoch bard, was determined to avenge the death of these two young men and at last, with the reluctant help of Sir James MacDonald of Sleat, in whose castle of Duntulm the two had been fostered, an expedition was organised under James's brother, Gilleasbuig, the warrior poet, otherwise known as *An Ciaran Mabach*, and seven of the murderers were killed. Their heads were cut off and washed at *Tobar nan Ceann* (The Well of the Heads) beside Loch Oich before being sent, as a reproach, to Glengarry (Lord MacDonnell and Aros), who regarded himself as High Chief of Clan Donald at that time, but had done nothing to avenge the killing of a Clan Donald chief.[34] (The account given on the Well of the Heads monument beside Loch Oich is incorrect.)

Alasdair Buidhe, previously Tutor of Keppoch, assumed the chiefship, although two of his sons were implicated in the murders, which further confirms the indifference of the clan, apart from *Iain Lom*, to the loss of their young chief. Coll was the grandson of *Alasdair Buidhe*, but if there had been any unease within the clan over the murders it is unlikely that it would still remain after twenty-six years. Balhaldy says of Coll:

> He was a gentleman of good understanding, of great cunning, and much attached to King James, but indulgeing himself in too great libertys with

respect to those with whom he was att variance, his followers became excessively licentious, and thought they had a good tittle to ruine and undoe their Chief's enemys, by all the wayes they could.[35]

Philip, again, relates that Coll was '…a man whom love of plunder would impell to any crime'.[36] Dundee himself also regretted his plundering propensities but seems to have been most understanding of his difficulties.[37]

These however are Lowland views. Balhaldy, although the grandson of Lochiel, cannot really be counted as a Highlander; he had not been brought up in the Highlands, his father having become rich as a merchant in Stirling, and it is unlikely that he was a Gaelic speaker as his father had had little or no Gaelic. At the battle of Killiecrankie he describes how:

> The brave Earl of Dunfermling proposed to gather about fifty or sixty Highlanders, whom they observed straggleing through the field of battle looking after their dead friends, and to attack them [the Earl of Leven's men]. Though none of the companey could speak Gaulick,… yet Mr.Drummond of Balhaldys haveing some acquaintance among them, made a shift to get so many of them together…[38]

I cannot agree with Hopkins' interpretation of this as meaning that Alexander Balhaldy spoke Gaelic.[39] Surely he managed to get them together because he knew them and not because he could speak their tongue.[40]

Coll's fellow Gaels, however, regarded him in quite a different light. To them plunder and booty were not such a problem, if a problem at all; Coll was, after all, the great champion of the Highlands and the hero of Mulroy, the last clan battle, fought only the year before, and contemporary poets – the son of *Iain Lom* and *Dòmhnall Dubh Shuileach* – preferred to judge him more on the basis of his military exploits.[41] We have to remember that he was constantly under threat from Macintosh who held a charter to Keppoch lands. The Keppoch chiefs belonged to those who held their lands by the sword and not 'by sheepskin'. Their clansmen had lived on their land for centuries and yet were subjected to the constant threat of finding themselves under a new overlord or even of being evicted to make room for the favourite tenants of that overlord.

When Coll first assumed the chiefship he had gone to Inverness in an attempt to settle his differences with Macintosh amicably but had been thrown into gaol (on Macintosh's instructions) and left there to regret his peace-making gesture for three months. After his release, obtained when he petitioned central government,[42] the pressure from Macintosh continued to build up and in 1685 Macintosh was given a commission of fire and sword against Keppoch. This resulted in Macintosh entering Brae Lochaber in 1688 with government support. He was defeated by Coll at the battle of Mulroy, fought near where the Roy joins the Spean. This celebrated victory made Coll famous throughout the Highlands, but at the end of the same summer government troops again entered his territory and burnt the crops and the houses. Coll was obliged to take to the hills with his people. The appalling weather of the 1688–89 winter made their situation even worse and it is therefore not surprising that Coll was obliged to raid to feed his clansmen or that he sat down before the town of Inverness, a town against which he naturally bore a grudge, and demanded 4,000 merks before he would release the hostages he had taken. A chief's first duty was, after all, to care for his people. Dundee appreciated this, which makes it all the more likely, as already suggested above, that any protests he may have made to Coll outside Inverness were made diplomatically. But however this may be, Coll's raiding proclivities were certainly very useful. Dundee is said to have called him *Colla nam Bo* (Coll of the Cows) because he could find cattle to feed the army when no-one else could. At Dalcomera he was '*Kapochus aureus*', so his coat must have been well covered with gold lace, and he appeared with his twin brothers and 'two hundred men of fierce aspect'.[43]

It is only after he has presented all the MacDonalds that Philip introduces Lochiel. We have already dealt with Lochiel's background and character and with his appearance on the field of Dalcomera and it is interesting to see that Philip gives him no special treatment, nor does he represent him as a host, as Balhaldy does. Lochiel had with him as his second-in-command his eldest son, John, the father of the future Gentle Lochiel and himself very far from being a faint-hearted supporter of James. Also with Lochiel was Alexander Drummond of Balhaldy, his son-in-law and the father of his memorialist.

Close behind them came the MacMartins of Letterfinlay, whose land lay to the east of Loch Lochy, like a buffer state between Lochiel's and Keppoch's. The field of Dalcomera formed the most southern end of it and the old MacMartin burial ground can still be found between Dalcomera and the Lochy river (or rather, where the river used to be). The MacMartins, being relatively few in numbers, had attached themselves to the Clan Cameron, often being referred to as the MacMartin Camerons or even as plain Cameron. It is often said that smaller septs attached to large clans were given the most difficult and dangerous tasks to do and the MacMartins certainly helped to ward off the predatory Macintosh, always seeking to advance into Keppoch's lands and beyond. There were close ties between the MacMartins and the Keppoch MacDonalds. Coll's mother had been a MacMartin and the MacMartins had helped Coll at the battle of Mulroy.

Donnchadh Mac Mhartainn Mhic Dhonnchaidh, the 4th Chief, had been Lochiel's foster-father and it was his great-grandson, *Martainn Og*, who led his clansmen onto the field on behalf of his aged father. His appear-

ance particularly impressed Philip and indeed he must have been a remarkable sight for, in addition to rising '...high above his whole line', as so
many of Philip's chiefs do, '...his dark locks hang around his face and
cover his cheeks, and his eyes shine like the stars, while his neck rivals the
white flowers...Whenever he turns his head and neck his arms rattle, and
the hollow rocks seem to moan, and as he treads the plain the earth groans
under his weight'. He wore the *fèileadh mòr* with garter ribbons of saffron
and a red-gold tunic, embroidered by his sister, with a double line of purple
round his shoulders.[44]

After the MacMartins came the Camerons of Glendessary, to the west
of Loch Arkaig, bringing with them members of the scattered Clan Gregor.
The Gregarach from bad luck and the intrigues of other clans, notably the
Campbells and the Colquhouns of Luss, had been outlawed and had lost
their lands.

As we have already seen the Drummonds of Balhaldy were themselves
MacGregors; they, however, were accompanying Lochiel. The
MacGregors who appeared with Cameron of Glendessary are likely to
have included the Glenstrae and Glengyle branches. Donald Glas, the
Chief of the Glengyle Gregarach, had been appointed to lead the clan as
his nephew, Gregor of Glenstrae, had had far less experience and was
himself aware of his inferiority in this respect. Donald Glas would have
had some of his sons with him, including no doubt Rob Roy, but probably not his eldest son as a chief joining an insurrection often left his eldest
son behind as an insurance policy and to protect the clan at home from
its enemies. Balhaldy says nothing at all about the presence of MacGregors
at Dalcomera and Philip describes them merely as 'the tribe of Lonoch
[the Lennox] and the widely spread clan of M'Gregor'.[45]

Rob Roy is pictured sometimes as a romantic freebooter and brigand,
in the style of Robin Hood, and sometimes as an heroic and honourable
saviour of his clan, but the truth, as so often is the case, probably lies somewhere between the two, or perhaps it would be more correct to say that
it lies in an amalgamation of the two. The dice were so heavily loaded
against the Gregarach that their chiefs had little choice, if they were to
feed their people, but to engage in freebooting and cattle lifting. Cattle
lifting, provided it was carried out in accordance with certain strict
unwritten laws, was quite an honourable occupation for a Highland
gentleman, but Lowland lairds living in the fat lands below the Highland
line did not, of course, see it that way. The Gregarach had had particularly bad experiences of the Stuart monarchs who had all, apart from Mary,
Queen of Scots, persecuted them. James VI, two days before he went south
in 1603 to claim the English throne, issued an Act proscribing the clan
and forbidding them to use their name or to carry arms. He made it known
that his desire was to extirpate Clan Gregor and root out their posterity
and name.

The Grants of Glenmoriston and of Glen Urquhart are next introduced, their forces amounting to between 60 and 150 men. The Chief of Grant, much of whose land lay around the River Spey, had decided in favour of William; he remained anti-Jacobite in subsequent Risings. His clansmen in the west, however, clung firmly to the Jacobite cause and at Dalcomera, being few in number, placed themselves under the banner of Glengarry. The Glenmoriston men were led by Iain Grant the Younger, later known as *Iain a' Chreagain* (Ian of the Rocks) because when Dundee's Rising ended he was obliged to hide in his native glen in a rough fort he built on Creagan Darach, a formidable rocky height above Bhlàraidh,[46] on which oak trees still grow, as its name suggests. Philip is quick to point out that Glenmoriston is '...*non ille degener* [*Grantius*]' (not that degenerate Grant), that is, Grant of Grant who was supporting William.[47]

The Glenmoriston Grants came from a deep wooded glen through which the River Moriston runs to Loch Ness from the west. The river mouth is guarded by the huge promontory of Sròn na Muic (the pig's nose) to its south, matched on the north side, though less spectacularly, by the heights above Achnaconeran. The lower glen is narrow for the first five to six miles, full of birch and alder and oak, and white with bird cherries in the spring. Silver ribbons of water slip down the sides of the glen or fall from high rocks into still pools; after long or heavy rain or after heavy snows they roar through their stony chasms, casting the spume up to where their fall began. There is some good grazing land, notably beside the loch and at Dalcataig and Libhisi (Leveshie), and also on the hillside above Bhlàraidh which once held the homes of three of the Men of Glenmoriston who succoured the Prince. Tradition tells of a great battle between the Caledonians and the Norsemen fought at Bràighe Bhlàraidh which the Caledonians won.[48] Further westwards the glen widens out into a broad strath round Inverwick and Dalchreichart with the Kintail hills as a backdrop.

The Glen Urquhart Grants are believed to have been led by James Grant of Sheuglie but there is doubt in some minds as to whether he survived to fight at Killiecrankie. According to family and local tradition he was present at the battle where, scoffing at the enemy as '*bodachan*' (old men), he was brought to his knees by a bullet which struck his targe, whereupon he sprang to his feet crying 'Och, but the *bodachan* are in earnest' and continued the fight. His targe with two bullet holes in it is said to have been preserved at Lochletter (one of the Sheuglie houses) until the beginning of the nineteenth century, when it is alleged that it was fraudulently removed to Glenmoriston. This no doubt explains why William Mackay claims that it had been carried at Killiecrankie by *Iain a' Chreagain* (Young Glenmoriston).[49] James is believed, by tradition and the Sheuglie family, to have been killed in 1691 during the Raid of Inchbrine, another cattle raid involving the Camerons.[50] Hopkins, however, cites *A true and partic-*

ular Information of the death of Grant of Shewglie and what occasioned the same impartially related which describes Sheuglie dying not at Inchbrine in 1691 but before the battle of Killiecrankie, during the raid about which Glengarry made such a fuss.[51] (See also p.68 above.) There is no indication as to who wrote this account or when it was written although the date must have been 1691 or later as there is talk of the indemnity given by William to those who had engaged in Dundee's campaign.

The Inventory of Lochiel Charters reveals however, that James Sheuglie was still alive in October 1689 (Killiecrankie was in July). This document is a claim for cattle carried away from James Grant in October 1689, made in 1713 by Alexander (his son) against John Cameron of Lochiel (Sir Ewen's son).[52] One would also expect that, had Sheuglie been killed by the Camerons, Glengarry, when protesting about the death of a MacDonald during the Glen Urquhart raid, would have made a fuss about the death of a Grant too, particularly one of the Grant gentry, as he could hardly ignore the death of a gentleman of a clan whose members were fighting under his own banner.

On the other hand I have in my possession a family tree drawn up by a descendant of the Grants of Sheuglie which shows James Grant's brother Robert as having been killed at Auldearn and his two grandsons, James and Alexander, as having fought at Culloden, the former being mortally wounded there, but it says nothing about James himself being at Killiecrankie which, if he was there, seems odd. Unfortunately this family tree gives very few dates and certainly no date for James Grant's death. Mackay in his account says he was still alive on the 14th May 1691 but does not say on what evidence he bases this.

Philip is of no help to us here; he mentions Glenmoriston and Grant of Urquhart as being present at Dalcomera but then confuses one with the other and tells us that Grant of Urquhart comes from Glenmoriston.[53]

MacNeill of Barra, whose multi-coloured tartan had so caught Philip's eye, led his fierce sea-going clan from the island at the southern tip of the Uists. In 1591 *Grainne Ni Maille*, the famous Irish sea reiver, married to Sir Richard Burke, had prepared twenty galleys to repulse the MacNeills when they raided the coast of Ireland, but had failed to destroy their power as sea-raiders. They traced their descent back to Niall of the Nine Hostages, High King of Ireland in the latter half of the fourth century and their chiefs lived in the great castle of Kismul, built on an off-shore rock in Castle Bay. As late as 1675 stones had been dropped down its murder-hole onto the King's Messenger when he tried to collect a debt, yet in spite of their disregard for authority their 38th Chief (if we begin counting from Niall of the Nine Hostages, which Sir Iain Moncrieffe of that Ilk disputes[54]), *Ruairidh Dubh*, had received a Crown Charter for the clan lands from James VII in 1688. It was he who led his clansmen to join Dundee. They had remained neutral during the campaign of Montrose but had been with Charles II at the battle of Worcester in 1651 and were to turn out again in the '15 and the '45. Ruairidh himself, and probably his ancestors as well, carried out all the charitable acts expected of a good chief. Martin Martin, writing at the end of the seventeenth century, describes how he cared for widows, found wives for widowers, replaced a tenant's milk cows if he lost them in severe weather and took those too old to work into his own household.[55]

The MacNeills of Barra seem to have attracted stories pointing to their leaning towards self-aggrandisement. There is the well-known tale of the piper on the battlements of Kismul Castle announcing to the world that MacNeill had dined and the story that at the Flood, when Noah built his ark, MacNeill had a boat of his own! Edmund Burt produces a story about a Spanish ship wrecked on the coast of Barra. MacNeill called a meeting to discuss what should be done with her:

> ...one of the members proposed if she was laden with wine and brandy, she should be confiscated as an illicit trader upon the coast, but if she was freighted with other merchandise, they should plunder her as a wreck.
>
> Upon this, one of the council... objected that the King of Spain might resent such treatment to his subjects, but the other replied, 'We have nothing to do with that; McNeil and the King of Spain will adjust that matter between themselves.'[56]

Hugh Fraser of Lovat hesitated about joining Dundee but Fraser of Culduthel, near Inverness, was there and so too was Fraser of Foyers from the east bank of Loch Ness where the famous waterfall slides down into the loch. There were the MacNachtons of Dunderawe and the MacLachlans and Lamonts from Kintyre and Dougal of Craignish from Knapdale at the north of that peninsula. Although MacLeod of MacLeod stayed at home the small sept of the MacLeods of Raasay were represented; their Chief led them onto the field wearing oxhide tunics and carrying oblong shields instead of the usual round targes.[57]

The MacLeans of Duart were not present at Dundee's gathering so Philip must have seen Sir John and his cousin Sir Alexander riding across the field at Dalcomera with their plaids flying at some other time.

The lands of Duart are in Mull; Duart Castle stands on a high promontory at the eastern corner of the island looking out over the Sound of Mull towards Morvern. The combined power of the Lords of the Isles and the MacLeans in earlier centuries is evident from the castles which adorn both sides of the Sound – the MacLean castles of Duart itself on the Mull shore and of Drimnin, Caisteal nan Con and Glen Sanda on the Morvern shore and the MacDonald castles of Aros on Mull and of Ardtornish and Kinlochaline in Morvern, all built before the forfeiting of the Lordship of the Isles. No ship could enter the Sound without being observed from one or other of these castles and the warning beacons would blaze down the coasts and across to the opposite shores, helping to preserve the power of these two seafaring clans and thus of the Lords of the Isles themselves, whose *birlinn* and *longfhada* had ploughed the seas round the western islands since Somerled first freed them from Norse domination in the twelfth century.

As continuing allies of the Lords of the Isles, having fought for them at Harlaw in 1411, the MacLean clan expanded considerably, especially in the fifteenth century, but about the middle of the sixteenth century the 11th MacLean Chief, *Eachan Mòr*, ceased to support the MacDonald claimants to the Lordship (now defunct) and *Lachlan Mòr*, the 13th Chief, fought the MacDonalds for possession of lands in Islay. He was defeated and killed by them at Traigh Ghruineard in 1598. This strand is at the head, i.e. the south end of the great oblong sea loch of the same name which thrusts a long arm into the north coast of Islay; it drains at low tide leaving only small swirls of shallow water on its bare sand. The MacDonalds chased the MacLeans up the west bank as far as the chapel, Cillnaomh (Kilnave), where they barred them in and set fire to the place.

This was the beginning of the decline of the Clan MacLean (*dol sìos Chloinn Ghill-Eathain*) and it ushered in a period when debts and the role played by the Campbell chiefs in the 'management' of these debts had a major effect on the fortunes of the clan; one ploy used by the Campbells was to buy up debts, thus giving themselves power over their new debtors. *Iain Lom* describes Campbell procedures succinctly in three lines of his *Oran do Mhac Gille Eathain Dubhaird* (Song to Sir John MacLean of Duart) written in about 1680:

> *Tha sgrìob ghiar nam peann gearra*
> *Cumail dìon air MacCailein,*
> *'S e cho briathrach ri parraid 'na chòmhradh.*[58]

(The sharp stroke of short pens protects Argyll, he who is as eloquent in conversation as a parrot.)

In spite of these difficulties, however, the clan fought for Montrose and were in Charles II's army at Inverkeithing in 1651 where 700 of them and their chief, *Eachann* (Hector) were killed. These included eight foster-brothers of *Eachann*, all struck down trying to protect him. There were not enough men left to till the land of Duart and this dearth persisted to 1672 and beyond.[59]

When Sir Ailean, the 18th Chief, died in 1674 his son and heir Sir John was only four. The stratagems of the Campbells had been such that by that time the very existence of the clan was in peril and all their lands in

Duart, Morvern and Tiree were in Argyll's power. Attempts are also thought to have been made on the infant Sir John's life and he eventually had to seek shelter with the Earl of Seaforth, where he remained until he was old enough to attend the university.

Iain Lom laments the inability of the MacLeans to stand up to Argyll:

Ghlac an fhireadh gréim teanchrach
Air deagh chinneadh mo sheanmhar;
'S lag an iomairt ge h'ainmeil an seòrs' iad.

Dhfhalbh ur cruadal 's ur gaisge
Le Eachann Ruadh 's le Sir Lachann,
Th'anns an uaigh far na phaisgeadh 'san t-sròl iad.

'S Lachann Mór a fhuair arram,
Chaidh a bhualadh an Gruinneord,
Cha tugt' uachdranachd Mhuile ri bheò dheth. [60]

(The ferret has seized my grandmother's goodly clan in a vice-like grip; feeble is the struggle put up by them although they are a famous family. Your hardihood and valour vanished with the going of *Eachann Ruadh* and Sir Lachlan, who are in the grave where they are swathed in silken shrouds.
And *Lachlan Mór* who won renown, he who was smitten at Gruineard, never while he lived could the lordship of Mull be taken from him.)

One of the MacLean bards, *Anndra Mac an Easbuig*, writing on the same subject at some time after 1674 enlarges on the difficulties that arose on the death of Sir Ailean and, remembering Duart in earlier times, says:

An dràsd, mar aisling
A bhà an cadal,
Bhà siod againn
Ged thàrlaidh fad air folbh e:

Mhaighean farsaing
Bu shàr-ghasd aitreabh
Gun dion gun fhasgadh
Gun spàrr gun alt gun chòmhla.

Gun cheòl pìoba,
Gun òl fiona –
Còir an gnìomhadh:
'S leòr dhomh mhiad de dhòrainn.

...
'S 'n lùchart laghach
'M bu dlùth tathaich
Cùirt Mhic Gill-Eathain – ...[61]

(Now, like a dream which occurred in sleep, it was there beside me, although it was far away, its wide plains of delightful dwelling, all without roof or protection, without beam or joint or door.
No pipe-music, no wine-drinking – quite proper things to do; so much anguish is enough for me.
...
This fine palace, once visited by many, is the court of Maclean...)

In 1680 Charles II, who had been asked to arbitrate between Argyll and Sir John, decided in Argyll's favour (probably under persuasion from Lauderdale). Argyll therefore received the Duart estates and Sir John was given an annuity as a consolation prize. His support for the Stuarts was therefore all the more remarkable in that he was landless at the time of both Killiecrankie and Sheriffmuir because of the decision of a Stuart king. He was nineteen in 1689.

Sir Alexander MacLean of Otter came from Morvern where his father was minister, subsequently becoming Bishop of the Isles. Alexander was born not later than 1655. Philip describes him as a brother to Sir John but he was actually a cousin, using 'cousin' in the widest sense of the word as their kinship was through *Lachlann Lubanach* and *Eachann Reagannach* in the fourteenth century. As he was at least thirty-four in 1689 and Sir John only nineteen, he was almost a generation older than his cousin.

He obtained the lands of Otter in 1686 when their Campbell owner was forfeited for his involvement in Argyll's rebellion of 1685, but he lost Otter again after Killiecrankie.[62]

His elder brother *Anndra Mac an Easbuig* (son of the Bishop) who was born in 1635 and whom we have already encountered lamenting the decline of the MacLeans, had fought in Montrose's wars and was a Captain in Dundee's army at Killiecrankie. In 1705 he wrote a lament for the death of his younger brother Alexander

Fear cruaich curant gun ghiorag
'N àm na tuasaid nach tilleadh,
'S tu buain urram gach spionnaidh le seòl.
'N àm dhuit dol do na blaraibh
'S ann air thus bhith bu ghnàtha leat:
Sin an t-sùil nach biodh sgàthach d'an còir.[63]

(Hardy, courageous and fearless one who would never retreat in time
of combat, earning by your cleverness a reputation for all strength
When you went to battlefields your custom was to be in front; that is
the eye that was never fearful when close to them.)

The Stewarts of Appin were one of the many branches of the royal house
that descended from an illegitimate son, in this case from John, Lord of
Lorne, murdered in 1463. In 1689 their Chief, Robert Stewart, was a
minor and away at college but the clan was brought out by the Tutor of
Appin, John Stewart of Ardsheal and Robert quickly left his books to join
them. According to Philip, two hundred clansmen came to the field,
carrying blue banners with yellow figures on them.[64] They came from the
shores of Loch Leven, under the shadow of Beinn a' Bheithir, the great
curved mountain that turns its back on the lands of Appin and looks
towards Ben Nevis and the Mamore hills, with Gleann a' Chaolais cutting
a deep green groove into its heart. And they came from the soft land of
Appin itself on the shore of Loch Linnhe with Ardgour and Kingairloch
across the water and the long island of Lismore dividing the currents
between them. They had fought alongside Montrose and were to come
out again in the Risings of 1715 and 1745.

Other clans represented included the MacLeans of Ardgour, Torloisk
and Coll and two clans from Kintyre under MacDonald of Largie and
MacAlister of Loup. The two latter had helped the MacLeans in their
attempt to seize control of Kintyre from the Campbells, of which more
later. There were also MacLeans and MacDonalds from Islay and Jura.

One particularly interesting contributor to Dundee's Rising is Rachlin,[65]
a variant of Rathlin, the large island off the coast of Co. Antrim. It was a
fertile source of Gaelic warriors as it was populated almost exclusively by
MacDonalds, Redshank families, who had prospered there under
Somhairle Buidhe (see pp.114–15). Ties with Co. Antrim had been very
close since *Fergus Mòr Mac Eirc*, King of Dalriada in the north of Ireland,
crossed the sea in about 500 A.D. to found another Dalriada in Argyll.
The people of this settlement eventually spread north and east to occupy
the whole of Alba.

As the day advanced the great field of Dalcomera which, it will be
remembered, could not be filled by the hosts of Agamemnon or of Xerxes,
nevertheless filled up with clansmen, horses, targes, tartan plaids, swords,
banners, camp fires, pipes and pipers, chiefs on horseback and on foot,
all the paraphernalia of Highland war. The close friends of Dundee who
had followed him all the way from Dudhope drew round him now or
watched him as he rode amongst his Highland soldiers, assessing their
numbers and their equipment, talking to their chiefs, inspiring them all
with his presence. The music of the great pipes rose up into the clear air,
exciting in their hearers the same atavistic joy that they still excite in the

most mundane of us today, shaking even the great hills to the east, their tops still shrouded in blankets of snow. The whole heather-clad plain with the bright figures on it seemed to form the stage of some giant amphitheatre with its auditorium in the hills around it. The banners of the chiefs fluttered in the wind and above all of them, moving this way and that in the vivid throng, was the royal standard, smoothing out its colours in the brisk air, the tawny lion[66] borne proudly beside Dundee by our poet himself. Whether he carried the standard throughout the campaign we do not know, but he certainly carried it at that first gathering for he tells us:

Regia et ipse meis portabam signa lacertis.[67]

(And I myself was bearing in my arms the royal standard.)

And he goes on to describe how Dundee among his Highlanders:

...as a bright sun, glows in their midst, or shines as the moon at the full among the lesser stars.[68]

Notes

1. *Grameid*, Book IV, lines 31–3.
2. Somerled Macmillan: *Bygone Lochaber, Historical and Traditional,* Printed for Private Circulation, 1971, p.257.
3. *Miscellany of the Scottish History Society*, Edinburgh, 1958, vol.ix, p.211.
4. *Grameid*, Book IV, line 34.
5. ibid., Book IV, line 32.
6. *Burt's Letters from the North of Scotland*, op. cit., pp.168.
7. ed. Henry Paton: *The Lyon in Mourning or a Collection of Speeches, Letters, Journals, etc. related to the affairs of Prince Charles Edward Stuart.* By the Rev. Robert Forbes, A.M., Bishop of Ross and Caithness, 1746–75, Edinburgh (Scottish Academic Press), 1975, vol.III, p.45.
8. W. Drummond Norie: *Loyal Lochaber*, Glasgow, 1898, p.101.
9. *Grameid*, Book IV, lines 233–4.
10. ibid, Book IV, lines 311–2.
11. ibid., Book IV, line 156.
12. ibid., Book II, line 294 and Book III, 222–4.
13. Edward Dwelly: *The Illustrated Gaelic to English Dictionary*. Glasgow (Gairm), 1988, p.581.
14. The aketon was fastened at the right side back and tied very tightly because weapons would do less damage if the internal organs of the wearer were firmly supported. The double-handed swords used were slashing not stabbing ones and linen would stand this sort of attack better. The aketon as made at Finlaggan on Islay by the TV Time Watch team and displayed in the Visitor Centre there has far less material in it and is quilted, the channels being stuffed with sheep's wool or linen fibres. There are gaps at the underneath part of the armholes, presumably to give greater freedom of movement. It is heavy, although how it might compare in weight with the tightly-pleated version as described by Dwelly I do not know, but I would suspect that Dwelly's version is heavier.
15. Alan G. Macpherson: *The Posterity of the Three Brethren. A Short History of The*

Clan Macpherson, published by the Clan Macpherson Association, Canadian Branch, 1993, p.59.

16. *Highland Songs of the '45*, ed. and translated by John Lorne Campbell, Edinburgh (John Grant), 1933, pp.154 and 156.
17. *Grameid*, Book IV, lines 82–84.
18. *Bàrdachd Shìlis na Ceapaich*, op.cit., pp.70 and 72.
19. *Grameid*, Book III, line 332.
20. ibid. Book III, lines 333–4.
21. Balhaldy, pp.260–1.
22. ibid., p.255.
23. Angela Countess of Antrim: *The Antrim MacDonnells*, Belfast (Ulster Television Ltd.), 1977, p.28.
24. *Chronicles of the Frasers*, op.cit., p.408.
25. *Grameid*, Book IV, lines 96–102.
26. Balhaldy, p.321.
27. *Book of Clanranald*, op.cit., p.175.
28. *Orain Iain Luim*, p.218, lines 2785–7.
29. Balhaldy, p.248.
30. *Grameid*, Book IV, line 10.
31. *Orain Iain Luim*, p.194, lines 2481–86.
32. *Grameid*, Book IV, lines 112–13.
33. Norman H. MacDonald: *The Clan Ranald of Lochaber*, op.cit., pp.19–22.
34. *Orain Iain Luim*, notes to Murt na Ceapaich, pp.271–2.
35. Balhaldy, pp.237–8.
36. *Grameid*, Book II, lines 303–4.
37. See pp.22–3 above.
38. Balhaldy, p.269.
39. Hopkins: *Glencoe*, op.cit., p.160.
40. Balhaldy, on pp.156–8 he gives a poem which he had translated from the Gaelic himself, which could contradict my theory about him. However it should be said that the ability to translate a Gaelic poem does not necessarily imply an ability to converse in Gaelic or look at things through Gaelic eyes.
41. Dòmhnall Dubh Shuileach: Latha Blar na Maoil Ruaidhe (The Day of the Battle of Mulroy) in: *Patrick Turner's Collection of Gaelic Songs*. Edinburgh, 1813, p.143. Mac do dh'Iain Lom: Oran air Latha Raon Ruairidh (Song on the Day of Killiecrankie) in: *Patrick Turner's Collection*, op. cit., p.141–2.
42. Alan I. Macinnes: *Clanship, Commerce and the House of Stuart 1603–1788*, East Linton (Tuckwell Press), 1996, p.43.
43. *Grameid*, Book IV, lines 120–6.
44. ibid., Book IV, lines 179–199.
45. ibid., Book IV, line 209 and note 2.
46. Bhlàraidh. The nominative should be Blàraidh. The aspirated form, given on all Ordnance Maps, is perhaps a residue of Coille Bhlàraidh or Bràighe Bhlàraidh, or it might just be a result of the Victorians' love of throwing aitches about to make things look more interesting.
47. *Grameid*, Book IV, line 371.
48. Alexander MacDonald: *Song and Story from Loch Ness-side*, Inverness (printed for the Gaelic Society of Inverness), 1982, pp.75–6.
49. William Mackay: *Urquhart and Glenmoriston. Olden Times in a Highland Parish*, Inverness, 1893, p.202. This targe was included in the National Trust for Scotland's exhibition at the Culloden Visitor Centre during the 250th commemoration of the 1745–46 Rising in 1996. According to the catalogue it was made in about 1700 and was carried during the 1719 Rising by Grant of Glenmoriston

(Iain a' Chreagain). A roundel hanging beside it said, however, that it was borne by Iain Ach Chreagan (sic) at Killiecrankie, preserved by the Sheuglie family and returned to the Glenmoriston Grants. It was lent to the exhibition by Ian Grant of Glenmoriston. See: *The Swords and the Sorrows. An Exhibition to commemorate the Jacobite Rising of 1745 and the Battle of Culloden 1746*, National Trust for Scotland, 1996, p.58, 4:5. The records are thus confused as regards not only Sheuglie's death but also the ownership of the targe.

50. ibid., pp.220–222. This view is also expressed in a private memorandum by a member of the Sheuglie family.
51. Hopkins: *Glencoe...* op.cit., p.150 and p.172 note 157. SRO: GD 112/43/17/8.
52. SRO: GD1/658, p.71.
53. *Grameid*, Book IV, lines 370–6.
54. MacNeil of Barra: *Castle in the Sea*, London and Glasgow (Collins), 1964, p.15.
55. Martin Martin: *A Description of the Western Islands of Scotland*, Edinburgh (The Mercat Press), 1981, p.97.
56. *Burt's Letters from the North of Scotland*, op.cit., p.272.
57. *Grameid*, Book IV, lines 321–326.
58. *Orain Iain Luim*, p.142, line 1764–6.
59. Macinnes: *Clanship...*, op.cit., pp.14, 30–31 and 109.
60. *Orain Iain Luim*, p.142, lines 1770–8.
61. *Eachann Bachach and other MacLean poets*, ed. Colm Ó Baoill, Edinburgh (Scottish Gaelic Texts Society), 1979, p.60, lines 707–719 and 724–726.
62. ibid., p.234–8.
63. ibid. p.68 and 70, lines 825–830.
64. *Grameid*, Book IV, lines 292 to 303.
65. ibid., Book IV. 10–14.
66. ibid., Book IV, line 501.
67. ibid., Book IV, line 442.
68. ibid., Book IV, lines 447–8.

Duart Castle, with the Sound of Mull and Ardtornish Point beyond
By kind permission of Sir Lachlan Maclean

CHAPTER SIX

Edinglassie

He [Dundee] seemed formed by Heaven for great undertakings,
and was in ane eminent degree possessed of all those qualitys that
accomplish the gentleman, the statesman, and the souldier.

> John Drummond of Balhaldy

THE GATHERING AT Dalcomera had taken place on the 25th
May. They spent that night at the camp and left on the 26th at about mid-
day. Dundee had had news of Mackay's movements in the east and now
hoped to intercept him somewhere in Atholl and to establish himself in a
dominant position in that strategically important area. He could not wait
for the MacLeans, who were busy in Kintyre, and had to go off without
them. According to Philip they left the camp after a long speech from
Dundee (well blown up with our poet's favourite bombastic turns of
phrase) of which few of his hearers will have understood a word. His words
incite to war and to glory and if he did express these sentiments, in more
moderate terms, he will probably have done so to the few friends and the
clan chiefs and gentry who could understand him.[1] Then they set off with
Glengarry in the van and Fraser of Foyers bringing up the rear.[2]

Their quickest route would have been to march up past Stronaba to
where Glen Fintaig Lodge now stands near the present A82 and from
there up Glen Gloy, Glen Turret and so to the top of Glen Roy, going
on to Garvamore and Cluny. (This route will be discussed in detail later
on.)

By the 29th they had reached Raitts Castle beyond Kingussie,[3] near
where the Raitts Burn joins the Spey. This castle was built by the Comyns
but nothing remains of it today. James MacPherson of Ossian fame built
his house of Balavil on or near the site and died there in 1796. The 29th
May was both the birthday and the Restoration Day of the late King and
Dundee celebrated it in romantic fashion with a bonfire which he set alight
himself. Wearing his usual scarlet coat and holding a cup of wine he drank:

> To the due honour of the late King, to his natal day, and the day of the
> happy restoration of Charles, to the success of his pious brother, to the
> health of the King and his restoration to his sceptre, with glad lips I
> drink this full cup.[4]

Keppoch was sent off to take Ruthven Castle and Dundee proceeded through Alvie to Rothiemurchus, Abernethy Forest near Nethy Bridge and Cromdale. In Glenlivet they at last caught sight of Mackay and prepared for battle, their trumpeters sounding *The King shall enjoy his own again*.[5] Dundee was seen 'pressing back his flowing locks within his gleaming helmet',[6] probably not an easy task. He must have discarded the black fur covering which he wore on his helmet outside the walls of Dundee.

They drove Mackay from his position three times and chased him as far as Edinglassie, a distance of fifteen miles as the crow flies, passing Tomintoul to the west. Any hopes Dundee had had of crushing Mackay at this early stage in the campaign were wiped out at this point when they heard that Mackay had been joined by Ramsay, coming up from the south; their combined force was too large for Dundee to take on. He was therefore obliged to retreat. During the retreat he fell ill. Philip does not mention this fact, nor does Balhaldy, but MacSwyne, who carried dispatches between Dundee and Ireland, reported that 'The Viscount fell sick...The next two days [after the first day of the retreat] the Viscount did not march six miles in all'.[7] Mackay let it be known that Dundee was ill 'of a flux', which suggests dysentery and this is accepted by most modern historians but it could well have been wishful thinking on the part of Mackay. Had Dundee indeed been suffering from dysentery one would expect many of his men to suffer in the same way, since it is a highly infectious disease.

In the meantime Keppoch, having taken Ruthven Castle as instructed, could not restrain himself from burning Dunachton, a property belonging to Macintosh. This again provoked a rebuke from Dundee, according to Balhaldy:

He told Keppoch, in presence of all the officers of his small army, that he would much rather choise to serve as a common souldier among disciplined troops, than command such men as he, who seemed to make it his business to draw the odium of the country upon him: That though he had committed these outrages in revenge of his oun private quarrell, yet it would be generally believed that he had acted by authority: That since he was resolved to doe what he pleased, without any regard to command, and the publick good, he begged that he would immediatly begone with his men, that he might not hereafter have ane opportunity of affronting the Generall at his pleasure, or of making him and the better disposed troops a cover to his robberys.[8]

Keppoch, instead of wrapping his plaid around him and departing in dudgeon with his men, actually apologised, saying, innocently, that he had thought Macintosh fair game as he was an enemy of the King. But he solemnly promised not to do anything in the future without Dundee's permission. Once again Philip says nothing about this rebuke, merely noting the burning of Dunachton and saying that Dundee could not prevent Keppoch from 'breaking out, and wrapping the whole district in flames'.[9] Keppoch was evidently a problem and Dundee always showed himself to be anxious to avoid any unnecessary damage or bloodshed. But, once again, whether Dundee really harangued the Glen Roy chief as fiercely as Balhaldy suggests remains highly doubtful.

The army, which had not made much headway in the past day or two in any case, paused to rest in the woods of Abernethy. While they are there it might be as well for us to examine the question of what had brought them there. What had caused them to flock to the banner of a Lowlander and to prefer the rule of James to that of William?

The answer, as far as their leader is concerned, is not hard to find. To appoint a leader amongst the Highland chiefs was always difficult, since none of any consequence was prepared to subordinate himself to any other. Yet finding a leader outside the Gaelic world required the existence of a very special person. Montrose of the house of Graham had been such a person and Prince Charles Edward was to be another.

Montrose's name and his victories were already enshrined in Gaelic verse and the fathers of many of those gathered at Dalcomera had fought under his banner and sung his praises to their children. Lochiel, the Cameron Chief, 'had Montrose alwaise in his mouth'.[10] Dundee was also of the house of Graham, a collateral of the Great Montrose, a soldier of experience. He did not suffer from the disability of the Earl of Mar and his main adherents at the beginning of the 1715 Rising, that is, that the Camerons and MacDonalds, the principal clans involved with Montrose and Dundee, had been reluctant to join Mar as they feared 'to trust leaders of whom they knew nothing, and whose banners were not mentioned in the war songs of their bards'.[11] If there were any doubts in the minds of the chiefs as they went to the gathering in Lochaber, they would soon have been dispelled once the personality of Dundee had played on them for but a short while. He was a man used to command yet sensitive to the opinions and customs of others, able to make up his own mind but yet aware of and deferring in some things to those of greater experience, aloof to place-seekers yet charming and approachable to those whose ambitions lay not merely in the accretion of power and wealth, although we must not think of Dundee or the Chiefs as being totally unambitious in these respects. Knowing his descent the Gaelic world will have expected much of him and its hopes must have been exceeded when meeting the man himself.

The question as to why they were prepared to risk their lives for James is a more complicated one. We have already seen how a government force was sent in support of Macintosh against Coll MacDonald of Keppoch

only a year before Dundee's campaign began and how MacLean of Duart
was deprived of his lands in 1680 by a decision of Charles II, but even
apart from these and other particular cases the reputation of the Kings of
Scots had not been a good one in the Highlands. Once these kings came,
by the end of the eleventh century, to represent a feudal monarchy, they
wished to extend as far as they could their power and thus their ownership of land. Consequently they made repeated attempts to integrate the
Highlands and Islands into the Kingdom of the Scots. In the fifteenth
century, in the time of James I, the western Highlands and the islands
were still ruled by the Lords of the Isles and took little account of the
Kings of Scots, sitting in their palaces far away in the east. The Lords of
the Isles, descendants of Somerled and High Chiefs of the Clan Donald,
had a stabilising influence amongst the clans and also preserved and
consolidated the old Gaelic culture brought from Ireland, a culture which,
to the south of the Highland line, had been gradually eroded since the
death of Macbeth by pressure from still further south and by intermar-
riage with Saxons and Normans.

In 1427 James I invited many northern chiefs to Inverness but when
they arrived, in good faith, he had them imprisoned and some of them
executed. The Lord of the Isles sought revenge for this violation of the
rules of hospitality, not to say diplomacy, but was crushed by James in a
battle in Lochaber in 1429. James I's successors continued to be in a state
of war with the Lordship until, in 1493, James IV declared its lands and
powers forfeit. Not surprisingly this did nothing to pacify the Highlands,
which made James V even more determined to unite the kingdom and put
an end to unrest once and for all. His response to a rebellion by *Dòmhnall
Gorm* of Sleat, who claimed a right to the Lordship, extinct by then for
more than forty years, was to embark upon a sea voyage round the northern
and western coasts of his kingdom. His armada, carrying artillery amongst
its other armaments, set out from Leith in May 1539 and comprised twelve
ships, the King's ship being luxuriously furnished to ensure that life on
board was much the same as at the royal courts on dry land. It was, of
course, also intended to impress the chiefs the King intended to visit.
He was away for a long time, long enough to sail from Leith past
Arbroath and Aberdeen, the Moray Firth and the shores of Caithness and
so to Orkney; then along the north coast to Cape Wrath and to Lewis,
Harris, the Uists and Skye, where he anchored in the harbour of
Portree (*Port an Righ* – the port of the king), sailing off subsequently to
Coll, Tiree and Mull, Kintyre, Arran and Bute, the mainland of Argyll
and finally Dumbarton. On his way he took prisoners or hostages,
along with the sons of some of the chiefs, who were to be put to school in
the Lowlands. These included the ancestors of some of the chiefs gathered at Dalcomera, for instance, of Clanranald, Glengarry and MacLean
of Duart.

His grandson, James VI, was no lover of the Gael. He wrote:

As for the Highlands I shortly comprehend them all into two sorts of people: the one, that dwelleth in our mainland, that are barbarous for the most part yet mixed with some show of civility; the other that dwelleth in the isles and are all utterly barbarous...[12]

He was anxious to 'extirpate the Irish [Gaelic] tongue', thinking that this would bring what he regarded as civilisation to the natives of the north. This view was shared by virtually all his Lowland subjects; it had been an aspiration since long before 1600 and was to remain one into the nineteenth, even twentieth century. James VI also 'planted' Ulster, expelling the native Irish from their lands and putting Scottish Lowlanders and English in their place. He tried to do the same in Lewis, but the inhabitants gave the planters such a bad time that they were glad to get back to their lands on the mainland. The Statutes of Iona, which James forced upon the western chiefs by very much the same means as those his grandfather had used, did nothing to enhance his popularity. They limited the households of the chiefs and the number of *birlinn* (galleys) they could possess, obliged anyone owning more than sixty cows to send his eldest son to the Lowlands to be educated, restricted the import of wine and ordered the setting up of change houses to prevent sorning, that is the tradition whereby travellers could demand hospitality from those on their route, remaining as guests for as long as it suited them; this was a great drain on poor households and the change houses were the one benefit the Statutes brought. They also stated that bards were to be treated as common thieves and driven from the country; bards with their praise poems and inflammatory verses extolling the virtues and greatness of their chiefs were regarded by James as inciters of unrest. Fortunately little attention was paid to this statute. Again, those who were forced to subscribe to these Statutes included the ancestors of members of Dundee's army, e.g. MacLean of Duart, MacDonald of Sleat, MacDonald of Clanranald, MacLean of Lochbuie, MacLean of Coll.

Charles I seems to have agreed with his father. He called the Highlanders 'that race of people which in former times hath bred so many troubles'. He was not so ruthless as to suggest their extirpation but hoped they would all go and live in Nova Scotia.[13] He must, however, have thought the Gaels useful, if not altogether desirable, when he considered bringing an Irish army to England and when he contemplated the successes of Montrose and Alasdair MacColla.

Charles II, after his first stay in Scotland in 1650 to 1651 when he was crowned King of Scots, did not visit the country again. The terrible admonitions and lectures he had had to listen to there from Argyll and the Presbyterian divines made him loth to risk another visit, although he may have felt more drawn to the Highlanders who fought with him at Inverkeithing and at Worcester. James Fraser tells us:

> Never was Prince more taken up with an army as our King was, especially with the Scottish Highlanders whom he tearmed the flour of his forces, and still sounded their praise in every society, especially before the general officers...[14]

It was during his reign that the Highland Host was entrusted with the work of policing the areas of Dumfries and Galloway where dissent from the King's church settlement had caused unrest which Dundee himself was employed to deal with. There was thus in Charles's reign some slight change in direction from earlier reigns when Highlanders needed to be suppressed or even expelled to protect the health of the nation, but Charles had no true understanding of Highland problems.

The one Stuart monarch before 1685 to grasp some of these problems was Mary, Queen of Scots. Speaking of the Gregarach who were obliged to live as caterans and brigands, having lost their lands largely due to the machinations of the Campbells, she declared: 'They cannot live without some rowmes and possessions' and twice wrote to Menzies of Weem asking him to let them remain on their original lands and to give them good tacks on the usual terms. She also gave the clan a general pardon.[15]

James VII, in the instructions he wrote for his son in 1692, recognized the loyalty of the Highlanders, but warned against Gaelic separatism in Ireland. He too recommended the extirpation of the Irish (Gaelic) tongue.[16] He was however sympathetic to the Highlander's dislike of subinfeudation, a feature of feudalism which involved land being handed over to some favoured courtier, oblivious of the fact that it had for centuries belonged (in fact if not in law) to the people living in it. Nor did James view with any kindness the practice of issuing commissions of fire and sword to one magnate empowering him to punish the misdemeanours of another, which usually ended in the former seizing the lands of the latter. The Campbells had made great use of this device, often engineering unrest so that they might be given the chance of crushing the authors of it and taking over their lands. The chiefs, particularly those who held no charters for their lands, found these practices very oppressive and were anxious to arrive at a situation where all lands were held directly from the King. James's more reasonable approach to these questions may well have gone a long way towards gaining Highland support. John MacLean, in his consideration of how Highland history is reflected in the work of the Gaelic bards, suggests that the chiefs may well have regarded the 'Glorious' Revolution as an attempt by the aristocracy to revive their waning power, which James had tried to reduce, thus benefiting many clans who had been freed from Argyll's domination as a result. One example of this had been James's refusal in 1685 to consider the Duke of Gordon's claim to be the feudal superior of the Cameron chief.[17]

But against the past delinquencies, in Highland terms, of Stuart monarchs we have to set another more potent factor; the adherence of Argyll to William's cause. The Campbell chiefs, as we have already seen, had aggrandised themselves at the expense of other chiefs. Had they gained power and land by right of conquest their expansionist policies might have been better understood, but instead, although not strangers to the sword, they had used legal twists and subtleties which were not understood by most Highlanders, or had created disturbances so that they might profit from putting an end to them. They seemed to be trying to create a new Lordship, with themselves at its head instead of the MacDonalds, a return to power of 'King Campbell', who had been temporarily eclipsed by the involvement of the house of Argyll in the rising in Scotland in 1685 in support of Monmouth's rebellion. This would have lost Lochiel much of his land and would have brought the complete and final ruin of the MacLeans of Duart, whilst Clanranald and Glengarry would have again been overwhelmed by debts and territorial claims. Keppoch too might have been in difficulties in prosecuting his unending quarrel with Macintosh. This all seems reason enough for embracing James's cause. General Mackay in his account of pro-James activities in Scotland and Ireland states that he asked Viscount Tarbat why the Highlanders had joined Dundee and was told:

> ...that it was neither the love of King James, nor hatred of King William, which moved them to it, or at least some of the wisest of them, as Lochiel Chief of the Camerons, whose cunning engaged others, who were not so much interested in his quarrel, but that it was out of the apprehension of the Earle of Argyles appearant restauration and favour, whose predecessors, during their greatness, had always quarrels with almost all the families of the Macdonalds...and because Lochiel had some of the late Earl of Argyles lands, which were forfeited in the reign of King Charles...and that several of those combined Highlanders did hold their lands of the Earle...[18]

There remains the question of religion. The bulk of Dundee's army was either Catholic or non-juring (Episcopalian) with a small percentage of Presbyterians. Judging by the religious allegiances of the chiefs there were more non-jurors in it than Catholics, but it is difficult to determine this with any accuracy as some of the Catholic clans, notably Clan Donald, were very large. The Catholics would naturally support James, their Catholic King, rather than his Protestant opponent. The Episcopalians had, during the Civil War, mostly either supported Charles I (a martyr of their sister church in England) or had remained neutral: they had welcomed the Restoration of Charles II and could not turn aside now from his brother, provided that their religion was assured. In a letter written just before he embarked for France James had commented on the state of the country:

> I hope it will please God to touch their [his subjects'] hearts out of his infinite mercy and to make them sensible of the condition they are in and bring them to such a temper that a legal Parliament may be called, and that amongst other things which may be necessary to be done they will agree to a liberty of conscience for all Protestant dissenters, and that those of my own persuasion may be so far considered, and have such a share of it, as they may live peaceably and quietly, as Englishmen and Christians ought to do, and not to be obliged to transplant themselves, which would be very grievous especially to such as love their country; and I appeal to all who are considering men and women and have had experience, whether anything can make this Nation so great and flourishing as Liberty of Conscience.[19]

Many remained unaware of or doubtful about these sentiments and remain so even today and Dundee was constantly impressing James's true wishes upon his contacts (see Chapter VII). He would have had more recruits at the beginning of his campaign had the King's desire for religious tolerance been well known, but it had, of course, been obscured by the reactions of English magnates, anxious about losing their lucrative posts at court to Catholics and belief in it was to be destroyed by the power of William's propaganda machine. Many Episcopalians remained neutral until they realised that William had no intention of preventing the imposition of Presbyterianism in Scotland. By the time they did realise this it was too late to be of help to Dundee.

But over and above all these factors there remained the traditional attachment of the Highlander to the *cinneadh* (kindred) of the clan and thus to the *ceann-cinnidh* (head of the kindred) which, when applied to the chief of a realm and not just a clan, naturally disposed them to support the representative of a ruling house rather than an outsider. This attachment had already found expression in the support given to Charles I, although here again it has to be remembered that a desire to reduce the power of the house of Argyll was a major factor.

But we left our people, some pages ago, resting in the woods of Abernethy and it is time to go back and see what was happening to them there. Dundee had sent Philip off with a party of cavalry to guard the fords over the River Spey, probably because he knew that *Eachann Og* (Hector MacLean of Lochbuie), from the south of the island of Mull was on the opposite side of the river trying to join him; Hector was Sir John's

Lieutenant-Colonel. Philip returned with Lochbuie and his 300 men who had already had a victory over a small body of Williamite troops and who entered the camp very pleased with themselves and loaded with booty.[20] This was on or about the 7th June. As they were all returning to Lochaber they were joined by Alexander of Otter with 200 men belonging chiefly to the MacDonalds of Largie and of Gallachellie and, shortly after their return, MacDonald of Sleat with 700 men and Clanranald with 600;[21] these are Balhaldy's figures.

The spirits of the Jacobite army were high, for they believed that they had only retreated to gather in a much larger army, which was, in essence, true. To Dundee, however, the retreat must have been extremely disappointing; he may well have thought that he had left Lochaber for good to begin his campaign in earnest and instead he must now face a period of inactivity.

By the 14th June they were all back at Dalcomera, waiting for more recruits to come in, for King James's promised army from Ireland and for whoever else Dundee could persuade to join him.

Whether the retreat had had any deleterious influence on future recruiting is hard to say. The Chisholms from Strathglass had certainly set out to join Dundee on his way to Edinglassie but when they heard that he was retreating they went home again and stayed there. It is not unlikely that some other people who had been on the point of joining were discouraged by the way things appeared to be going. *Iain Glas*, the Earl of Breadalbane and chief of the Glenorchy Campbells, was uncertain about the prospects at this stage but later felt that Dundee had a good chance of winning; but his change of heart came too late.

It was never very easy to keep a Highland army together. Highlanders were not prepared to sit about doing nothing; if there was no action they became bored and restive and there was then always the danger that they might go back home and not reappear. Also they were anxious to leave their booty at home and to see how the sowing or harvest were progressing. Montrose had found that the only constant element in his army was the Irish contingent as it was too far for them to go home, even if they had had ships to go in and most of them in any case had their wives and families with them.

The only thing Dundee could do at this juncture was to dismiss most of his men on the understanding that they would rejoin him immediately when needed. This would please them and would also relieve Lochaber of the burden of feeding them, which would have been a considerable one at any time but was made even worse by the lateness of the spring and the difficulties in exchanging stock for grain caused by the awful weather. Balhaldy also records that all the towns from which they might have obtained victuals were in the hands of the enemy.[22] Dundee kept with him his own friends and members of his old troop, along with the MacLeans and the MacDonalds of Largie who had only just joined and there was a certain amount of coming and going as new contingents came in from the west. Many of the Camerons and the Keppoch and Glengarry MacDonalds were near at hand and in an emergency Dundee would have to rely on getting in the rest of his original forces as quickly as he could.

Thus deprived, for the moment, of the chance of continuing his campaign with arms Dundee settled down to the task of furthering it with his pen.

Notes

1. *Grameid*, Book IV, lines 471–506.
2. ibid., Book IV, lines 517 and 523.
3. ibid., Book IV, lines 551–2.
4. ibid., Book IV, lines 572–591.
5. ibid., Book IV, lines 764–5.
6. ibid., Book IV, 775.
7. ibid., p.209, note 4.
8. Balhaldy, p.243.
9. *Grameid*, Book IV, lines 720–1.
10. Balhaldy, p.114.
11. Duncan Campbell: *The Lairds of Glenlyon*, Strathtay (The Clunie Press), 1984, p.231.
12. Quoted in Max Hastings: *Montrose. The King's Champion*, London (Gollancz), 1977, p.27 and in Fitzroy MacLean: *Highlanders*, London (Adelphi), 1995, p.116.
13. Charles to Aith, 17.6.1629. Historical Manuscripts Commission, Montrose, 3rd Report, 401.
14. *Chronicles of the Frasers*, op.cit., p.379.
15. Ronald Williams: *Sons of the Wolf*, Colonsay (House of Lochar), 1998, pp.20–21.
16. Bruce Lenman: *Jacobite Risings in Britain 1689–1746*, London (Methuen), 1984, p.49.
17. John A. MacLean: *The Sources, particularly the Celtic Sources, for the History of the Highlands in the 17th Century*, Ph.D. Aberdeen, 1939. pp.254 and 397.
18. Hugh Mackay of Scourie: *Memoirs of the War Carried on in Scotland and Ireland 1689–1691*. By Major General Hugh Mackay, Commander in Chief of H.M.Forces, Edinburgh, 1833. Presented to the Bannatyne Club by James M. Hog, Patrick F. Tytler and Adam Urquhart, p.18.
19. Quoted in Jock Haswell: *James II*, London (History Book Club), 1972, p.298.
20. *Grameid*, Book V, lines 387–9.
21. Balhaldy, p.248.
22. ibid., p.248.

CHAPTER SEVEN

Letters from the Highlands

Gairidh mi an tula,
Mar a chaireadh Muire,
Caim Bhride 's Mhuire,
Car an tula 's car an lair,
'S car an ardraich uile.
...
Bial Dia dh'orduich,
Aingheal Dia bhoinich,
Aingheal geal an car an tealla,
Gon tig la geal gu beola.

Carmina Gadelica

(I will build the hearth,
As Mary would build it.
The encompassment of Bride and of Mary,
Guarding the hearth, guarding the floor,
Guarding the household all.
...
The mouth of God ordained,
The angel of God proclaimed,
An angel white in charge of the hearth
Till white day shall come to the embers.)

transl. Alexander Carmichael

THE HOUSE AT STRONE – and there is still one there, although not the one that Dundee knew – sits up on a spur of land on the west bank of the River Lochy looking across the river and over the relatively flat land immediately beyond it to the heights of Ben Nevis and Aonach Mòr. These great hills, in June still with patches of snow upon them, are not here obscured so much at their base by the ridge of land that hides them at Dalcomera. Their impact is great. They shut out the eastern world and give their chill winds and the freshness of the snow in their corries to the western air. In the pale Highland nights of June, when there is no real dark, only a gently deepening grey, they melt into the skies above them and draw down their veils of mist until the morning breaks or cut outlines in the clear sky amongst the pale stars.

Dundee must have become very aware of their moods and changes, if indeed his preoccupations permitted him to notice them at all, as he sat, sometimes hour after hour, alone or with silent friends or one attendant to mend the fire, writing and writing into the night, taking a few minutes' rest from time to time by propping his head on his clenched fists, while the peats on the hearth glowed and fell apart and the candle flickered at his elbow.[1] Philip describes how 'forgetful of rest and sleep, [he] loads his breast with nocturnal care',[2] a picture reminiscent of Wm. Sanderson's description of Montrose: '...he leids his soldiers sleep, whilst his noble and unwearied soul sits awake with resolves of warlike affairs'.[3]

There are extant twenty letters which Dundee wrote between the 19th May and the 26th July and these letters contain many references to others which have not survived. When we remember that between the 26th May and the 14th June he was absent from Lochaber with little, if any opportunity for writing, it becomes evident that a great deal of the rest of the time available to him was spent pen in hand.

Of these twenty letters fifteen were written to urge the recipient to join him; four to Lord Murray, eldest son of the Marquis of Atholl, seven to Cluny MacPherson and one each to MacLeod of MacLeod, Strathnaver, Breadalbane and to the Atholl heritors, Leonard Robertson of Straloch and John Robertson of Bleattoun. Some of these are long, occupying one or two printed pages, while longer still are letters forming a part of his correspondence with the King of which the two to Melfort occupy altogether eight printed pages.

Melfort, the King's Secretary of State and brother-in-law to the Earl of Perth, was worse than useless as far as Dundee was concerned. He paid little attention to Dundee's requests for supplies, embroiling him instead in his own difficulties with other courtiers and adherents who were anxious to get rid of him. But at least with Melfort he could let his hair down a little, which he could hardly do even with his closest friends, so vital was it to maintain morale in his army; it is only in his letters to James's Secretary that we are able to glimpse some of his trials, for instance, the straits he was in for money and arms:

> ...I have told the King I had neither commission, money, nor ammunition. My brother-in-law, Albar [Robert Young of Auldbar] and my wife found ways to get credit. For my own, nobody durst pay to a traitor.[4]

and:

> ...When we came first out, I had but fifty pounds of powder; more I could not get: all the great towns and sea-ports were in rebellion [supporting William] and had seized the powder, and would sell none. But I had on [one] advantage, the Highlanders will not fire above once, and then take to the broad-sword.[5]

He later complains that no gunpowder, not even four or five barrels, have been sent to him and he has only twenty pounds left.[6] Most of all he wonders that he has not heard from Melfort in three months.[7] He wrote this last complaint on the 27th June and is apparently referring to a letter from Melfort which he has just received. This suggests that up till then Melfort had not communicated with him since the end of April, that is not since well before Dundee set out for Lochaber, which seems an extraordinary state of affairs, even taking into consideration the difficulties involved in delivering correspondence, and suggests that Melfort either wished to play down the importance of Dundee's Rising, for some devious reasons of his own, or that he totally failed to appreciate the importance to James of a Rising on Scottish soil.

The letters to Melfort also reveal the situation of some of Dundee's supporters. He wrote on the 27th June:

> The Advocate [Sir George Mackenzie of Rosehaugh] is gone to England, a very honest man, firm beyond belief; and Athol is gone too, who did not know what to do. Earl Hume, who is very frank is taken prisoner to Edinburgh, but will be let out on security. Earl Breadalbin keeps close in a strong house he has, and pretends the gout. Earl Errol stays at home; so does Aberdeen. Earl Marshal [Marischall] is at Edinburgh, but does not meddle. Earl Lauderdale is right, and at home.

Adding, with exasperation but with the humour ever present in his writings: 'The bishops, I know not where they are. They are now the kirk invisible.' He continues with his list of supporters: Panmure, Strathmore, Southesk, Kinnaird, Airlie, Balcarres, Dunmore and Stormont, stressing how much they suffer and how likely it is that they will have to submit if they do not get help soon.[8]

Dundee worried about his supporters living in politically dangerous parts of the country and in his second letter to Melfort of the 28th June he writes:

> ...the honest suffer extremely in the low countries in the time, and I dare not go down for want of horse, and in part for fear of plundering all, and so making enemys, having no pay.[9]

His army was a volunteer force and could not therefore be denied plunder as compensation for lack of pay. This was not the way Dundee liked to wage war, but he had no choice. A similar anxiety about his army losing control and making James's cause unpopular is to be seen in a letter to Cluny MacPherson of the 22nd July:

> Our people coming from this countrey which doeth not abound in provi-

sions will want meat when they come into Badinoch. I am unwilling that they should go loose in your countrey (to seek provisions as they did last) [during the Edinglassie expedition] for fear of ruining it...[10]

A basic distaste for disorderly soldiery is to be seen in both these extracts – a sense of order instilled in him by his military training and perhaps also a natural trait of his character; his humanity also shines out; he does not want the countryside spoilt and its inhabitants brought to starvation or to all those other miseries that a riotous army can bring. It is notable that he did not burn and destroy any areas through which he passed as Montrose and Mackay did; the only signs of a burnt earth policy came from Keppoch.

In the group of fifteen letters which we might describe as 'recruiting letters' the earliest dates from before his arrival in Lochaber. He wrote it to his cousin Sir Lachlan Macintosh, Chief of the Clan Macintosh. This letter, written on the 22nd April has not survived, but a follow-up letter dated the 24th April is still extant. It was written from Coxton, Morayshire, probably from the home of Innes of Coxton, one of those who rode from Glen Ogilvie with him and runs:

Sir, I wrote to you the day before yesterday, concerning the present state of affairs, yet having the occasion of this bearer, I am so concerned that you make no wrong step to the prejudice of your family, or to you own dishonour, I would forbear to mind you of the just cause the King has, or the objections you have to him, and the happy occasion you have now by declaring for the King to oblige him and all honest men in such manner. As you will be sure to be established in all your ancient rights, and rewarded according to your deservings, you may assure your-self ever of all the good offices and services lays in the power of, sir, your affectionate cousin and most humble servant.[11]

This predated his meeting with MacDonald of Keppoch outside Inverness when, as I have already suggested above, he had supported rather than denigrated Keppoch for raiding Macintosh lands and for demanding money from Inverness and had thought that Macintosh had deserved his treatment at the hands of Keppoch because he had not responded to either of Dundee's letters. When Dundee wrote the letters to Macintosh he may have been ignorant of inter-clan disputes or he may have hoped that he could smooth things over between the parties until the King's affairs were in a sufficiently strong and stable state to weather the inevitable storms. Had Macintosh indeed been established in all his 'ancient rights', as Dundee suggests, it would have been greatly to the detriment of not only Keppoch but also Lochiel, with whom Macintosh also had a long-standing quarrel.

But as far as we know he did not write to Macintosh again and Macintosh himself did not merely remain neutral but tried to prevent other clans from rising. For instance, he gave orders falsely said to have come from the Duke of Gordon telling his [the Duke's] vassals to submit to the government. This is evident from Dundee's letter to Cluny dated the 20th July: 'That McKintosh is a lying rogue. The D[uke] of Gordon gave no comision to forbid you to rise.'[12]

Dundee began his correspondence from Lochaber on the 19th May, the day after he met Lochiel, when he sat down in the house at Strone and wrote to Cluny. This is the only letter that has survived from the period 18th–25th May. The lands in Badenoch of Duncan MacPherson of Cluny occupied a strategic position, lying across the main traffic arteries of the Highlands, which made his participation on the Jacobite side particularly desirable to Dundee. The letter runs:

> Sir, I hear M[ajor] G[eneral] McKay has been by threats and promises indevoring to engadge you in his rebellion against our Laufull Suverain King James, but I knou your constant Loyalty your honor and your conscience will secur you against such proposals. I have nou received Letters from Yrland by which I am seur nothing but want of fair wynd can hinder the landing of a considerable force in this contrey from thence, and that the King will be with us very soon. In the meantime he is pleased to apoint me to be L[ieutenan]t Gen[eral] and command the forces whereupon I am to requyr all honest men to attend the Kings Standart.
>
> I perswad myself you will not be wanting in so good ane occasion as this is of indevoring under God to restor our gracious monarch. I will not desyr you to apear in armes untill such time as you see us in body able to preserve you which I hop in God you will in a feu days see.
>
> There is on thing I forwarn you of not to be alarumed with; the danger they would make the world believe the protestant religion is in. They must make the religion the pretext as it has been in all times of rebellion. I am as much concerned in the protestant religion as any man, and will doe my indevors to see it secured. I am, Sir, your most humble servant.[13]

This letter incorporates three of the constantly recurring subjects of Dundee's correspondence at this time. Firstly he flatters the recipient by assuming that a man of such honour and loyalty cannot hold back. Secondly he presents an optimistic view of the general situation, hoping to persuade him that joining will be to his advantage in all ways and thirdly he assures him that his religion will be safe in King James's hands, for he knew well the doubt engendered in the minds of many Protestants by James's Catholicism and his determination to pursue a policy of toleration, which was regarded by many as likely to favour Catholics.

In the past the MacPhersons had supported the royal cause; 300 of them under Ewan Og (who died before his father and thus did not inherit the chiefship) joined Alasdair MacColla early on in Montrose's campaign,[14] so Dundee could reasonably suppose that he might get help in this quarter. On the other hand the MacPhersons had always been on good terms with their neighbours, particularly with Grant of Grant – who stood aside from all the royalist/Jacobite Risings – and while Ewan Og was leading his father's clansmen in support of Montrose his father, Andrew, was signing a 'bond of combination' with the Grants for their mutual protection.[15]

A further problem for Cluny was that he had recently been offered a commission in the army which he had been anxious to accept and was now loth to turn down. He did not actually reject it until the day before Killiecrankie.[16] In addition he had just married his daughter to the son of Sir Hugh Campbell of Calder (Cawdor) and the clan feared that for lack of a male heir he would entail the chiefship upon this son-in-law.[17] His relationship with the very people amongst whom he would have to recruit to meet Dundee's demands was therefore an uncertain one.

He may also have remembered that his father, Ewan Og, after he had taken part in Montrose's campaign was forced, with some of his kinsmen, as 'malignants', to 'mak their repentance in sackcloth in the Kirk of Auldearn…Thairafter…in the Kirk of Kingussie…and after thair repentance they are ordained to subscryve the Covanant and League at Kingussie'.[18] West Highland chiefs, unlike Cluny, had the advantage of not being under the thumb of their clergy. Cluny therefore dithered, still kept in touch with Dundee but did not positively commit himself. The orders falsely declared to have come from the Duke of Gordon (see above p.104) cannot have helped. Dundee was to write at least six more letters to him, bolstering him up with good news of Irish forces on the way, of Derry having fallen. On the 14th July he became more imperative and after giving news of good progress thought to have been made in Ireland he writes:

> Wherefore tis high time for you to draw to armes, which I desire you to do with all your men and folowers, and I shall give you notice where to join us.
>
> P.S. Sir, this I wryt to you to be communicat to all the gentrey of Badenoch, so call them together for from the head to the foot I will spair non that Joyns not. The gentrey must march themselves, and I expect 400 men and no expenses will be allowed. McIntosh, Grants, and all must come out.[19]

The MacPhersons and Macintoshes both belonged to the large clan federation of Clan Chattan, while the Grants of Strathspey, as we have seen, were Cluny's neighbours and, usually, allies. Grant of Grant had declared firmly in favour of William and Macintosh was at daggers drawn with Keppoch. He may also, if he had heard of it, been less than pleased that Dundee had encouraged Keppoch to plunder his lands.

Later in the month Dundee's letters become still more testy, even menacing; he writes on the 20th July:

It is nou no more time to look on when all your nighboors ar ingadged. I asseur you it will prove your uter ruin if you doe; so you will doe well to drawe to armes or be looked on as rebelles. If you sit this Sumonds, you shall not be often troubled with mor letters from me so I desyr a positive answer and I requyr you to call the contrey and intimat this to them.[20]

and on the 22nd July, after requiring Cluny to have provisions ready for 1,500 men for two days, he adds: 'I pray yow force me not to do things to yow, against my inclination.'[21] Cluny still did not move but he did eventually join the Jacobite army, though not until a day or so after Killiecrankie.

Another correspondent was MacLeod of MacLeod; he received at least two letters. Only the second one is extant; it was written on the 23rd June:

Sir, Glengaire [Glengarry] gave me ane account of the substance of a letter he receaved from yow: I shall only tell yow, that if yow heasten not to land your men, I am of opinion yow will have litle occasion to do the King great service; for if he land in the west of Scotland, yow will come too late, as I believe yow will thienk yourself by the news I have to tell yow.

There follows a most encouraging account of the campaign, of Ireland, of the King being ready to land in Scotland, of the clans gathered in or near Lochaber, of the possibility of Breadalbane joining.[22] But as far as we know MacLeod did not reply and certainly did not appear in support of James.

MacLeod of MacLeod, *Iain Breac*, (Pock-marked John) the 18th Chief, had succeeded his brother, *Ruairidh Mir* (Merry Rory) in 1664. The MacLeods had not supported Montrose but were present with Charles II at Worcester where 700 of them died, either in the battle or on their way home; they had little chance of getting there, travelling in their outlandish garb through a hostile country whose language they could not speak.[23] It was at a camp near Stirling, shortly before Charles II was crowned at Scone, that the famous *Padruig Mòr Mac Chruimein* (Patrick Mor MacCrimmon), hereditary piper to MacLeod, was presented to Charles and, inspired by the King's giving him his hand to kiss, played extemporaneously the well-known pibroch *Thug mi pòg do làimh an Rìgh*:

Thug mi pòg, is pòg, is pòg,
Thug mi pòg do làimh an rìgh.
Cha d'chuir gaoth 'n craicionn caorach
Fhuair 'n fhaoilt ud ach mi.[24]

(I gave a kiss, a kiss, a kiss,
I gave a kiss to the King's hand,
No one who blew into a sheepskin
Got that honour but myself.)

It is unlikely that he could have composed all the complicated variations on the spot but he may have played the *urlar* (ground) and then worked it up and played it in full in 1661 when MacLeod visited the King in London. The MacLeods had suffered such casualties at Worcester that the other clans agreed they should not be asked to take part in any further campaign until their losses had been made up.[25] But when *Ruairidh Mòr* visited London in 1661 the King made no mention of these losses. His apparent ingratitude incensed the clansmen and they did not forget it, for when an Englishman visited Skye a hundred years later he was told that the clan had decided at that time that they would not again fight for the Stuarts;[26] they never did. One tragic result of their appearing on the opposite side (Cumberland's side) in 1745–6 was the death of *Dòmhnall Bàn Mac Chruimein*, Patrick Mor's grandson – the sole casualty of the Rout of Moy and the composer of the haunting pibroch *Cha till, cha till, cha till MacChruimein* (MacCrimmon will never return) which foreshadows his own death.

Dòmhnall Gorm Og MacDonald of Sleat spent most of July in Skye trying to persuade *Iain Breac* to come out but he remained 'very faithful and well affected to Their Majesties' Government and Service' according to the account of the Proceedings of the Estates for 1689–90.[27] What he himself thought about it all is hard to tell. It is difficult to avoid thinking that he might have had some leaning towards Jacobitism, but he had spent much of his time since becoming chief in trying to pay off the heavy debts his father and brother had left him. He did not want to waste all the work he had done by taking part in a campaign of doubtful outlook and he remained deaf to the appeals of Melfort and Dundee and of his kinsmen amongst the MacDonalds. *Dòmhnall Gorm*, the elder Sir Donald, was his father-in-law. Presumably he felt that the increased power that would accrue to Argyll if King James were defeated would not seriously affect him. But he found it difficult to preserve his neutrality.

At some time towards the end of 1688 or in the first half of 1689 he expelled his harper, *An Clàrsair Dall* (The Blind Harper), *Ruairidh Mac*

Mhuirich, from Dunvegan Castle and settled him on a farm at Totamor in Glenelg. His name appears in the Dunvegan records for the last time in July 1688. Ruairidh was an enthusiastic Jacobite and Iain may have feared, with some reason, that he would stir up Jacobite sympathies in the clan and make it all the more difficult for him to hold to the political course he had chosen.[28] In a poem which Ruairidh composed at about this time he says: '... *an rìgh-s' thàinig a dh'annas oirnn,/gur faileas e no ceò*'[29] (this king who is newly come upon us is no better than a shadow or a vapour) and goes on to speak of the time when King James will come into his inheritance. In another poem he also praises several of those involved with Dundee, such as Lochiel, Keppoch and Glengarry.[30] In speaking here of Keppoch he seems to be referring to his reputation as a cattle reiver when he says: '...*b'annsa dol d'a bhualadh/na buaile 'n fhir-theud*' (Better go to strike at him [Macintosh] than at the Harper's cattle-fold).[31] Coll of Keppoch was busy during the summer of 1689 finding enough cattle to feed Dundee's army and in June, when food was particularly short, raided even into Jacobite territory, including Kintail, so Ruairidh had good reason to be anxious about the safety of his beasts.

The likelihood that his Jacobitism was the reason for Ruairidh's departure from Dunvegan is supported by the fact that in Glenelg he was given the tenancy of his land free, whereas at Dunvegan he had had a tack of land at Claggan, near the castle, for which he paid. Pipers and harpers to a chief usually held their tenancies free in return for their services, so it is not clear why Ruairidh did not do the same. Perhaps he was regarded or regarded himself as too high up the social scale to accept payment in any form, although all pipers and harpers were regarded as gentlemen. MacLeod may have given him free tenancy of the Glenelg land to make up for his banishment from the castle. That is, MacLeod had no personal quarrel with him, merely found his absence expedient in the prevailing political climate. Without him it was that little bit easier to hold to his neutral course in spite of his sitting between the two territories of the Sleat MacDonalds who might 'infect' his clansmen with Jacobitism.

One of the most important of those who received 'recruiting letters' was Lord Murray, the eldest son of the Marquis of Atholl. Dundee thought that he had gained Atholl as an ally and, as we have already seen, had persuaded him to leave Edinburgh with him, but at the last moment Atholl changed his mind or lost his nerve. But Dundee did not write Atholl off entirely, although the Marquis had conveniently felt a sudden deterioration in his health and had gone off to Bath to take the waters. There he felt safe from having to make any more decisions and could leave matters to his son. He seems to have been genuinely uncertain of the right course to take. Browne, however, casts a less charitable gloss on his thought processes, referring to '... Athole who, ever since the cold reception he had met with from William, had been wonderfully loyal [to James] ...'[32]

But Dundee did not give up; he turned his attention to the son, John, Lord Murray (later 1st Duke of Atholl). Four of the letters he wrote at this time were to him. The Atholl family was split in its politics as it was to be during the '45 and John, who had a severely Presbyterian wife (the daughter of the Duke of Hamilton, President of the Convention), supported William, whereas his brother James was a Jacobite; so too was Patrick Stewart of Ballechin, his father's steward.

While Dundee was away on his expedition to Edinglassie Murray came to Blair Castle to review the situation and called his tenants together. They did not respond as he had wished to his talk in favour of William but turned aside to the river, scooped up some water and drank a health to James instead. But some tenants submitted, including Menzies of Weem and the young Struan Robertson who had originally intended to join Dundee. Murray put a small garrison into Blair Castle and went back to the Lowlands, leaving Ballechin in charge and satisfied that he had settled matters.

Blair Castle was in another strategically important position lying, like Cluny's land, athwart the central highway of the Highlands and Dundee could not allow it to slip from his grasp. He needed it as a staging post, as a stronghold from which to control traffic and armies moving north and south and as a beacon to demonstrate James's power. Accordingly on the 10th July he sent Halyburton of Pitcur to Blair with orders to take the castle which he proceeded to do with the help of Ballechin and most of the Marquis's tenantry. Ballechin continued to write to Murray as if he were a loyal steward which, according to his own way of looking at things, he was, since he was merely interpreting the state of mind of his master, Atholl, as it had been when he had last seen him.

Murray appeared in Atholl again and Ballechin refused to hand Blair over to him, so Murray found himself in the disagreeable position of having to besiege his own castle. In this situation it must have been very galling to receive a letter from Dundee dated the 19th July beginning:

My Lord, I was very glad to hear that yow had appoynted a randevous of the Atholl men at Blair, knowing as I doe from your Lordships oune mouth your principles, and considering your educatione and the loyaltie of your people, I ame persuaded your appearance is in obedience to his Majesties commands by the letter I sent yow, which is the reason why I give you the trouble of this line, desiring that wee may meet, and concert what is fittest to be done for the good of our country and service to our lawfull King... To satisfie the people as to their consciences, hes he [James] not given his royall promise, in his declaratione, that he will secure the Protestant religion as by law established, and put them in possessione of all their priviledges they have at any time enjoyed since the restoratione of King Charles the Second, which should satisfie the

Episcopall and Cavaleer party? He promises to all other dissenters
liberty of conscience, which ought to please the Presbitereans; and, in
generall, he says he will secure our religione in Parliament to the satis-
factione of his people. .[33]

He ends with a very rosy report on the situation in Ireland: 'the King is
now maister of all Ireland, and hes ane army of 6,000 men...rady to transport'.[34]

There was no reply to this letter or to the short letter of the same date
confirming that Blair Castle had been taken over. Dundee made his final
attempts with Murray on the 23rd and 25th July when he was already in
Badenoch. In the former letter he tried to explain that the taking of Blair
Castle had not been meant as an affront to Murray and in the letter of the
25th he warned Murray to delay no longer:

> ...for you know, my Lord, what it is to be in arms without the King's
> authoritie. Yow may have the honour of the whole turn of the King's
> affairs; for, I assure yow, in all humane probability, turn it will.[35]

But there was still no response. Dundee used Blair Castle as his headquarters immediately before the battle of Killiecrankie.

To John Gordon, Lord Strathnaver, son of the 14th Earl of Sutherland,
who wrote advising him, for his own and his family's sake, to have nothing
to do with James, he replied on the 15th July:

> ... My Lord, I am extreamly sensible of the obligation I have to you,
> for offering your endeavours for me, and giving me advice in the
> desperate estate you thought our affairs were in. I am persuaded it flows
> from your sincere goodness, and concern for me and mine, and in
> return, I assure your Lordship I have had no less concern for you, and
> was thinking of making the like address to you, but delayed till things
> should appear more clear to you.

He then lists all the false information he thinks Strathnaver may have been
given and continues:

> ... So, my Lord, having given you a clear and true prospect of affairs,
> which I am afraid among your folks you are not used with, I leave you
> to judge if I or you, your family or myn, be most in danger...[36]

Strathnaver's letter must have irritated Dundee so much that he could
not, even for the sake of his cause, bring himself to adopt the usual cajoling,
flattering style of his 'recruiting letters'. Only sarcasm could relieve his
feelings. That is the last we hear of Strathnaver.

There remains to be considered Dundee's correspondence with Breadalbane of which only one of the letters written is extant. The Earl of Breadalbane, Chief of the Glenorchy Campbells, was alleged to be '...as cunning as a fox, wise as a serpent, but as slippery as an eel'.[37] He was at first uncertain of the prospects of the campaign, believing that Dundee had little chance of success, He was not a consistently loyal and honest person like Dundee and had already made overtures to William which he had hoped might result in his being named Chancellor, but as these had been unsuccessful he thought he might try his luck with James, if there were no danger attached to it. He was a natural rival of the house of Argyll for the leadership of the Clan Campbell and a successful campaign in support of James would further his ambitions here; but he did not want to join with Jacobite clans if another ravaging of the lands of Argyll was part of their programme. He would have been an invaluable asset to Dundee, almost making up for the loss of Atholl. Until the situation became clearer to him he was content to remain quietly at home, reportedly suffering from an attack of gout while his agents sounded out possible recruits for Dundee's army. As we have seen Dundee was not taken in by this plea of ill-health and reported to Melfort on the 27th June: 'Earl Bredalbin keeps close in a strong house he has, and pretends the gout.'[38] Breadalbane had already used the excuse of ill-health to avoid sitting at the Convention. Later on he decided that Dundee's prospects were much more promising than he had at first thought and Dundee seems to have had a fairly strong belief that he would join him. The one extant letter suggests that correspondence between them was not infrequent and that Dundee was sufficiently sure of him to tell him quite a lot about his plans. Breadalbane seems to have persuaded him that there was some hope of Lord Lorne, the eldest son of the 9th Earl of Argyll, retrieving the glory of his house by coming to the support of James, but this hope was to be sadly disappointed, indeed it is hard now to see how it could ever have been entertained. Lorne's father had been executed for his part in the 1685 rebellion and this had lost his descendants the earldom for the time being. He himself had been living in Holland, came to England with or soon after William and, his title now restored to him, had administered the coronation oath to William and Mary. His continued support for William was such that he was in due course (1701) made 1st Duke of Argyll. Breadalbane seems to have had some scheme afoot to return his chief to favour either with one king or the other, but it is impossible to see what this scheme was without having the other letters in this correspondence. Dundee could not resist having another dig at him over his supposed gout: 'What a glorious work you would bring about siting with soar foot at the fyr seyd'.[39] Did Breadalbane intend by some devious means to further his own ambitions within the Clan Campbell by restoring the power of Argyll? Or was his intention to embroil Argyll in a Jacobite Rising during which he (Breadalbane) would hold aloof until he could see which would be the winning side? It is interesting to speculate on the influence Argyll's defection from William might have had on Dundee's other supporters, all implacably opposed to the ever-growing power of the house of Argyll. Dundee already had doubts about the situation existing between Argyll and MacLean of Duart. It will be remembered that the Duart lands had been handed over to Argyll in 1680, but Argyll had subsequently been forfeited for his part in the 1685 rising. Now Dundee writes:

> The business of the M'cleans I fear too. They have been so fordward for the kings service and so francly joyned with me that I can not in honor indevor any thing to their prejudice but it will be easy for the king to make up that ane other way.[40]

As it was Breadalbane sat successfully on the fence. In 1690–2 he carried on negotiations between the Williamite government and the Highland chiefs with a view to persuading (bribing) the latter to remain quiet. These negotiations broke down and their failure led to the government adopting a policy of massacre rather than bribery. Whether Breadalbane actually had any hand in the Massacre of Glencoe however is a question that still remains unanswered.

It is melancholy to contemplate the fact that all these letters, consuming a great deal of Dundee's time and energy, came virtually to nothing. None of these people were prepared to join him, unless a Jacobite victory and the return of James became a very certain prospect. There was still no real information about the troops promised by James and there seemed nothing left to do but keep up with the endless correspondence and sifting of reports, inspire his companions with an optimism which he could show but may not have felt and do what he could to prepare the men present at Dalcomera – they were a shifting population – for the fight to come.

Notes

1. Chambers: *History of the Rebellion...*, op. cit., vol.III, pp.68–9.
2. *Grameid*, Book III, line 521.
3. Wm. Sanderson: *A Compleat History of the Life and Reign of King Charles*, 1658.
4. *Letters*, p.242.
5. ibid., p.242.
6. ibid., p.247.
7. ibid., p.242.
8. ibid., pp.243–4.
9. ibid., p.247.
10. ibid., p.260.
11. ibid., p.236.
12. ibid., p.256.
13. ibid., p.237.
14. Macinnes: *Clanship...* op.cit., p.149.

15. Macpherson: *Posterity*... op.cit., p.28.
16. Macinnes: *Clanship*... op.cit., p.167.
17. Hopkins: *Glencoe*, op. cit., p.137.
18. Macpherson: *Posterity*... op.cit., p.33.
19. *Letters*, p.250.
20. ibid., p.256.
21. ibid., p.260.
22. ibid., pp.238–9.
23. I.F. Grant: *The MacLeods*, Edinburgh (Spurbooks), 1981, p.296.
24. *Chronicles of the Frasers*, op.cit., p.379. Alexander Nicolson: *History of Skye*, Portree (MacLean Press), 1994, p.129.
25. Canon R.C. MacLeod: *The Island Clans during Six Centuries*, p.89.
26. *The Highlands of Scotland*, 1750, ed. Andrew Lang, p.46.
27. *Proceedings of the Estates, 1689–90*, ed. E. Balfour Melville, Scottish History Society, p.286.
28. *An Clàrsair Dall. The songs of Roderick Morrison and his music*, ed. William Matheson. Edinburgh (Scottish Gaelic Texts Society) 1970, lvi-lix.
29. ibid., p.20, lines 255–6.
30. ibid., p.32–44, lines 401–604.
31. ibid., p.40, lines 543–4.
32. James Browne: *A History of the Highlands and of the Highland Clans*, London, Edinburgh and Dublin (A.Fullarton & Co.), 1850. vol.2, p.122.
33. *Letters*, pp.253–4.
34. ibid., p.255.
35. ibid., p.261–2.
36. ibid., p.250–1.
37. MacKy: *Memoirs of Secret Service*, p.119. Quoted in William A. Gillies: In Famed *Breadalbane*, Strathtay (The Clunie Press), 1987, p.163.
38. *Letters*, p.243.
39. ibid., p.258.
40. ibid., p.258.

CHAPTER EIGHT

Sea-girt Ireland

Ho, brother Teig, dost hear de decree,
Lillibulero Bullen a la!
Dat we shall have a new Deputy?
Lillibulero Bullen a la!
Ho, by my soul, it is a Talbot,
Lillibulero Bullen a la!
And he shall cut all de Protestant t'roat!
Lillibulero Bullen a la!

Thomas Wharton

MEANWHILE in Ireland, as is so often the case, things had not been going well. In December 1688 James VII was still in exile in France, but with the intention of going to Ireland as soon as he could and with the hope of so conducting affairs there that he could proceed to Scotland with a large army and thus eventually regain his throne.

We often find in history that a sudden glorious or disastrous turn of events is precipitated by some trivial circumstance and in this case it might not be an exaggeration to suggest that the downfall of James in Ireland was the result of the Earl of Antrim's wish to recruit into the regiment he was asked to form only men who were at least six feet tall. His regiment was to take over garrison duty in Derry from Mountjoy's regiment which had been ordered to Dublin to replace three Irish regiments which the Lord-Deputy, Tyrconnel (Richard Talbot, 1st Earl), intended to send to London to help James deal with William's invasion. Mountjoy had to march south shortly after the 20th November 1688 and as Antrim was not ready this left Derry temporarily without a garrison. Owing to difficulties in finding six-footers it was not until the first week in December that Alexander MacDonnell, 3rd Earl of Antrim, aged seventy-six at the time, advanced towards Derry to take over garrison duties with his completed regiment of 1,200 Redshanks – a name given to the barelegged Highlanders or gallowglasses (*gall oglach* – foreign soldier) who moved between the west of Scotland and the MacDonnell lands in Antrim. In the more distant past they had formed mercenary bands which had gone across to Ireland to fight for one Gaelic captain or the other and later supported the sixteenth century descendants of the Lords of the Isles. They sometimes also helped Irish chieftains against the English. It was said that when *Somhairle Buidhe* (Yellow-haired Sorley) – somewhat ridiculously Englished into Sorley Boy – needed reinforcements he only had to light a beacon fire on Fair Head by Ballycastle and galleys full of fighting men would quickly row across from the south of Kintyre. Ties between Ireland and Scotland had always been very close; the Scots had, of course, originally come from Ireland and shared a culture and a language. In the seventeenth century however these ties gradually began to loosen, largely due to the buffer of Protestant planters, Lowland Scots and English, which James VI placed between the Scottish and the Irish Gaels in the hope of reducing Gaelic power.

Alexander, the 3rd Earl, had inherited the earldom, (but not the Marquisate) from his brother Randal in 1682. The family was Catholic, descended from the *Somhairle Buidhe* mentioned above, who was a scion of the MacDonnells of Dun Naomhaig (Dunyveg) – *Clann Iain Mhoir* – and had consolidated MacDonnell dominance in the Glens of Antrim and in the Route to the south of Coleraine. Alexander was also the cousin of that same Alasdair MacColla who, under the direction of the Marquis of Antrim, brought a force of 1,100 men to join Montrose in 1644. In 1642 Alexander had commanded a regiment in the Irish Confederate Army, which sounds very like high treason, but relations between the Irish and Charles I at that time were so complicated, with the King hoping to bring over an Irish army to help him against Parliament whilst at the same time pretending that he was going to do no such thing, that Alexander managed to avoid the worst of the possible consequences and eventually even had his estates returned to him. He was seventy when he inherited the earldom, a kindly man with a well-developed sense of humour, speaking fluent Irish, but lacking the charm and quicksilver qualities of his elder brother. In 1688 when he enters our story he was Lord Lieutenant of Co. Antrim.

Whether his regiment was in the end actually made up entirely of six-footers seems unlikely. In command of it were forty-three officers, twelve of them MacDonnells and the rest mainly Irish, including a member of the Talbot family, that is, the family of the Lord-Deputy Tyrconnell, a Catholic appointed to the post by James.

There was no real reason for Derry to fear their arrival, after all it was just a routine change of garrison and all might have been well had they arrived when Mountjoy's regiment left. But in the meantime there was the Comber letter. This was an anonymous letter, addressed to Lord Mount-Alexander, found lying in the street in the village of Comber, Co. Down, now more famous for its early potatoes than for having any hand in King James's affairs. The writer warned Lord Mount-Alexander to be on his guard as on the 9th December all Irishmen would turn on the Protestants and kill every one of them. It is unlikely that there was any substance behind it; it must have been written solely to stir up alarm and

despondency in an already unstable society. It was, however, firmly
believed by Protestants, who had never forgotten the tales they had heard
of the horrors of Phelim O'Neill's Rising in 1641.

A copy of the letter reached Derry on the 7th December and grave
doubts arose as to the advisability of admitting within Derry's walls a regiment led by a Catholic Earl, officered by Irish and Scots-Irish and with
its ranks composed of wild, barelegged Highland Scots and Scots-Irish of
Catholic persuasion. It should be remembered that Derry was a Protestant
city, founded in 1613 by London companies, hence its alternative name
– Londonderry.

The city fathers were faced with a terrible choice. Today the establishment of William of Orange on the throne is such an unalterable fact of
history that it is hard fully to appreciate the problems they had to consider.
Should they obey their King (James) and admit Antrim and his soldiers,
remembering the awful fate prophesied for all Protestants in the Comber
letter, or should they refuse Antrim entry, thus making themselves into
traitors and supporters of a usurper who, however apparently pleasing to
a Protestant mind, might not win in the end? What would happen to them
then?

While these points were being debated news came that Antrim's soldiers
were in sight on the opposite bank of the Foyle and already beginning to
cross the river in boats. At this moment, a decision still not having been
reached, thirteen apprentice boys took the initiative and rushed down to
pull up the drawbridge and slam shut the gate, with the Redshanks only
a few yards away. The Apprentice Boys still parade in Derry every year to
commemorate this simple act which was to have such far-reaching results,
not only for James and for Dundee but for Ireland down to the present
day.

The closing of the gates did not however immediately lead to a siege.
Antrim and his regiment, stunned by having the gate they were just about
to enter slammed in their faces, hung about for a time and then, seeing
no hope of entry, returned to the east bank of the river. Derry itself, its
inhabitants still fearful that its action might turn out to have been treachery
to the winning side, remained unmolested for the time being and took the
opportunity of pushing out as many Catholics as it could. The situation
remained unresolved until March while all the political shifts and influ-
ences as between Dublin and Derry, Dublin and London and Derry and
Scotland played on one another and daily unsettled Ireland more. As we
have seen, the Convention met in Edinburgh in early March and Dundee
retired to Dudhope Castle to await instructions from his King.

James landed in Kinsale in early April and travelled across Ireland to
Dublin, through sleet and freezing winds. In the north of Ireland the
Protestant inhabitants of many of the smaller towns began to hasten to Derry
and Enniskillen for protection, while rumour and the Irish armies around

them grew. Derry itself repaired its defences and reorganised its forces.

On the 8th April, the day before Dundee's son was baptised and three days before William and Mary were declared King and Queen in Edinburgh, James set out for the north at the head of the combined Irish forces, confident that once Derry caught sight of its rightful King the city would be prepared to open its gates to him and his army. But it was not so prepared and after some parleying and preliminary firing of cannon James realised that a siege was unavoidable and left his commanders to carry on as they thought fit while he returned to Dublin. Only now and at about the time that Dundee raised the standard on Dundee Law did the siege proper begin. It continued through April and then through May; on the 4th June the Irish blocked the Foyle with a boom to prevent the city being relieved from the sea.

By the time Dundee returned to Lochaber from his expedition to Edinglassie and settled down to six weeks of waiting, conditions within Derry's walls had become much worse as stocks of food declined and the inhabitants were subjected to constant pounding from the besiegers' artillery which, though it could not breach the walls, destroyed many houses and killed many people within them. For those besieging the city however conditions were not much better, for they also suffered inter- mittently from a lack of food and in addition to this had no shelter, apart from the cover of trees and some inadequate and mud-filled trenches. The weather was appalling; bitterly cold at first, the cold being later replaced by continuous rain. All were dispirited. But not in Scotland. There Dundee was continuing with his recruiting, with organising his clan army, training his men, writing incessant letters to magnates he hoped would join him, bearing the whole weight of the King's affairs in Scotland. But amidst all this one anxiety constantly gnawed at him. When would Derry fall? For the army that James had promised him from Ireland (he was hoping for 5,000–6,000 men) could not embark until the siege was over.

He constantly refers to Derry in his 'recruiting' letters, assuring the recipients that the city has already fallen or is about to do so, and that they can therefore expect a great turn-up in the King's affairs; that is, they would be very unwise to miss all the honour and glory that could accrue to them by being on the right side. Philip's frequent and topographically strange references to Ireland reflect the preoccupation of his leader. He talks of 'Dalcomera…looking towards the shores of sea-girt Ireland',[1] of 'Corpach [extending] to the Irish Sea'[2] and describes how Dundee 'sitting silently by the mouth of the gliding Roy…turns not his eyes from rainy Ireland'.[3]

The Irish army outside Derry was very poorly served by its quarter- masters. Many of the soldiers had no weapons or only defective ones. The gunsmiths and swordsmiths in Dublin and elsewhere were nearly all Protestants and could not therefore be encouraged to get much of a move on. As the siege proceeded the Irish also faced a worsening food situation as nearly all the cattle in the areas to which they had access had already been eaten. There was also the problem that, although Lieutenant-General Richard Hamilton was officially in command he was for a time harassed by the appointment of Conrad de Rosen as Major-General. Rosen was a French officer of Russian origin. He had learnt soldiering on the continent of Europe during the Thirty Years War, not a theatre of war likely to encourage one's kindly instincts. This experience, added, no doubt, to the natural harshness and brutality of his character, made his approach to the Derry situation very different from that of the humane Hamilton. On the 2nd July Rosen issued instructions that Protestant families in any way related to those in Derry or to any others in rebellion elsewhere should be rounded up and left outside the walls of Derry, the idea being that the people of Derry could hardly leave them outside to starve but would have to let them in, thus making further demands on the dwindling food supplies and so shortening the length of the siege. Families were rounded up from as far as Belfast and Carrickfergus in the east and Sligo in the west and the Irish officers and men ordered to herd them to the walls were said to have wept while they did so. Hamilton however managed to put a stop to Rosen's plan and the unfortunate victims were taken back to their homes. James, when he heard of it, called Rosen 'a barbarous Muscovite' and he was recalled.

Meanwhile Major-General Percy Kirke had been given the task of relieving Derry. He had been very active in the suppression of Monmouth's rebellion but had now abandoned his former master and signed on with William. He took up his new post on the 28th April, but was so dilatory and, when he did at last pull himself together, so plagued by bad weather, that he did not reach Derry until the 7th June, by which time the boom was, of course, in place. Instead of making energetic attempts to destroy it or circumvent it in some way Kirke sat quietly in Lough Foyle doing very little at all for six weeks, while the position of both besieged and besiegers deteriorated.

Throughout June Dundee heard constant reports of the city's fall which were always contradicted soon afterwards. In a letter to Melfort dated the 28th June he wrote:

> ...I have so often written over al that Derry was ours, that now, say what I like, they hardly believe, and when I talk of relief out of Ireland they laugh at it...[4]

He had already told MacLeod of MacLeod on the 23rd June that in Derry:

> ...hors flesh was sold for sixpence a pound, and for cannon bullets they were shooting lumps of brick wrapped in pewter plates.[5]

On the 23rd July when he was already on his way to Blair Castle and Killiecrankie he finished a letter to Lord Murray with the words:

P.S. My Lord, upon my word of honour, I can assure yow Derry was taken this day 8 dayes...[6]

By this time the wretched inhabitants were glad to be able to buy a mouse for 6d or a rat for 1/0d or a quarter of a dog for the unheard-of price of 5/6d; the dog was particularly valuable because it had become fat from feeding on the bodies of the Irish slain! The besiegers were unable to attack the city because they had too few pieces of artillery and were also short of men as a result of wounds (poorly treated), sickness (due largely to poor food and appalling weather conditions) and the many desertions. The only way in which the crisis could be resolved seemed to be either for the Irish to withdraw or for the people of Derry to lose their nerve or die of starvation.

But the King was not expecting the Irish to withdraw. He still thought that a little more time would bring a capitulation. On the 7th July he wrote to Dundee from Dublin:

...We doubt not of the continuance of your zeal, and we have sent you one regiment to your assistance, and all the Scotts officers, excepting Buchan and Walcob, whom we could not dispence till the siege of Derry was over, which is now near done, and so soon as that is over, we shall send them to you with all speed; and shall with all care send, from time to time, to your assistance, tho ther is great difficulty in the passage.[7]

This 'one regiment' turned out to be 300 men, instead of the 5,000–6,000 Dundee was hoping for, poorly equipped, according to report. Balhaldy described them as 'new-raised, naked, undisciplined Irishmen'.[8] They had embarked at Carrickfergus on the 10th July in three frigates. Unfortunately they met two Glasgow privateers and in the ensuing fracas some of their officers were killed and they had to alter tack and sail for Duart on Mull, where they were welcomed on the 12th July by the MacLeans. They did not reach Inverlochy until the 20th July because of contrary winds, having lost their supply ships and thus all the 'meale, beefe, butter, cheese and other necessarys' which King James had sent with them.[9] Their overall commander, Thomas Buchan, had had to remain in Ireland, as is evident from the King's letter quoted above. Their Colonel was James Purcell. All we know of him is that he landed in Ireland from the continent in the spring of 1689 to support the King. He may have been attached to James's court at St Germain-en-Laye, or he may, like Sir John MacLean, have been intending to go to Hungary (see p.126 below). It seems unlikely that he was a kinsman of the celebrated Henry

Purcell, England's greatest composer; he was certainly not a close kinsman. Henry's eldest brother, Edward, was in King James's army in England and also in Ireland and remained loyal to James for some time after William landed, but eventually felt himself obliged to take the oath to William;[10] so the Purcell family were hardly enthusiastic Williamites, although Henry's music flourished under the benevolent eye of Mary.

In its section on this regiment King James's Irish Army List mentions only Colonel Purcell and Major Denis Kelly, of whom we know nothing. The rest of the page is left blank. There is no indication of who the other officers were or where the rank and file came from.[11] They could have been recruited from any part or all parts of Ireland, unlike the Irishmen Sir John MacLean brought with him, who probably came chiefly from Co. Antrim.

Iain MacAilein, one of the MacLeans who stood beside the Irish at Killiecrankie said of them:

> *Bha re sgèith sin buidheann èiginn*
> *Dh'fholbh à Eirinn còmhla,*
> *Re mionaid èabhla phàigh an èirig*
> *Fèin le gleus an còmhraig;*

> (At that wing a terrible [makeshift] host
> who left from Ireland together,
> with a minute of fire they paid for themselves,
> with the method of their combat;)

but he added:

> *...Cha robh am faicinn bòideach;*
> *...*
> *Bu chosamhla an gleus ri treudan bhèistean*
> *Na ri luchd cèile còire.*[12]

> (...the sight of them was not lovely;
> ... their get-up was more like herds of beasts
> than men of justice and reason.)

What Dundee thought of his Irish army is not recorded. 300 untrained, heterogeneous souls as compared with the 1,100 picked men Alasdair MacColla had brought to Montrose – men who had trained and fought together and who were fighting under a Gaelic captain, which Purcell's men were not. And 300 instead of five to six thousand! But, as Balhaldy assures us: '...the brave Lord Dundee was not to be discouraged by accidents of this nature'.[13]

Meanwhile in Derry where rats, mice and dogs had become even more valuable food commodities there was at last, shortly after the Irish regiment embarked at Carrickfergus, a movement towards a resolution of the siege. Six commissioners set out on the 13th July to negotiate a surrender; just what the King and Dundee had been longing for. The greatest stumbling block to an agreement however was Derry's demand that the surrender should not come into force until the 26th July, there being a truce in the intervening period. They were still hoping that Kirke might come to their rescue before then and the Irish, of course, wanted to have the siege abandoned before he did. He had recently removed himself from Lough Foyle to Lough Swilly in the west, intending to make an attack from there. The Irish were prepared to agree generous terms (anything to get the whole affair over), but they would not wait until the 26th, insisting that the surrender must be on the 15th July, so the commissioners returned to Derry empty-handed.

At this point William of Orange lost all patience with Kirke and asked Schomberg to take a hand. Friedrich Hermann Schomberg was a German who had served the Dutch, the Swedes, the French and the Elector of Brandenburg, some of them twice, and had now attached himself to William. He was in his seventies and a very experienced, efficient and distinguished commander, the very man to force Kirke at last to do what he had been sent to do, that is, break the boom and relieve the city. Schomberg immediately applied himself to this task, with what results we shall see later.[14]

Notes

1. *Grameid*, Book IV, lines 31–4.
2. ibid., Book III, line 15.
3. ibid., Book III, lines 284–5.
4. *Letters*, p.247.
5. ibid., p.239.
6. ibid., p.261.
7. Quoted in *Grameid*, p.236–7, Note 1.
8. Balhaldy, p.257.
9. ibid., p.257.
10. Maureen Duffy: *Henry Purcell*, London (Fourth Estate), 1994, pp.111–2 and 144–5.
11. John D'Alton: *Illustrations, historical and genealogical, of King James's Irish Army list (1689)*, Dublin, 1861, ii. 766.
12. ed. Colm Ó Baoill: *Gair nan Clàrsach*, Edinburgh (Birlinn), 1994, p.190.
13. Balhaldy, p.258.
14. The background facts to this chapter are taken from: Angela Countess of Antrim: *The Antrim MacDonnells*, op. cit., p.38; Patrick Macrory: *The Siege of Derry*, Oxford (University Press), 1988, pp.257–89; J.G. Simms: *Jacobite Ireland 1685–91*, London (Routledge and Kegan Paul), 1969, pp.95–113.

CHAPTER NINE

Island Chiefs

Athair a chruthaich an fhairge,
'S gach gaoth shéideas gach àird',
Beannaich ar caol-bharc 's ar gaisgaich –
Cum i féin 's a gasraidh slàn.
A Mhic, beannaich féin ar n-acair,
Ar siuil, ar beartean, 's ar stiùir;
'S gach droinip tha crochta ri'r crannaibh,
'S thoir gu cala sinn le 'd iùl.
                    Alasdair Mac Mhaighstir Alasdair

(Father, Creator of Ocean,
Of each wind that blows on the deep,
Bless our slim bark and our gallants,
Herself and her crew safe keep.
And Thou, O Son, bless our anchor,
Our sails, shrouds, and helm do thou bless,
Each tackle that hangs from our masts,
And guide us to port in peace.)
                    transl. Alexander Nicolson

WHILE THESE AFFAIRS were going forward in Ireland, to the great discomfort of both sides and while the great Irish army that was to support Dundee still remained on that side of the water, Dundee himself turned his mind, whenever he had the leisure to do so, to the problem of how best to train the men he had and prepare them for the battles that must lie ahead. According to Philip he spent some of the time between his arrival in Lochaber on 17th/18th May and the gathering on the 25th in directing military exercises:

Burning for war he strengthens his forces, and of his own accord gives the signal for battle, in which alone is his hope and joy. He thinks the days are dreary, and the hours lost, when unspent in the pursuits of war. With him there is no pampering of himself, no sluggish ease or luxury, no listless sleep, but practising for the battle, he reviews his troops, and turns out his foaming squadrons on the plain. He deploys his compact columns, and wheels them again into formation, displaying

the image of the future battle on the heavy and dusty plain. Mounted
on horseback, he teaches the toilsome task of Mars, and how to meet
the fire of the enemy, and the heavy charge of swift cavalry, and how
to charge by horse and foot. Yet the time seemed long till the sun should
arise on the appointed day.[1]

But as clansmen were arriving intermittently during this week it is likely
that his training was directed largely at the horsemen he had brought with
him and even they must have been short of horses after the number they
had lost in the bogs of Rannoch.

Balhaldy, however, places these military exercises after the Edinglassie
expedition and he tells us that Dundee at first intended to drill his
Highlanders in accordance with the methods of warfare he had himself
learnt on the Continent. Lochiel, however, dissuaded him, saying that it
would be worse than useless to try to train Highlanders in an alien way of
fighting.[2] It says much for Dundee's adaptability that, after having spent
most of his adult life as a servant of conventional methods of warfare, he
at once realised the wisdom of Lochiel's advice and abandoned his original plan.

Apart from any Camerons/MacMartins who might have been available,
being the nearest clan to his camp, the clansmen he had with him after
Edinglassie, as he had sent the bulk of them home to return when needed,
were from the islands; it was not as easy for them to go home and come
back again promptly when required. Even so the island chiefs came and
went to some extent. MacLean of Lochbuie had turned up during the
Edinglassie expedition and Alexander MacLean of Otter, Clanranald, the
MacNeills of Barra and the MacDonalds of Sleat appeared not long afterwards, but Lochbuie was sent off to Mull with the prisoners from Perth
and the Sleat MacDonalds returned to Skye in an attempt to get the
MacLeods and Mackinnons to rise. It therefore seems that any organised
plan of military exercise would have been difficult, except with the cavalry
and they certainly may have needed training most, as many of them will
have had no experience of war. As far as the clansmen were concerned,
however, it may well have been Dundee himself who was most in need of
training since the Highlanders conducted their battles in a very different
way from that which he had learned on the Continent.

Their main tactical weapon was the 'charge' or in Gaelic 'a' dol sìos'
(going down). They first had to find sloping ground to give them cothrom
a' bhràighe (the advantage of the brae). They could then take the offen-
sive, rushing down upon their enemy. As someone, probably Lord George
Murray, was later to say: 'Even a haggis, God bless her, can charge down-
hill', but this basic ploy became a major feature of Highland battles once
chain mail and armour had been abandoned, and was refined, with spec-
tacular results, by Alasdair MacColla. Alasdair had tried out his ideas in

Ulster at the Battle of the Laney, near Ballymoney, in 1642; this was an encounter during Phelim O'Neill's Rising and was fought between Archibald Stewart of Ballintoy and four Gaelic captains, two of them being Alasdair himself and his brother Ranald. Stewart was heavily defeated.

The first modification Alasdair made was to incorporate firearms in the charge and the second to alter the formation of his men after the charge had begun. They would begin the charge, fire a volley at about twenty to thirty paces, throw their muskets down and then gather into groups of between twelve and fourteen men. The smoke from the muskets would confuse the enemy and prevent them from seeing clearly what was happening and the small, tight groups would have a greater impact at the points they attacked and give better protection to the attackers than would a continuous but thin line of men. The equipment employed in the charge – the targe, the basket-hilted broadsword (*claidheamh mòr*, claymore) and the musket, did not come into use until the seventeenth century. Before then a huge, two-handed sword (*claidheamh dà làimh*) was used which did not leave a hand free for a shield of any kind. Soldiers were also weighed down by the armour they wore which seriously affected their mobility.

The targe in its simplest form was a round shield of wood and leather. It was sometimes beautifully ornamented with metal and sometimes had a metal spike screwed into its centre front. Or it would have a metal boss at the centre; these bosses were each said to give out its own peculiar note when struck and clansmen then knew where their leader was. With its protection and with the lighter, single-handed sword, the Highland soldier was able to fight without armour, usually in his shirt and plaid or, should the weather be hot, in his shirt alone, He was therefore far more mobile than his predecessors or than his southern opponents. Many Highlanders would also carry the *biodag* or dirk, a long dagger worn on the right side.

The Highland charge continued its successful career until 1746 when the Duke of Cumberland is said to have trained his men to defend themselves more effectively against the sword and targe by aiming not at their opponent but at the man to their opponent's left, i.e. at his less well-protected side. There seems to be some doubt, however, whether this manoeuvre could be successful.[3]

So while the rest of Europe made 'progress' in their armaments and the way in which they were deployed, abandoning their archers (who had won Agincourt for the English) and their swords for the awkward pike and for muskets which were difficult and tedious to load and fire, the Highlanders hung on to their tried and tested methods, admitting the musket but only as an introduction to their charge. In this they were singular not only amongst European armies but even amongst the Gaels themselves, as the Irish Confederate Army had given up their old ways by then and gone over to pike and musket.[4]

The Highland charge, as managed by Alasdair MacColla, played a major part in all Montrose's victories and *Iain MacAilein*, one of the MacLean bards, gives a stirring description of it:

'N àm dhol sìos, 'n àm dhol sìos,
'N àm dhol sìos bu deònach
Luchd nam breacan, luchd nam breacan
A leigeadh le mòintich
A' folbh gu dian, a' folbh gu dian
Gun stad re pris, an òrdugh,
An dèidh a' ghunna an claidheamh ullamh
Gun dad tuilleadh motion.[5]

(When charging down, when charging down,
when charging down, undaunted,
the men in plaid, the men in plaid
who would rush down the hillside,
pressing on keenly, pressing on keenly,
stopping for nothing, in order,
after the gun the sword ready
without any more motion.)

Dundee also learnt from Lochiel that Highlanders must be led by their own chiefs, since if they were mixed with regular troops under strange officers they fought no better than anyone else.[6] The old Gaelic battle order was doubtless also made clear to him. There was no leading from behind; the chief and his nearest kinsmen stood in the front line, the cadets of the clan immediately behind and the rest of the clan behind them. This must have fed Dundee's desire to lead his army into battle instead of directing it from the rear, a desire which was to cause great anxiety to the chiefs before Killiecrankie.

The island chiefs who were his main support during the weeks of waiting after Edinglassie had not been present at the Dalcomera gathering, but they had by no means been idle.

As early as the 6th April, before Dundee had raised his standard, let alone started off for Lochaber, Alexander MacLean of Otter, the cousin of Sir John MacLean of Duart, arrived in Dublin to ask Tyrconnell, the Lord-Deputy, for help. He promised a large Highland army and begged for 2,000 regulars from Ireland and supplies to support them. Three regiments were formed – the Earl of Antrim's and Cormac O'Neill's, both raised in Antrim, and the Scottish Brigadier-General Ramsey's. Major-General Thomas Buchan was to command them but they could not be sent to Scotland then as they were needed at the siege of Derry, amongst other places.

Sir Alexander of Otter (he had been knighted by James in Dublin along with *Dòmhnall Gorm Og* of Sleat) himself raised two companies of Irish; they were intended as the nucleus of a clan regiment which was to include MacLeans, MacLeods and Stewarts.[7] It is possible that he raised these companies entirely in Co. Antrim, which would account for Philip's references to Rachlin (Rathlin Island) amongst the places from which those present at the gathering came.[8]

Sir John MacLean of Duart and young Donald of Sleat (*Dòmhnall Gorm Og*) had both been on their way to the Hungarian wars against the Turks. Joining in European wars as mercenaries was a good way of gaining military experience and Dundee himself had obtained his own knowledge of military matters initially in this way. Hearing that James was leaving France for Ireland they abandoned Hungary and joined James instead, leaving Dublin with him on the 8th April for the north and Derry. They subsequently became involved in the attempt to gain Kintyre for the Jacobite cause.

The Campbells had crushed Kintyre after the end of Montrose's campaign when Alasdair MacColla retreated with his Irish army down the whole length of the peninsula and began to ship his men back home to Ireland. Unfortunately Alasdair had not got them all away when the Covenanting army under David Leslie caught up with them and besieged them in Dunaverty Castle; they were eventually obliged to surrender, having been cut off from their supply of water. Although promised quarter they were slaughtered to the last man. Kintyre was left completely in the hands of the Campbells. Dundee was very anxious to wrest it from them since Argyll would then have a hostile country at his back and would be less able to move against him; however, as the rising in Kintyre began so early it was probably instigated from Ireland and not by Dundee.

Although its southern tip is on a line of latitude well to the south of Glasgow, indeed, a little to the south of Ayr, Kintyre remained a Gaelic area, saved from Saxon influence by the narrow band of water between it and Arran and between Arran and the mainland. It had close ties to the western islands and, particularly, to Ireland. From the Mull of Kintyre it is only a short sea voyage to Co. Antrim and on a reasonably clear day one can see the houses on Rathlin Island, off the Antrim coast, and in Ballycastle itself.

Kintyre is a thin strip of land attached to the mainland by only about one and a half miles of dry land at Tarbert (*tairbeart*, isthmus). Magnus Barefoot had his ship hauled across here as Malcolm III of Scots had agreed that the Norse should rule any land round which they could sail with rudder in place. Magnus particularly wanted Kintyre because its land was so much more fertile than the islands and he is said to have sat at the tiller of his ship while it was rolled overland to make his compliance with the conditions more evident.

Kintyre is battered on both sides by wind and rain and the frequent storms give its fields a peculiarly pure and intense green, while its wide skies, for it has no high mountains, reveal Arran hiding the more crowded world to the east and on the other side Gigha with green Islay and Jura of the deer floating on the western sea. Its ruined castles and abbeys, its standing stones and cairns, its grave slabs where ancient warriors lie in their aketons and helmets, their great two-handed swords slanting across their bodies, make it at once a place of mystery and a rich treasury for archaeologists and historians.

On the 2nd May *Dòmhnall Gorm Og* of Sleat landed in Cara, a small island off the west coast of Kintyre and south of the much larger island of Gigha. He was joined a few days later by the two MacLeans. Sir Alexander made MacNeill of Gallachallie from Gigha his Lieutenant-Colonel and sailed off to Mull with Sir John and with his two companies of Irishmen.

MacNeill of Gallachallie was to organise the Kintyre clans with the help of *Dòmhnall Gorm Og*, MacDonald of Largie, MacAlister of Loup, MacAlister of Tarbert and MacDonalds, MacLeans and MacNeills from Islay and Jura.

The Kintyre Jacobites began their campaign well by capturing Skipness Castle, an impressive fortress at the north-east corner of the peninsula, but were then easily defeated by Captain William Young at Dunskeig Bay, to the west of Tarbert. This was on the 15th May. Hearing of their plight the indefatigable Alexander of Otter sailed from Mull on the 21st with his Irishmen and a hundred MacLeans given him by Sir John. He rescued most of the Jacobites and got back to Mull with them on the 31st. But there was little rest for Alexander's men there as they soon set off again to join Dundee, reaching him shortly before he got back to Lochaber from Edinglassie on the 14th June.[9]

MacLean of Lochbuie, as we have already seen, had joined Dundee when he was actually on his way back from Edinglassie, while Sir John MacLean, who had been further delayed by illness, reached Morvern across the Sound of Mull from Duart on about the 24th June and came on from there. A day or so before this the Sleat MacDonalds arrived in Lochaber along with Clanranald and MacNeill of Barra.[10] *Dòmhnall Gorm Og* must have left again fairly soon, however, as he spent much of July in Skye trying to get the MacLeods and Mackinnons to join him, while MacLean of Lochbuie was sent back to Mull by Dundee at the end of June in charge of the prisoners taken at Perth. They must have been a great burden all this time, particularly for the amount of food they will have eaten, but it was very important to hold on to prisoners as they might be exchanged for prisoners taken by the other side. They did not do so well for food in Duart as the Mull people were themselves very short. Sir Alexander went off to Braemar on the 10th July to help John Farquharson of Inverey, the Black Colonel, who was having difficulties with his neighbours. The only other departure from Dalcomera at that time was of

Halyburton of Pitcur; he was sent off on the 9th July to help Stewart of
Ballechin who had orders from Dundee to take Blair Castle and hold it
for James in despite of Lord Murray.[11]

It is at this point that we lose our faithful poet and standard bearer. His
lines end as King James bids godspeed to Purcell and his Irishmen. Several
blank pages follow, the first of which is headed and numbered ready to
take a fair copy of lines perhaps already written and corrected. Did Philip
write the rest? Or did he find the tale too agonising to reduce to Latin
verse?

Fortunately for us the story is taken up by a Gaelic poet, the redoubtable
Iain Lom (John the Sarcastic) who, it will be remembered, had not rested
in 1663 until the murder of the young Chief of Keppoch and his brother
had been avenged. Iain enters the stage at the very point where Philip
leaves it, as though sent by heaven to fill out the records of the time.

At about the date the negotiations on the surrender of Derry collapsed
Sir Donald of Sleat, *Dòmhnall Gorm*, and his son, *Dòmhnall Gorm Og*, were
getting ready to leave Skye again, having failed to persuade the MacLeods
and Mackinnons to come with them. Iain and other Keppoch MacDonalds
who had gone to Skye in May were now returning with them. Their presence amongst the Sleat MacDonalds may have had something to do with
the appointment of Keppoch as Lieutenant-Colonel to the elder Sir
Donald.[12]

Iain was born somewhere around 1624 so he would have been in his
early forties at the time of the Keppoch murders. Twenty years before
that, in 1645, tradition ascribes to him a journey up the Great Glen to
Cill Chuimein (Fort Augustus) to warn Montrose that he had not only
Seaforth's army in front of him to the north but also an army behind him,
for the Campbells, burning to avenge the harrying of Argyll, were gathering at Inverlochy. Montrose hardly knew whether he could trust Iain at
first and set a watch on him, but consideration must have inclined him to
believe the story, for he turned about, went up the bank of the River Tarff
and then turned off southwards, away from the Corrieyairack Pass and
over the hills into Glen Roy. It was January and the mountains were under
a thick blanket of snow; there were no habitations on the way and no
means of obtaining food, apart from the oatmeal they might have in their
sporrans, unless they caught and killed a deer or a hare, though even then
there was no time to stop and cook it and the flesh had to be eaten raw as
they stumbled on with little rest and no sleep. They arrived in the dark
on the height above Inverlochy Castle. The Campbells below them took
them only for a small raiding party until the King's trumpets sounded at
dawn and they knew that the King's Lieutenant himself was there above
them. Just before the battle began Alasdair MacColla noticed Iain leaving
the ranks and offered him a sword, saying, 'Iain, will you leave us?'. But
Iain refused to take part, for who would chronicle the deeds of Clan Donald

on that day if he were killed? His great poem *La Inbhir Lochaidh* – The Battle of Inverlochy – is fierce, triumphant, vengeful, bloodthirsty verse, ending with the chilling lines:

Sgrios oirbh mas truagh leam bhur càramh,
G' éisdeachd anshocair bhur pàisdean,
Caoidh a' phennail bh'anns an àraich,
Donnalaich bhan Earra-Ghàidheal.[13]

(Perdition take you if I feel pity for your plight, as I listen to the distress of your children, lamenting the company which was in the battlefield, the wailing of the women of Argyll.)

But we hear nothing from him about the terrible journey which preceded the battle except for a reference to Culachy, above Cill Chuimein, which was near the start of their route.[14] This reinforces the assumption that he must have taken part in the march to Inverlochy, and that it must therefore have been he who took the warning to Montrose.

In describing the arrival of the MacDonalds of Sleat at Dundee's camp Balhaldy again attempts a verse translation of Philip's lines, in which he is far from being as successful as in his earlier attempt when describing the weather in the Great Glen, He tells us how Sleat:

Marched o'er the ample field and of his line,
In his bright train five hundred warriours shine,
Well arm'd and fierce, whom from the Skeyan shoar,
In long flatt-bottom'd boats, he wafted o'er.[15]

The Latin gives *'Insula quos longis transmisit Skya carinis'*,[16] (whom the Isle of Skye has sent over in long ships) and I feel that Balhaldy must have inserted 'flat-bottom'd' in an attempt to fill out his line, with which he was evidently having difficulty, as there is nothing in the text to warrant it. The 'long ships' were probably *birlinn* or galleys which are convenient Gaelic and English terms respectively to encompass the various ships of the western coast and islands developed from the Viking longships. Strictly speaking the *birlinn* had fewer oars (12–18 per side) than the galley or *longfhada* (18–24 per side), but the two words have come to be interchangeable. Both had sails as well as oars. They demonstrated and consolidated the wealth and power of the island and west coast chiefs. They were the main means of transport and so of trading. They kept the seaways clear of pirates and other undesirable travellers, helped by the *tairsearan fairge*, the ocean constabulary based on Ha'sgeir, a tiny rocky island to the north-west of North Uist (not to be confused with Heisgeir, of the Monach Isles) and served as warships when manned by the fighting men of the clans. Their importance to the life of the west of Scotland is evident from the fact that in the 1350s when John of Islay, Lord of the Isles, married Margaret Stewart, the daughter of Robert the Bruce, he took 60 birlinn with him to Glasgow and altogether 108 attended from the west coast and the islands.[17]

James VI destroyed many of them in his efforts to bring the isles more firmly under his control and the Statutes of Iona which he forced upon the island chiefs forbad them to keep more than one ship each, although it seems doubtful whether this rule was ever strictly observed. Even so the *birlinn* saw a gradual demise, although it was still very much in use in the early part of the eighteenth century when *Alasdair Mac Mhaighstir Alasdair* wrote his splendid poem *Birlinn Chlann Raghnaill* – Clanranald's Galley – from which are taken the lines at the head of this chapter. It describes a hazardous journey across the sea to Carrickfergus on the north-east Irish coast.

The last of these beautiful ships were destroyed by the British Navy after the collapse of the 1745 Rising and when, in 1989, it was decided to build a replica of Clanranald's galley not a single plank from any galley was available to help the designers and builders. They had to base their work entirely on written descriptions and on carvings and drawings.[18]

The arrival of the Sleat MacDonalds on the mainland and their march to Dalcomera are described in *Iain Lom*'s *Oran air Feachd Rìgh Seumas* (A Song to King James's Army). It also plots the march of the whole army to Killiecrankie and describes the battle there. It is not absolutely certain that this song was written by Iain; it may have been the work of his son, also a considerable poet and known merely as *Mac do dh'Iain Lom* (the son of Iain Lom) but it is certainly included in Mackenzie's edition of his work[19] and is under his name in the Turner collection of Gaelic songs.[20]

He begins by telling us that it is time to leave the district as all the beef has been eaten.[21] What he means by the 'district' is not made clear but Mackenzie assumes it to be the head of Loch Eil, although this location is not mentioned until the third verse.[22] As Iain describes it they left the 'district' on the Tuesday morning and pitched camp in the evening.[23] The next morning (Wednesday) they set out 'on the journey to the house where our plan lay',[24] which must be Dundee's house at Strone. On Wednesday night they halted and lit fires.[25] This is said in such a way that one can infer they did so more than once, that is, Wednesday and Thursday nights. It is only after this that Iain tells us: 'From the head of Loch Eil we marched and halted when the sun set. At the head of Loch Lochy we pitched camp and rested.'[26] So they got to Loch Lochy on the Friday night. Mackenzie takes the lines 'From the head of Loch Eil we marched and halted when the sun set' as though they stood at the very beginning of the poem, assuming perhaps that they are displaced chronologically for poetic effect. She has thus managed to persuade us that the journey described started at the head of Loch Eil on the Tuesday, and that they then took the next three days to march to Loch Lochy – a distance of only fifteen miles! If, however, we take it that the lines are in their correct chronological position and describe activity on the last day of the march only, the Friday, the situation becomes very different. Then the journey would have begun on Tuesday morning, but probably in Skye. Nothing is said about crossing the Sound of Sleat, but they drew up '*Aig leathtaobh an t'saile*',[27] which MacKenzie translates as 'on one side of the shore', in this case, she says, the shore of Loch Eil, but '*an t-saile*' could equally well mean the shore of the Sound of Sleat or could even be given its literal meaning 'of the sea'. They did not make any further progress that day and when the evening came they pitched camp ready to start off again the next morning.[28] They probably camped twice more, on the Wednesday and Thursday, the second time at Kinlocheil. On the following day, the Friday, they marched from there to Loch Lochy, i.e. Dalcomera. Assuming that their landing was somewhere in the region of Mallaig this would mean that they marched between twelve and thirteen miles on Wednesday and on Thursday and fifteen on Friday, which seems a much more reasonable speed for Highlanders than taking three days to cover fifteen miles!

Iain also tells us, in Mackenzie's translation, that when they pitched camp on the first night (the Tuesday) 'our commander marched out from us. The words of our Colonel to Sir Donald were to be at the ready in accordance with the order'.[29] The commander and the Colonel are presumably one and the same. Mackenzie believes the Colonel to be Dundee, while Millar thinks he is Keppoch.[30] Both overlook the fact that the Colonel and commander of the Sleat MacDonalds at this juncture was the elder of the two Sir Donalds – *Dòmhnall Gorm* – and that he fell ill after reaching the mainland and had to return to Skye.[31] We also need to remember that a great deal of confusion is caused by there being two Sir Donalds at the same time, the elder Sir Donald, the 3rd Baronet. *Dòmhnall Gorm*, and the younger Sir Donald, *Dòmhnall Gorm Og*, who had been knighted in Dublin by King James and was therefore already Sir Donald before he inherited the baronetcy. By taking this into account it is possible to read the second verse of the poem as meaning that the Colonel, the elder Sir Donald, left the camp and as he went gave orders to 'Sir Domhnall', his son, to be at the ready. One could incidentally disagree with the translation of '*dh'imich ar ceannard uainn a mach*' as 'our commander marched out' when 'went out' or 'departed' would seem more usual. Perhaps Mackenzie was influenced by her belief that the colonel was Dundee and described his departure in a more military and positive way than the Gaelic actually warrants. Poor *Dòmhnall Gorm* would not have felt like marching and Dundee, with his Irish army about to arrive, with letters still to write, with Mackay's reported marches and counter-marches in the east and with the coming and going of various contingents of his army, would have had little time to take a two-day jaunt to Mallaig, or even a one-day jaunt to Kinlocheil, particularly as he had just had to ride down to Inverlochy, on the 14th July, to give orders regarding the expected Irish.[32] Millar's suggestion that the colonel is Keppoch, who had accepted a Lieutenant-Colonelcy from the elder Sir Donald, is unlikely. Had he been with the other Keppoch MacDonalds accompanying *Dòmhnall Gorm Og* one might argue that he left them at this juncture to go ahead and raise his clan ready for the army's departure from Lochaber. He certainly did not manage to do so, as he and the Keppoch MacDonalds were not present at Killiecrankie,[33] apart from those who were involved in this march from Skye to Dalcomera.

On the evening of Friday the 19th July when they arrived at Dalcomera Iain and his companions had a good welcome from those already at the camp. There they '*shuidich [sinn] campa/Latha roimh Dhi-dòmhnaich 's dà latha 'na dhèidh*' (pitched camp and rested for the day before Sunday and two days after it).[34]

Notes

1. *Grameid*, Book III, lines 620–638.
2. Balhaldy, pp.250–2.
3. The Chevalier de Johnstone: *A Memoir of the 'Forty-Five*, London (Folio Society), 1958, p.82. James Michael Hill: *Celtic Warfare 1595–1763*, Edinburgh (John Donald), 1986, p.1. John Telfer Dunbar: *History of Highland Dress*, London (Batsford), 1979, p.191. David Stevenson: *Alasdair MacColla and the Highland Problem in the Seventeenth Century*, Edinburgh (John Donald), 1980, pp.82.
4. Pádraig Lenihan: Celtic Warfare in the 1640s, in: *Celtic Dimensions of the British Civil Wars*, ed. John R. Young, Edinburgh (John Donald), 1997.
5. Ó Baoill: *Gair nan Clàrsach*, op.cit., pp.184–5.
6. Balhaldy, p.251.
7. Hopkins: *Glencoe...* op.cit., p.140.
8. *Grameid*, Book IV, line 12.
9. *Letters*, p.239.
10. ibid., p.239.
11. ibid., p.261.
12. Hopkins: *Glencoe...* op. cit., p.143.
13. *Orain Iain Luim*, p.24, lines 270–3.
14. ibid., p.20, line 194.
15. Balhaldy, p.248.
16. *Grameid*, Book IV, line 110.
17. John MacAulay: *Birlinn. Longships of the Hebrides*, Cambridge and Isle of Harris (The White Horse Press), 1996, pp.61–3. Reliquiae Celticae, op. cit., p.159.
18. Wallace Clark: *The Lord of the Isles Voyage. Western Ireland to the Scottish Hebrides in a 16th century galley*, Naas, Co. Kildare (The Leinster Leader Ltd.), 1993, pp.2–13.
19. *Orain Iain Luim*, pp.184–189.
20. *Patrick Turner's Collection...* op cit., p.70.
21. *Orain Iain Luim*, p.184, lines 2338–9.
22. ibid., p.307. note to Oran air Feachd Righ Seumas, p.194, line 2360.
23. ibid., p.184, lines 2344–8.

24. ibid., p.184, lines 2354–5.
25. ibid., p.184, lines 2358–9.
26. ibid., p.184, lines 2360–3.
27. ibid., p.184, line 2346.
28. ibid., p.184, line 2348.
29. ibid., p.184, lines 2349–51.
30. ibid., p.308, note to 2350. A.H.Millar: translation of Oran air feachd Righ Seumas in: *Scottish Historical Review*, vol.III, p.65 sqq.
31. Hopkins: *Glencoe*, op cit., p.156.
32. *Letters*, p.250.
33. *The MacDonald Collection of Gaelic Poetry*, Inverness, 1911, p.75. Latha Raonn-Ruairidh, 1689 by Mac Alasdair Ruaidh, verse 9 - Fir Ghlinnecomhann, 's a Bràighe.
34. *Orain Iain Luim*, p.184, lines 2362–3.

Sir John Maclean
By kind permission of Sir Lachlan Maclean

CHAPTER TEN

Lochaber No More

'...so great was the confidence they reposed in his [Dundee's] conduct, that they resigned themselves entirely to his pleasure without searching into his designs. Though the Highlanders are in general a high-spirited and proud people, and of unruly and stubborn temper, yet the authority he had over them was surprising.'

John Drummond of Balhaldy

THE ARRIVAL of *Dòmhnall Gorm Og* at Dalcomera on the 19th July was followed on the 20th by the coming of Purcell's Irish regiment to Corran Ferry, below Inverlochy.[1] Ferrying more than 300 men across the Corran Narrows where the tide runs very strongly would take time. Even a modern ferry has to travel some way north-east up Loch Linnhe before it is able to turn into the current and get down to the pier on the east side. If the Irish did actually get to the camp at Dalcomera before it was broken up their stay would have been brief. According to Balhaldy they joined Dundee as he was heading for Badenoch which he reached on the 23rd July.[2]

When they landed at Inverlochy their overall commander was Brigadier-General Alexander Cannon, replacing Buchan. Their Colonel James Purcell was accompanied by several Scots, including the Earl of Buchan, Lewis Viscount Frendraught, Sir William Wallace of Craigie and Sir George Barclay. Another Scot, this time a Highlander, was *Ruairidh MacMhuirich* of Balilone.

The MacMhuirichs were descended from *Muiredhach Ó Dálaigh*, bard to *Cathal Crodhearg*, King of Connaught. In 1213 or thereabouts Muiredhach had had an unfortunate encounter with the King's Steward who demanded rent from him, although he felt that, as an important official at the royal court, he should be required to pay none. In his rage Muiredhach split the Steward's head open and had to leave Ireland in a hurry. He took shelter with Donald of the Isles and became the principal bard at his court. This became an hereditary appointment and amongst the descendants of Muiredhach was *Lachlan Mòr* who recited his famous *Brosnachadh* (incitement to battle) before the battle of Harlaw, which the Lord of the Isles won. The hereditary position of the MacMhuirichs ended with the demise of the Lordship of the Isles, but Neil MacMhuirich, younger brother of John, bard to the last Lord, went to South Uist during the 1490s and became bard to the Clanranald MacDonalds. In 1506 the MacMhuirichs were granted land at Balilone in Bute, but less than forty years later, in 1543, *Dòmhnall MacMhuirich*, the 11th Chief of Clan Mhuirich, involved himself in a conspiracy to restore the Lord of the Isles in the person of *Dòmhnall Dubh*, son of Angus of the Isles. When this attempt failed MacMhuirich was obliged to repeat his ancestor's flight, but in reverse, and seek shelter in Ireland. He acquired land there at Balilone in Co.Antrim amongst the Scots-Irish MacDonalds. Whether the name of the place was a strange coincidence or whether he renamed it is not clear.

Dòmhnall Mac Mhuirich, Ruairidh's father, was an officer in the band of Irish and Scots-Irish brought to Scotland by Alasdair MacColla in 1644. When this campaign came to an end Donald managed to get back to Ireland with Alasdair, but one of his sons perished in the massacre of Dunaverty, to which we have already referred.

Ruairidh, the 18th Chief of Clan Mhuirich and the 10th of Balilone, born five years before his father's death in 1665, continued his father's support of the Stuarts by accompanying the contingent of Irish crossing to help Dundee.

When Dundee's army was disbanded Ruairidh found refuge in the islands for a time and then went to France. He joined the Scottish Gentlemen Volunteers formed with the permission of James VII as part of the French army. When this unit disbanded Ruairidh went to Russia and became an officer in a Cossack Guards Regiment in Peter the Great's army, eventually becoming Colonel. So the young Scots-Irishman who set out from Ireland to Lochaber in his thirtieth year became a member of one of the fiercest bands of warriors in the army of the Tsar. Towards the end of his life he returned to Ireland and Balilone and died there in 1730.[3]

Dundee had set a provisional general rendezvous for the 28th or 29th July, but with the arrival of the MacDonalds of Sleat and the landing of Purcell's regiment, which made the gathering together of a sizeable army more feasible and with the alarms and excursions attending Mackay's movements in the east, it seemed essential to move at once. His intention was not merely to hold Blair Castle as a strategic point in his plan of defence and attack but to raise Braemar and Atholl for the King. He had already despatched Sir Alexander MacLean of Otter, MacNeill of Gallachallie and Halyburton of Pitcur to carry through preliminary skirmishes to this end and now, hearing that Mackay was moving northwards in the direction of Blair, he gathered the whole camp at Dalcomera together, sent out for the absent, waiting clans and left the camp on the 23rd July. On the day before this he wrote from Strone ordering Cluny to have provisions ready 'near to the place of Clunie for 1,500 men for 2 days' and 'to meet

me tomorrows night (without fail) at Garva'.[4] It will be remembered that
Iain Lom was camping at Dalcomera 'on the day before Sunday and two
days afterwards', that is, up to and including Tuesday the 23rd. This
suggests that they may not have left very early on the Tuesday, yet Dundee
was to be at Garva that night and in fact got as far as Cluny Castle, but
perhaps only with the cavalry. The camp was broken up so quickly that
even Lochiel, the nearest to it, could only gather about 250 of his clansmen
and had to leave his son, John, to bring up the rest.

Dundee hurried away from Dalcomera, away from the junction of the
two rivers and from the high mountains that he had grown to know so
well. It was only two months since the day of his arrival. Then the glens
had been full of snow and ice, now they were green in the warmth of July
and the heather moving towards the time of its flowering. Then he had
known nobody, apart from the friends he had brought with him; now he
was acquainted with all the leaders of his clansmen, even if in some cases
the acquaintance had necessarily been brief. The chiefs, from being merely
names on paper or names heard without knowledge of their characters or
faces or whence they came, had become physical presences, bringing with
them something of the aura of their lochs and mountains, their tall galleys,
their sounding pipes and the surge of far-off seas on sand and pebbles. He
in his turn had developed for them into a known and loved personality
who:

> ... knew so well to adapt himself to the humours and inclinations of the
> people whom he commanded, that there was a general harmony and
> agreement among all the officers of his little army.[5]

Sir John Dalrymple of Cranstown gives a remarkable account of his habits
when the army was on the march:

> ... he walked on foot with the men, now by the side of one clan, and
> anon by that of another. He amused them with jokes; he flattered them
> with his knowledge of their genealogies, he animated them by a recital
> of the deeds of their ancestors and of the verses of their bards.[6]

If there is any truth in this it suggests a much vaster knowledge of Gaelic
than one would expect. His life up to 1689 had been spent entirely in the
Lowlands and in Dumfries and Galloway, apart from his service abroad,
but his home in Glen Ogilvie was close to the highland line and there
would surely have been Highlanders in his household, outdoor servants
to take him into the high hills, serving girls and nursemaids to sing
Highland songs and tell stories from their own Gaelic world. Sir John
Dalrymple also records that Dundee:

... had inflamed his mind from his earliest youth by the perusal of antient poets, historians, and orators, with the love of the great actions they praise and describe. He is reported to have inflamed it still more, by listening to the antient songs of the highland bards.[7]

It is generally believed that there was something like an iron curtain between the Highlands and the Lowlands until the middle of the eighteenth century and although this was to some extent true there were many incursions, welcome or otherwise, on both sides and Lowland gentlemen were wont, for instance, to flock to the lands of Highland chiefs to hunt, at which time they were expected to don some kind of Highland garb. John Taylor, the Water-Poet (he had been a waterman on the Thames), wrote of his journey to Scotland in 1618 that he found on the Braes of Mar a gathering of:

... truely noble and right honourable Lords...and hundreds of others knights, esquires and their followers...For once in the yeere, which is the whole moneth of August, and sometimes part of September, many of the nobility and gentry of the kingdome (for their pleasure) doe come into these high-land countries to hunt...As for their attire, any man of what degree soever that comes amongst them must not disdaine to weare it: for if they doe, then they will disdaine to hunt, or willingly to bring in their dogges: but if men be kind unto them, and be in their habit; then are they conquered with kindnesse...[8]

But Dundee would have needed to learn a great deal of Gaelic from the Highlanders he met, whether at home or while hunting, before he could behave as Dalrymple suggests. It is interesting that very similar behaviour is attributed to Prince Charles Edward, who is said to have walked along beside his men and entertained them with the Gaelic he had been able to pick up since he landed in Scotland. We do know of him, however, that he sometimes used Gaelic phrases and that he had appointed one of his officers, probably the poet *Alasdair Mac Mhaighstir Alasdair*, as his Gaelic tutor. There is nothing however in what we hear of Dundee to suggest that he made any progress in Gaelic and indeed he had far less time to do so than the Prince.

The Gaelic poets wrote verses in praise of him. *Mac Alasdair Ruaidh*, the brother of Alasdair Mac Alasdair, the Glencoe Chief killed in the massacre, described him as:

Og sgiobalta suairc thu,
Sàr bhuachaill' an tréud thu,
'Gan cumail a gàbhadh,
Toirt dhaibh àit' air an réidhlean.[9]

(You were young, active and mild. You were an excellent shepherd of
the flock, keeping them out of danger and giving them a place on the
smooth plain.)

Iain Lom also gave him twelve lines in *Latha Raon Ruairidh*, the Battle of
Killiecrankie, whereas in *La Inbhir Lochaidh*, the Battle of Inverlochy, he
does not even mention Montrose, keeping all his admiration for the Clan
Donald. He calls Dundee *'an Gramach a b'fhearr nadur'* (the good natured
Graham)[10] and *'A shar Cleibhears nan each Bu cheann-feadhn' thu air feachd'*
(Noble Clavers, rider of horses, a worthy captain of a host were you).[11]
Always he is *Cleibhears* or *an Gramach* or *Dundighe*.[12] They never give him
a Gaelic soubriquet. In spite of this everyone writing about him inevitably
tells us that the Highlanders' name for him was *Iain Dubh nan Cath* – Dark
John of the Battles. No reference is ever given for this and I have certainly
found no instance of such a name in any contemporary Gaelic verse. I
wonder whether there could possibly have been confusion with *Iain Ruadh
nan Cath*, the red-headed 2nd Duke of Argyll, who, not much more than
twenty years after Dundee's campaign, became the hero of Oudenaarde,
Ramillies and Malplaquet. Soon after this, in 1715, he commanded the
Hanoverian army in the inconclusive battle of Sheriffmuir. His military
exploits would have been bruited about the Highlands at a time when
Dundee's were still not forgotten. The Duke was a Highlander and a
Highland Chief and one would expect him to be given some Gaelic soubriquet, whereas Montrose and Dundee were not and therefore did not
acquire one.

Keppoch did not join Dundee as he moved eastwards. Hopkins says
that 'Keppoch apparently failed to join though the army marched through
his lands of Glen Roy'.[13] Though they certainly marched through part of
Glen Roy they may have missed the most populated part of it, that is, the
lower part of the glen. To help us determine this we have to return to *Iain
Lom*'s Song to King James's Army where he tells us:

> *Dh'fhalbh sinn a muigh cho ro stàtail*
> *Gus an do ràinig sinn bràighe Ghlinn Ruaidh;*
> *Mach ri Gleann Turraid is monadh sin Dhrumainn*
> *Dh'imich gach duine bha guineach 'san ruaig.*[14]

(We set out in very stately order till we reached the head of Glen Roy.
Out by Glen Turret and over that moor of Drummond marched each
man who was vindictive in the battle.)

Mackenzie's note on these lines does not make the matter at all clear; it
could be interpreted in several ways:

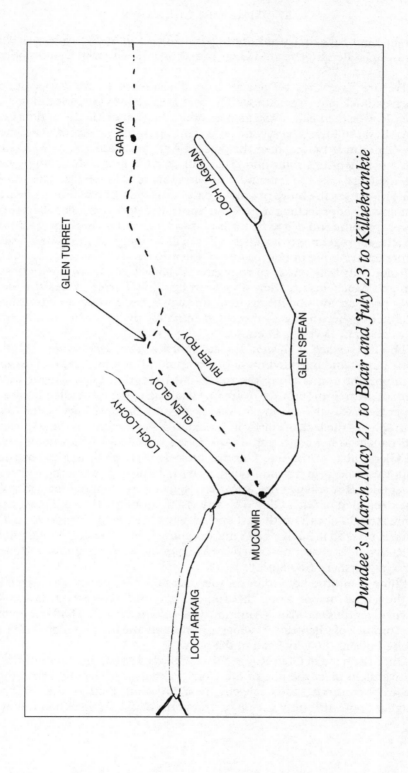

Dundee's March May 27 to Blair and July 23 to Killiekrankie

Iain Lom says that from the head of Loch Lochy the clans marched through Glen Roy beyond Glen Turret over the moor of Drummod...[15]

There are two ways of getting from Dalcomera to Melgarve on the Corrieyairack and so to Atholl. The first is to go into Glen Spean and up Glen Roy to the head of the glen at White Falls, passing the end of Glen Turret on the way. The second is to slant up north-east from Dalcomera to Glen Fintaig Lodge, near the present A82, and then go up Glen Gloy; one must then turn right into Glen Turret and, after a short while, bear left, eastwards, up the remainder of Glen Roy to White Falls. The second route by-passes the more populous part of the glen. It will thus be evident that anyone approaching from Glen Spean will not enter Glen Turret but merely pass the end of it as he turns eastwards near Turret Bridge, whereas anyone approaching from Glen Gloy will actually go into Glen Turret before entering the upper reaches of Glen Roy.

It depends how one is to translate '*ri*'. '*Mach ri Gleann Turraid*', says Iain and Mackenzie renders it as 'Out by Glen Turret'. Does she mean 'by = past' or 'by = by means of or through'? And should it be translated by either of these forms or more appropriately by 'to' or 'in the direction of' as given in Dwelly's Dictionary?

The line '*Mach ri Gleann Turraid is monadh sin Dhrumainn*' (Out by Glen Turret and over that moor of Drummond) marks these two features as important points along the route and I feel that Glen Turret would seem of greater importance to anyone wanting to get from Glen Gloy into upper Glen Roy than to anyone merely passing the opening to Glen Gloy.

In spite of the lack of clarity in Mackenzie's comment on these lines the end-papers to her collection of *Iain Lom*'s songs show the second route, via Glen Gloy, as the one Dundee took. It was certainly a major route from west to east in his time when, as we have already seen, the routes up lower Glen Roy and up Glen Spean to Laggan were of merely local interest. The deep cleft of Glen Gloy is clearly visible from the field of Dalcomera, going straight ahead north-east and drawing the eye upwards into it. The route is marked in Moll's 1725 map as going from Mucomir (Dalcomera) to Ruthven. It is also described by Moir in his work on tracks and highways in Northern Scotland.[16]

Philip is of little help to us on this occasion. He merely says, speaking of the earlier march along this route, i.e. to Edinglassie: '*Transieratque procul vallis confinia Roae*' (And now [the tartaned host]... had left behind the confines of Glen Roy)[17] which presumably means that they were past White Falls at the very head of the glen.

Once the head of Glen Roy at White Falls is passed, the track continues eastwards to meet the line of the Corrieyairack at Melgarve. From there the army continued to Breakachy, near the south bank of the Spey and roughly opposite Cluny Castle on the north bank. Dundee had followed this route before when heading for Edinglassie and for his celebration of Restoration Day beside Raitts Castle further down the Spey. He wrote a letter to Murray, possibly from Cluny Castle, on the evening of the 23rd.[18] There is nothing to suggest that Cluny met him at Garva as he had been asked to do or even that he produced the provisions requested. At Blair the army was found to have 'suffered much by the want of provisions' according to Balhaldy[19] and in describing their march to Blair from Dalcomera he writes:

> He [Dundee] had gained so much upon the affections of his small army, that, though half-starved, they marched forward as cheerfully as if they had not felt the least effects of want.[20]

If Dundee did indeed write his two letters to Murray of the 23rd and 25th from Cluny Castle it will probably not have been in the presence or at the invitation of its owner. He may have gone to Cluny Castle with his cavalry only and may have stayed for three nights there or in the vicinity, waiting for the rest of the army to catch up with him. Perhaps only the horse got to Cluny by the evening of the 23rd and the clans did not begin their march from Dalcomera until that evening or even the following morning, the 24th. This would fit in with *Iain Lom*'s statement that they camped at Dalcomera 'for the day before Sunday and two days after it'. It is about thirty-five miles from Dalcomera to Cluny Castle. Even a Highland army could not go that distance on foot over that terrain in one day but they could have done it in two. When Dundee went to Edinglassie he was at Raitts Castle (about ten miles further than Cluny) by the 29th May (probably by the evening before), having left Dalcomera at mid-day on the 26th May. This means that they did forty-five miles in two and a half days, assuming that they came on the same route. In July therefore the clansmen could easily have completed the thirty-five miles to Cluny by the 25th, even allowing for some delay in clearing the camp.

By late on the 26th July they were all at Blair Castle, still in the safe hands of Patrick Stewart of Ballechin and spent the night there. Balhaldy says that they arrived on the 27th, but the date on the letter to Cluny (26th July – see below) from Blair Castle and the events of the 27th make this unlikely.

Finding some relatively quiet room amidst the noise and bustle Dundee sat down, his officers coming and going with reports, and wrote a final blast to Cluny:

> Sir, My Lord Murray is retyred doun the contrey. All the Atholl men have left them saive Stratherel, Achintully, and Baron Read Straloch, and they will not byd my doun coming to morou. The rest of the heritors will be here to morou. They will joyn us, and I supose to morou

you will have ane answer so if you have a mynd to preserve yourself and
to serve the King be in armes to morou that when the letter comes you
may be here in a day. All the world will be with us blissed be God. I
am, Sir, your most humble servant.[21]

Sentries were posted and scouts sent out – Dundee's intelligence was
always very good, unlike Montrose's – and the great, ancient building
gradually fell silent under the soft, pale grey of a Highland summer night.

Notes

1. *Letters*, p.257.
2. Balhaldy, p.257.
3. W.M.Currie of Balilone: *With Sword and Harp, Clan Mhurrich (Currie). The
   Warrior Poets*, Milngavie (Heather Bank Press), 1977. pp.95–8.
4. *Letters*, p.260.
5. Balhaldy, p.276.
6. Dalrymple: *Memoirs of Great Britain...*, op. cit., vol. ii, Pt.II, Bk. II, p.74.
7. ibid., vol.ii, Pt.II, Bk.II, p.46.
8. *The Pennyless Pilgrimage...* of John Taylor, quoted in John Telfer Dunbar: *History
   of Highland Dress*, op. cit., p.34.
9. *The MacDonald Collection of Gaelic Poetry*, op, cit., p.74, verse 3.
10. *Orain Iain Luim*, p.186, line 2370.
11. ibid., p.192, lines 2454–5.
12. ibid., p.188, 1ine 2404 See also Mac Alasdair Ruaidh, in: *The MacDonald Collection
    of Gaelic Poetry*, op. cit., p.74, verses 1 and 3.
13. Hopkins: *Glencoe*, op. cit., p.156 See also note 7 to Chapter Eleven.
14. *Orain Iain Luim*, p.186, lines 2374–7.
15. ibid., p.309, note to line 2375.
16. D.S. Moir: *Scottish Hill Tracks, Old Highways and Drove Roads*, Part 2. Northern
    Scotland, Edinburgh, 1975, Route 59.
17. *Grameid*, Book IV, line 526. Philip is referring here to the march to Edinglassie;
    his narrative ends before the second march along this route.
18. *Letters*, p.261.
19. Balhaldy, p.262.
20. ibid., p.258.
21. *Letters*, p.262.

CHAPTER ELEVEN

Killiecrankie

Clara viri sic fama valet pro mille maniplis.

The Grameid

(Thus the bright fame of a hero is worth a thousand swords.)

BLAIR CASTLE is now a well-known landmark on the railway journey south from Inverness. It lies well back to the north of the railway line on a gentle rise amidst a wild countryside of forests, rivers, mountains and rich green upland fields. Its walls, harled and painted white, make it impossible to miss against the darker hills and trees behind it. Dundee would hardly recognise it today; it was remodelled after the '45, when it was bombarded by Lord George Murray, and altered again in the nineteenth century. Many of the rooms we know today were not there in his time, for instance, the entrance hall and the small drawingroom and those that were there lacked the eighteenth- and nineteenth-century plasterwork that now ornaments them. The whole place may well have been in chaos when he arrived for the castle had been in a state of defence for some weeks and filled with Ballechin's men. Blair was built by the Comyns in 1236 and Edward III of England stayed in it during one of his predatory visits to Scotland in 1336. Montrose had made use of it and so had Cromwell for it was, as Dundee rightly appreciated, in a pivotal position as far as the defence of the Highlands was concerned.

Two or three miles south down the line from Blair is the village of Killiecrankie and here anyone sitting by the window on the south-west side of the train and looking downwards at the right moment can see through the trees the steep precipice ending in the bed of the River Garry with a narrow path struggling through the gorge beside it. The name Killiecrankie derives from the Gaelic Coille Chnagaidh – the bunchy wood; part of it was known as Coill' a' Chreathnaich – the trembling wood, which suggests aspen trees. The area is still heavily wooded and there cannot be many more beautiful sights than the Killiecrankie gorge in spring, when the fresh, young leaves throw a green light over the water, or in autumn when the margins of the river and its towering sides turn bright gold and tawny red. Above it to the north-east are the smooth green slopes of Meall an Daimh and of Creag Eallaich below Carn Liath. Pennant in true eighteenth-century vein described it in 1769 as 'a scene of horrible grandeur'.[1]

There was a council meeting at Blair on the morning of the 27th July. Two possibilities had to be considered. Should they stay in or around the castle to keep it out of enemy hands, which was after all the main reason for their march from Lochaber, and wait until the rest of the army came up? Or should they give battle immediately. The Lowlanders and regular army officers were for the former alternative but the Highland chiefs, who knew the resilience (and impatience) of their men, favoured the latter. Glengarry was the first to come down on the side of immediate battle and he was supported by the other chiefs. Dundee finally asked Lochiel, who had remained silent, for his opinion and he agreed with his fellow Gaels, saying that he had not spoken before because

...he had already determined himself to submit to his Lordship's conduct, which was so exactly adapted to the genius of the Highlanders, that he needed no advice; but that since he had commanded him to give his opinion, it was in one word – 'To fight immediately, – for our men,' said he, 'are in heart; they are so far from being afraid of their enemy, that they are eager and keen to engage them, least they escape their hands, as they have so often done. Though we have few men, they are good, and I can venture to assure your Lordship that not one of them will faill yow. It is better to fight att the disadvantage of even one to three, than to delay it till M'Kay's dragoons and cavalry have time to joyn him. To pretend to stop them in the Pass is a vain project, for they have undoubtedly gott through it ere now, and to march up to them and not immediatly to fight, is to expose ourselves to the want of provisions, seeing we can spare no men for forageing; besides, we will discover that, even in our oppinion, we are unequall to the enemy, which would be of dangerous consequence among Highlanders. If the enemy shall be allowed time to march up and offer to attack us, and we retreat, it will be still worse. If your Lordship thinks proper to delay fighting, and wait the arrivall of our men, my oppinion is, that we immediately retreat again to the mountains and meet them; for I will not promise upon the event, if we are not the aggressors. But be assured, my Lord, that if once we are fairly engaged, we will either lose our army, or carry a compleat victorey... Their great superiority in number will give a necessary reputation to our victorey; and not only fright them from meddling with a people conducted by such a General, and animated by such a cause, but it will incourage the whole kingdome to declare in our favours.[2]

This advice was obviously what Dundee wanted. Delight grew on his face as Lochiel spoke. But Lochiel had one request to make, that Dundee should not engage personally in the fight as his life was too valuable to their cause to be risked. To this, however, Dundee would not agree. Mindful of the Gaelic manner of fighting which required the Chief and his family to expose themselves to the greatest danger, he wished to show the clans that he too was prepared to do as much, as he feared that otherwise he would not retain that ascendancy over them that he then had. They would not follow him willingly. He must, he said '... give one 'Sheardarg' [Scots for harvest day's work]...to the King.[3] The council gave in but with great reluctance.

Once the decision on giving battle had been agreed and knowing that by that time Mackay was probably already out of the Pass, they hastily gathered the army together and marched towards the heights overlooking Killiecrankie. It was about midday.

Mackay had reached Dunkeld on the night of the 26th and had left it early on the 27th. He rested at Pitlochry and marched on towards the Pass at 12.00 noon.

The Pass of Killiecrankie, roughly a mile long and squeezed into the narrow gorge of the river with high hills on either side, could not accommodate more than two, in places perhaps three men abreast. Mackay and his officers and the men too no doubt had an anxious time struggling through it. They did not know what snipers might not be hidden above them or what sort of reception they might have when emerging from the Pass into the wider landscape. One cavalry officer was picked off by *Iain Bàn Beag Mac Rath*, a famous Atholl hunter who, fortunately for Mackay's men, had only one bullet left. Lochiel had rightly rejected the idea of meeting them at the exit from this narrow defile because there was too little time to carry through such a manoeuvre properly. Even as things were the clansmen had to hurry to gain a strategic place on the slopes of Carn Liath and were almost running as they approached the final battle stance.[4]

There were about 2,000 men with Dundee. Mackay had 4,000, including two troops of horse and three small pieces of artillery, one of which fell apart when it was first fired. His men had flintlock muskets and plug bayonets, short knives carried in the belt which had to be rammed into the shaft of the musket before they could be used; when there they naturally prevented the firing of the musket. As can be imagined it was difficult to get them into the musket shaft quickly. (After the battle Mackay developed the ring bayonet which was permanently fixed to its staff and did not interfere with firing. It was used by Cumberland at Culloden.) Mackay moved quickly to the terrain around the present Urrard House. Its Gaelic name is Raon Ruaridh (Rory's upland field) and to Gaels the battle has always been known by this name. He waited there for the baggage. No Highlanders were in sight.

Meanwhile Dundee had left Blair Castle in the early afternoon on news of Mackay's approach. He sent a small contingent of Camerons along the road from Blair as a feint. The rest of the army crossed the Banvie Burn which runs close by the castle, crossed the Tilt and then turned east beside the Fender, going behind the Hill of Lude, which meant that they were not visible to Mackay for some time. They went round the edge of Loch Moraig and then down the Clune Burn to the lower slopes of Creag· Eallaich.

Mackay had taken up a position facing northwards, expecting Dundee to arrive along the road from Blair, but when he saw the Highlanders deploying above him he performed what he called a *'quart de conversion'* and turned his army ninety degrees to the right. He then marched up to a plateau above the house of Raon Ruairidh and arranged his men in a long line only three deep, anxious not to be outflanked.

Dundee arranged his men in their clan regiments. This was important as it encouraged the clans to emulate and outdo their fellow Gaels; it also meant that they were fighting under well-known commanders. As Mackay, with nearly twice the number, had stretched his lines out such a distance Dundee had to spread his very widely to avoid being outflanked in his turn, with the result that there were wide gaps between the blocks of clansmen.

On the extreme right were the MacLeans of Duart under the nineteen-year-old Sir John, including MacLeans from Islay, Jura and Kintyre and probably also from Coll. Next came the Irish regiment under Purcell, then the MacDonalds of Clanranald, also with a youthful chief, but the Tutor of Clanranald was with him. To their left were the Glengarry MacDonalds along with the Grants of Glenmoriston and Glen Urquhart who were fighting under Glengarry's banner.

In the centre and stationed a little back from the line were forty horse under Wallace of Craigie. That morning he had produced an order, signed by his brother-in-law, Melfort, giving him command of the horse in place of the loyal and experienced Dunfermline. This order Dundee apparently felt it best to accept – with what reluctance we can only imagine – although in his latest letter James had written:

> …in the meantime, what commissions we have sent, or what others we shall send, we leav to you to cancell or suspend as you shall think fitt, having reposed in you the trust of that affair,[5]

but to have ignored James's order might have soured relations with his latest recruits. Dunfermline must have appreciated the difficulties which might arise if the order were blocked and stood down without making a protest. Balhaldy records 'that noble Earl calmly resigned, much to the dissatisfaction of Dundee'.[6] This appointment was to have unfortunate if not fatal results.

To the left of the horse came Lochiel with 180 Camerons who were to be joined later by those Camerons who had been sent along the road from Blair and who sniped at the enemy's left wing for a time until they were dislodged. To the left of Lochiel came the MacLeans of Otter including Alexander's Irish, the Kintyre clans (MacDonald of Largie and MacAlister of Loup) and the MacNeills of Barra. The extreme left was held by the MacDonalds of Sleat with whom were those Keppoch MacDonalds, including *Iain Lom*, who had recently accompanied them from Sleat. Keppoch himself and Glencoe were not there.[7] Presumably they had not been able to gather their men in time. These two clans often raided together and as the general rendezvous had been set for the 28th or 29th they may well have been bringing in cattle to feed the army, expecting still to get there in time. (They both joined after the battle bringing 250 men between them.)

There were also various smaller bands of Gaels from small clans or septs, too few in number to form their own clan regiments. The Grants of Glenmoriston and Glen Urquhart have already been mentioned and there were also the MacLeods of Raasay who may have fought under the banner of Sir John or Sir Alexander or most likely *Dòmhnall Gorm Og*. The MacGregors were there in the shape of Alexander Drummond of Balhaldy who rode with the horse but it is doubtful whether the Glenstrae or the Glengyle Gregarach had any place in the battle line. W.H. Murray says the MacGregors stood with the Camerons, citing Terry, the *Memoirs of the Lord Viscount Dundee* and *The Grameid*, but Terry does not mention MacGregors at Killiecrankie, the *Memoirs of the Lord Viscount Dundee* merely says that they joined after the battle and *The Grameid*, of course, stops several days before the battle.[8] The Camerons of Glendessary, with whom the MacGregors had appeared at Dalcomera, did not come in until the 28th/29th, being amongst the many Camerons who lived at some distance from Dalcomera and were brought in by Lochiel's son John. The Glenstrae and Glengyle MacGregors may have been with them. The MacGregors of Roro joined at this time, as did the Appin Stewarts.[9]

Half the chiefs were from the islands or Kintyre: they had either stayed with Dundee after he sent the nearer clans home or had arrived before the date of the general rendezvous to make sure of being in time. Unlike the mainland clans they had to make allowances for the weather. Lochiel was the only truly experienced chief and sixty-three years old. Glengarry and Otter were both in their thirties with little military experience. The others were in their teens and early twenties.

MacKay's men waiting below at least had the advantage that the sun was not shining in their eyes on that hot July day. But above them was the unnerving sight of the Highland army poised to descend in one of those fierce charges which chilled the blood at the hearing. The wild cries that arose from time to time from these 'savages' (as they thought them) must have inspired in them a terror akin to that of the Romans when they heard the carnyx, the ancient Celtic war trumpet with boar's head and clapping metal tongue, blown at Mons Graupius. And above these cries were the eager notes of the pipes pushing up into the still, hot air all along the battle line.

We can only speculate on the pipers who may have been present. The most famous piping family, the MacCrimmons, were not represented as they were hereditary pipers to MacLeod of Dunvegan, who had not responded to Dundee's invitation to join the Jacobite army.

As both MacLean of Duart and MacLean of Coll were at the battle it would be reasonably safe to assume that one of the Rankin family of pipers was with them. The Rankins were hereditary pipers to MacLean of Duart and afterwards to MacLean of Coll. The Gaelic name of the Rankins is *Clann Mhic Fhraing* – children of the son of Frang (*Frangan*, Francis). They were a branch of the MacLeans of Duart and the first to be appointed as piper is said to have studied music in Ireland and to have founded a school of piping in Mull before the more famous piping school of the MacCrimmons was established in Skye. Pipers from these two areas are believed to have attended each other's schools. When the fortunes of the MacLeans of Duart declined the Rankins transferred their piping skills to the MacLeans of Coll.[10] It was Neil Rankin who played at dinner when Boswell took Dr. Johnson to visit the Laird of Coll. Johnson wrote:

> The bagpiper played regularly when dinner was served, whose person and dress made a good appearance, and he brought no disgrace on the family of Rankin, which has long supplied the Lairds of Col with hereditary musick.[11]

At what precise moment in the decline of the MacLeans of Duart their hereditary piper was lost is not clear. It may have been after 1689 or it may have been before that year. The MacLeans had been in difficulties since 1598 but it was not until Sir John's father died in 1674 that these difficulties became acute, culminating in the handing over of the Duart estates and thus of their rents to Argyll in 1680. But a Rankin is likely to have been at Killiecrankie, whichever of the MacLeans he was representing.

One of Lochiel's sons, Donald, was serving in Mackay's army. He had probably taken his oath to James but honour may have obliged him to retain his commission and Lochiel may also have thought it politic for him to remain where he was. It was good insurance to have someone in the family on the enemy side in these civil wars for then whichever side won there might be a chance of saving the clan lands from forfeiture. But it must have been hard for those most closely involved to have to fight against their own family, culture and beliefs. It seems surprising that any commanding officer could put his trust in an officer in this condition and

says a lot for the code of honour and obligation to which these unfortu-
nates were bound. Scanning Dundee's lines Mackay said to Donald:
'There's your father, with his wild savages; how would you like to be with
them?' to which Donald replied: 'It signifies little what I would like; but
I recommend you to be prepared, or perhaps my father and his wild savages
may be nearer to you than you would like before night.'[12]

As they all waited in the hot afternoon sun Mackay grew restive and
tried to provoke an attack by firing at the opposing line with his artillery.
The Highlanders had no means of replying to this; some of them were
killed or wounded and this increased the natural impatience of the others.
It was galling and dispiriting to have to stand still and see one's friends
fall. They stood ready for the fight, having cast their plaids and tied their
shirt-tails between their legs.[13] But Dundee was determined not to loose
them on Mackay until conditions were just right, particularly not until the
sun, which was shining in their faces, had sunk behind the western hills.
He rode up and down the lines, controlling and inspiring at the same time.
Few, if any, at any time could have exercised that degree of control over
such an army. He had been persuaded to remove his scarlet coat and put
on a silver and buff one. He may have worn a green scarf and Iain Lom
speaks of his *clogad bàn* (his white or bright helmet).[14] It has, however,
been suggested that he had abandoned his morion and was wearing a wide-
brimmed, plumed chapeau, whilst another writer believes that he may
have worn a white plume similar to the one he wore at Seneffe when he
saved the life of the Prince of Orange.[15] It will be remembered that on
Dundee Law, when hoping to pick up the loyal members of his old troop
of horse, he wore a helmet covered with black fur and during the
Edinglassie expedition he was seen making ready for battle by pressing his
long hair up under a gleaming helmet (*galea rutilante*).[16] ... It therefore
seems very unlikely that, at a far more important encounter than either of
these, he would not seek the protection of a helmet. Certainly his helmet
was buried with him; it was made of brass (see p.153 below) and would
have shone like bright, pale gold in the sunshine.

Between 7 and 8 o'clock that evening the sun dropped below the horizon
and allowed the Highlanders to have a clear view of their opponents.
Dundee gave the order to charge and the clansmen rushed down the hillside, holding their fire, as they had been trained to do, until within a few
yards of the enemy. During this time they had to bear enemy fire as best
they could with only the passive defence of their targes. Once they crashed
into the opposing lines however and attacked with their broadswords
Mackay's soldiers had no leisure either to reload their muskets or to fit
their bayonets onto them. The smoke from the clansmen's single burst of
musket fire as they drew near confused Mackay's men; they could not see
clearly what was going on and before the smoke had cleared the
Highlanders were in amongst them with their broadswords. In a very short

time they were smashed by the weight of Dundee's compact squares which, though they were of necessity precipitated only against portions of the line, were far heavier than the thin line they opposed and so not only broke through at the points attacked but threw the intact portions of the line into confusion. Alasdair MacColla would have been proud to see his tactics so well understood by both commander and commanded.

Many of Mackay's men did not wait until the clansmen reached them but turned tail and fled, some back down the Pass while others tried to reach the river and get across it, many being drowned in the process. Others found the ford to the west of the Clune Burn and crossed there. Mackay, seeing that the day was lost and that those who had run off were not likely to return, gathered together as many men as he could and slipped away over the hills to Castle Menzies where he spent the night.

The slaughter was great on both sides but above all on Mackay's. He lost more than half his army. It was observed the next day that most of the dead Highlanders fell during the charge when they were close to the enemy but had not yet fired on them.[17] These losses did not slow down the charge. They have been calculated by some at 900, a figure later given to the King as the total casualties.[18] If as many men as this were killed during the charge it would mean that Mackay's army of 4,000 was destroyed by a Highland army that had shrunk by the moment of contact to little more than 1,000 men. Casualties were, as usual, especially heavy amongst the gentry of the clans, as they always stood in the front line.

Young MacDonald of Largie was killed along with others of his family, so too were Glengarry's brother Donald and five close kinsmen of *Dòmhnall Gorm Og* of Sleat. Several MacLean gentry lost their lives, another brother of Glengarry, Iain, was wounded and half the Camerons were left dead on the field, but Lochiel himself survived unhurt. James of Capstil, a Sleat MacDonald, was killed and that night in Capstil his cows gave blood instead of milk.[19] A death attended by strange circumstances was that of Gilbert Ramsay, a young lawyer recently admitted as Advocate to the Faculty of Law in Leyden. He had thrown up his career in the law to join Dundee and was warned in a dream just before he awoke on the day of the battle that he would not survive it. Several gentlemen assured him that in such a case he could withdraw from the battle without loss of honour, but he refused to do so and was killed while riding after Dundee beside Alexander Drummond of Balhaldy.[20]

But the grief attending these deaths was as nothing when it was found that Dundee himself lay seriously wounded on the field. He had last been seen, his arm raised, urging his horsemen on towards the enemy. Wallace of Craigie had taken a turn towards the left, for some unknown reason, when he should have led them straight ahead and Dundee would seem to have been trying to correct this move. While doing this he became enveloped in a cloud of smoke and was not seen again until he was found by Pitcur and Balhaldy lying on the ground with a wound in his left side. The wound was so placed that it was thought the bullet had reached him while his arm was raised trying to urge on the horsemen behind him; this arm movement would have lifted his breastplate and exposed the area of the wound.[21] The inevitable story put about by some of his enemies was that he had been killed by a silver bullet, the only bullet capable of destroying a man in league with the devil, fired from the window of the house at Raon Ruairidh while he paused to water his horse in a wet hollow of the field. Even those totally unacquainted with warfare can appreciate that no commander would stop to water his horse during a cavalry charge!

Those who had followed Wallace were not seen again until after the battle. The sixteen gentlemen who followed Dundee included Dunfermline, Pitcur, Alexander Balhaldy and Ramsay. Johnston (see below) must have been another and probably also Philip of Almerieclose, although he is not mentioned. They observed Dundee as he was entering the smoke 'turn his horse towards the right and raiseing himself upon his stirrops, make signes by waving his hatt over his head for the rest to come up'.[22]

When he fell from his horse he was supported by someone of the name of Johnston. This may have been John Johnston, brother of the Earl of Annandale. A Lieutenant Nisbet who was a prisoner at Blair Castle after the battle deponed, once he got back to his own side, that at Blair:

> ...one named Johnston told [him] that he had catched the Viscount as he fell from his horse after his being shot. The Viscount then asking the said Johnston how the day went, and that he answered, 'the day went weel for the King' (meaning King James), but that he was sorry for his Lordship, and that the Viscount replied, 'it was less matter for him seeing the day went weel for his master'.[23]

John Johnston was present at Dalcomera and Philip calls him 'the Johnston youth' (*Johnstonia pubes*) and describes him riding onto the field there with Gilbert Ramsay, the cavalier who foresaw his own death.[24]

The sixteen gentlemen who had followed Dundee observed that Hasting's regiment was still in the field and, gathering together a few Highlanders, made an attack on it. But when Leven's regiment came to its aid the gentlemen were obliged to retire; these two regiments had had no-one to oppose them owing to the large gaps Dundee had been forced to leave in his line, hence their continuing presence after Mackay had decamped. As Dunfermline and his friends retired they found Dundee 'just breathing out his last'[25] and prepared to carry him off, but Leven fired on them, wounding Pitcur; he made light of it at the time but died from his wound two days later. They must have carried Dundee with them to get out of reach of the enemy for they then 'poured out a flood of tears on the hearse of their great General'. The use of the word 'hearse' suggests that by that time Dundee was dead. They wrapped him in plaids and carried him to Blair Castle.[26]

Colin Lindsay, Earl of Balcarres, who, it will be remembered, had originally intended to leave Edinburgh with Dundee but had delayed his departure, with unfortunate results to himself, tells us that during the night Dundee's body was stripped – a fate that often befell battle casualties – and that it was found almost naked on the field by an officer the next morning.[27] At the time of the battle Balcarres was a prisoner in Edinburgh and his account is therefore based on hearsay. As we have seen however, Balhaldy's account states that Dundee was carried to Blair Castle at some time subsequent to the end of the battle, which did not last very long, having begun at 7 to 8 o'clock in the evening; he must therefore have been removed from the field well before daybreak. This version must have been obtained at least in part from the writer's father and grandfather, both of whom were present on the field. We do not know who Balcarres' informants were but his description of events seems to have led to the fairly general belief (quite ignoring Balhaldy's statement) that Dundee was stripped, a belief also accepted by Mackenzie on the basis of *Iain Lom*'s lines:

> *Bu mhór cosgradh do làmh*
> *Fo aon chlogaide bàn,*
> *'S do chorp nochdaidh geal dàn gun éideadh air.*[28]

(Wearing your white [bright] helmet, you wrought great slaughter single-handed and now your naked body lies white and shameless, and all unclothed.)

Dundee's brother David wrote to General Cannon on the 19th September 1689 referring to the help which Lochiel and his son had promised in retrieving certain articles of Dundee's; this has been interpreted as suggesting that Camerons were involved in their disappearance. Both Linklater and Hopkins refer to this letter[29] but do not seem to have read it, otherwise they would surely have told us what the missing articles were. The last part of this letter is as follows:

> Sir, Lochiel and his son wer pleased to assur me they would do all they could to recover (?) what was in my brother's pocketts and now My Ladie writes that her own jewells of 400 £ sterl. value besyds the other things wer on him so I entreat yow mind them of ther promise and I doubt not but you will be assisting in this for my Ladie is extremlie impatient upon the head and lett me know what amount I may expect of them.[30]

There is no mention of the armour and clothing to which reference is sometimes made, only of the pockets and what was in them. Dundee's wife, already helpful in finding money to continue the campaign, must have sent him her jewels (or given them to him when he left her) so that he could realise their value whenever he needed to do so. And where else would they be entirely safe but on his person? He did not envisage a time when he would be unable to protect them there.

We cannot be sure what was meant by 'pocketts'. Were they pockets in clothing or those separate pockets performing the duty of the modern handbag which were in favour for so long (like Lucy Lockett's pocket which was also denuded of its contents)? And when and how were they and/or their contents lost? Was he indeed stripped, which, as I explain below (p.154) seems very unlikely? Or did the contents slip out of the pockets unnoticed when his friends undid his armour and some of his clothing to examine the wound and see whether anything could be done for him? Or when they were lifting him onto the plaids and carrying him to Blair Castle, probably in the half-light? Some documents were thought to have been found on the field the next day which he was known to have been carrying with him[31] and of the articles which fell out or were taken out of his pockets these papers would naturally have been ignored by any thief as being worthless. (Alas they might have been of great worth to us!) Or was he perhaps robbed while he was lying at Blair Castle and being prepared for burial?

Linklater says that his armour and some of his clothing was later retrieved from the Camerons by David Graham, but he does not give a reference and I am unaware of any document that might prove it. In any case Dundee was buried in his armour. His helmet and breastplate were revealed in 1884 when the 7th Duke of Atholl had the vault in which he was buried examined. He gave the breastplate to a blacksmith to 'tidy up' and the blacksmith, anxious to give it authenticity, put a bullet hole through it, unaware that the fatal bullet had gone in below the breastplate, as described above. The helmet seems to have been sold by the gravedigger to tinkers, who wanted it for its brass content. A letter from General Robertson of Lude, dated 25.3.1910, reveals that:

Lord Dundee's and Pitcurr's bodies were buried together in their armour, at the Kirk of Blair. In removing a seat there some years ago, the remains and armour were taken up, and the latter consigned to the uses of the blacksmith and tinker, by the clouded mind and unfeeling hands of rapacious destruction. On hearing of this, I with much difficulty recovered the front piece of Dundee's helmet, but so much mutilated by fire and the hammer, as scarcely to discover any of its ancient lustre.

Perhaps General Robertson misinterpreted the Duke's action in handing the breastplate to his blacksmith and perhaps when the Duke did so the helmet had already been sold by the gravedigger to the tinkers who were not interested in the breastplate as it was made of steel.

The breastplate and the front part of the helmet are now displayed in Earl John's room in Blair Castle, a room which, appropriately, also holds a portrait of the Great Marquis of Montrose. A copy of General Robertson's letter is pinned beside the helmet.

One would think that pieces of armour would be prized objects and the first things to be taken by battlefield marauders and this throws some doubt on the story that Dundee's body was stripped. It is also unlikely that he was left alone between the fall from his horse and his discovery by his friends. Johnston, having found his leader wounded but still alive, would hardly want to leave him without first finding someone else to take his place, and when his other friends found him they kept him with them, alive or dead, until reaching Blair Castle. *Iain Lom*'s reference to the '*chorp...gun èideadh air*' (body without clothes, or without armour) might have described the body when being prepared for burial or might have had some symbolic meaning.

A letter to King James purporting to come from Dundee and written after the battle was found by James (Ossian) MacPherson amongst the Nairne Papers in the Bodleian Library and was printed in MacPherson's *Original Papers*.[32] It is thought by some to be genuine and by others to be a forgery perhaps put about, if it was circulated at all, to mask the fact that Dundee was dead. On the back of it is a 'Speech to the army before battle'. Neither composition is in Dundee's handwriting but he could of course have dictated them. The speech ends:

> In God's name then, let us go on, and let this be your word: King James and the [Episcopal] Church of Scotland, whom God long preserve.

Dundee was a staunch Episcopalian but it seems strange, to the modern mind at least, that while fighting for a Catholic King with an army containing a good percentage of Catholics, he should have introduced this somewhat jarring religious note. If such a speech was ever made it must have been intended, like the Restoration Day speech and that given before leaving Dalcomera for Edinglassie, only for the ears of his friends – who were themselves mostly, if not all Episcopalians. As with his earlier speeches, the rest of the army, apart from the chiefs and the clan gentry, would not have understood him anyway.

The speech and letter even if not composed by Dundee are certainly contemporaneous with their alleged writer. The letter runs:

> To King James
>   Killiecrankie, 27 July 1689
> Sir, It has pleased God to give your forces a great victory over the rebels,

in which 3–4ths of them are fallen under the weight of our swords. I might say much of the action if I had not the honour to command in it; but of 5000 men which was the best computation I could make of the rebels it is certain there cannot have escaped above 1,200 men: we have not lost full out 900. This absolute victory made us masters of the field and enemy's baggage which I gave to your soldiers, who to do them all right both officers and common men, Highlands and Lowlands and Irish behaved themselves with equal gallantry what ever I saw in the hottest battles fought abroad by disciplined armies, and this Mackay's old soldiers felt on this occasion.

I cannot now Sir be more particular but take leave to assure your Majesty the kingdom is generally disposed for your service and impatiently wait for your coming: and this success will bring in the rest of the nobility and gentry, having had all their assurances for it except the notorious rebels. Therefore Sir for God's sake assist us though it be with such another detachment of your Irish forces as you sent us before especially of horse and dragoons and you will crown our beginnings with a complete success and yourself with an entire possession of your ancient hereditary Kingdom of Scotland. My wounds forbid me to enlarge to your Majesty at this time, though they tell me they are not mortal. However Sir I beseech your Majesty to believe whether I live or die I am entirely yours.[33]

Of course if the letter is genuine Dundee must have survived for some time after receiving his wound and must have dictated the above lines either on the field or, if Balhaldy is mistaken about the time of his death, at Blair Castle. There are certainly echoes of him in its style and composition and his usual modesty is evident in such phrases as 'I might say much of the action if I had not the honour to command in it', which is reminiscent of his letter to MacLeod of MacLeod:

I have also receaved...a...letter [from the King] [which is] so kind, that I am ashamed to tell.

He counts for great services, which I am conscious to myself that I have hardly done my deutie.[34]

There was little rejoicing after Killiecrankie. The amazing scale of the victory went almost unnoticed amidst grief at the losses sustained and the Highland bards concentrated on those who had fallen rather than on the marvellous prospects of victory to their cause which their deaths had opened up.[35] The death of Dundee was particularly lamented, as in *Iain Lom*'s *Oran air Feachd Righ Seumas*:

'S e do bhàs, a Dhùn-dighe, dh'fhàg ormsa trom-lighe,

Chur toll ann mo chridhe 's a dh'fhàg snigh air mo ghruaidh;
Bu bheag air son t'éirig na thuit de na beisdean.
An cogadh Righ Seumas ged dh'éirich leinn buaidh;[36]

(It is your death, Dundee, that has left grief upon me, that has pierced my heart and made the tears course on my cheek. Although we won the victory in the cause of King James, all the brutes that fell would be little as blood-price for your death.)

and again in *Cath Raon Ruairidh*:

A shàr Chléibhears nan each,
Bu cheann-féadhn' thu air feachd;
Mo chreach léir an tùs gleac mar dh'éirich dhuit.[37]

(Noble Claverhouse, rider of horses, a worthy captain of a host were you; my utter woe that you should fare thus at the outset of the fight.)

Although this latter song extolls the bravery and skill of Dundee himself and, of course, of the heroes of Clan Donald,[38] it lacks the exultant lilt of his *La Inbhir Lòchaidh* at which Montrose suffered few casualties:

Dhirich mi moch madainn Dòmhnaich
Gu bràigh caisteil Inbhir Lòchaidh;
Chunnaic mi 'n t-arm dol an òrdugh,
'S bha buaidh a' bhlàir le Clann Dòmhnaill.

Hi rim hó ro, hó ro leatha,
Chaidh an latha le Clann Dòmhnaill.[39]

(Early on Sunday morning I climbed the brae above the castle of Inverlochy. I saw the army arraying for battle, and victory on the field was with Clan Donald.
Hi rim ho ro, ho ro leatha, Clan Donald won the day.)

The Highland soldiers found their strength so reduced by the long march from Dalcomera with little food, followed by the hurried march from Blair, the hot hours of waiting on the hillside and the ferocious attack on a much larger army that they had no desire for anything but sleep and were brought back to the field after their pursuit of the enemy with some difficulty by Lochiel.[40] On the following day:

…the Highlanders went and took a view of the field of battle, where the dreadful effects of their fury appeared in many horrible figures. The

enemy lay in heaps allmost in the order they were posted, but so disfig-
ured with wounds, and so hashed and mangled, that even the victors
could not look upon the amazeing proofs of their own agility and
strength without surprise and horrour. Many had their heads divided
into two halves by one blow; others had their sculls cutt off above the
eares by a back-strock, like a night-cap. Their thick buffe-belts were
not sufficient to defend their shoulders from such deep gashes as allmost
disclosed their entrails. Several were cutt quite through, and some that
had scull-capes had them so beat into their brains that they died upon
the spott.[41]

At first sight it seems strange that they should have been so surprised and
horrified as similar injuries must have been inflicted by Highland armies
many times in the past. In this case, however, the Highlands had been
quiet for about thirty-five years, since the end of Glencairn's Rising and
most of the combatants at Killiecrankie would not have fought in any
major battle before.

Now they needed rest, which the completeness of their victory made
possible, and time to bury their dead; then they would march away to
continue the campaign as best they could without their admired and
beloved leader.

Notes

1. A.J. Youngson: *Beyond the Highland Line. 3 Journals of Travel in Eighteenth Century Scotland. Burt, Pennant, Thornton*. London (Collins), 1974, p.138.
2. Balhaldy, pp.263–4.
3. ibid., p.264.
4. *Orain Iain Luim*, p.186, lines 2386–9.
5. *Grameid*, p.236–7.
6. Balhaldy, p.268.
7. Mac Alasdair Ruaidh: Latha Raon Ruairidh, in *The MacDonald Collection of Gaelic Poetry*, op. cit.,p.75, verse 9.
8. W.H. Murray: *Rob Roy MacGregor his life and times*, Glasgow (Richard Drew Publishing), 1982, p.93 sqq. and p.265, note 2 to Chapter Eight. Charles Sandford Terry: *John Graham of Claverhouse Viscount of Dundee 1648–1689*, London (Constable), 1905, p.290. *Memoirs of the Lord Viscount Dundee*, op.cit., p.22. Hamilton Hewlett in: *Highland Constable. The Life and Times of Rob Roy MacGregor*, Edinburgh and London (Blackwood), 1950, does not begin his account of Rob until the 21st August 1689, after the Battle of Dunkeld, which suggests he does not believe that he was at Killiecrankie.
9. Balhaldy, p.283.
10. History of the Rankins, in: *The Celtic Monthly*, vol. XIX (1911), p.195. I am indebted to Hugh Cheape of the National Museums of Scotland for drawing my attention to this article.
11. *Journey to the Western Isles. Johnson's Scottish Journey*. Retraced by Finlay J. MacDonald, London and Sydney (MacDonald & Co.). 1983. p.149.
12. Stewart of Garth : *Sketches of the Highlanders...*, op. cit., vol.1, p.66.
13. Mac Alasdair Ruaidh in: *The MacDonald Collection of Gaelic Poetry*. op. cit., p.81.

14. *Orain Iain Luim*, p.192, line 2461.
15. Magnus Linklater and Christian Hesketh: *For King and Conscience*, London (Weidenfeld & Nicolson), 1989, p.214.
16. *Grameid*, Book IV, line 775.
17. Balhaldy, p.271.
18. *Letters*, p.265, letter to the King.
19. Martin Martin, op.cit., p.156.
20. Balhaldy, p.280.
21. ibid., p.269.
22. ibid., p.268.
23. Acts of Parl. Scot., Appendix to... p.56.
24. *Grameid*, Book IV, lines 444–5.
25. Balhaldy, p.269.
26. ibid., p.270.
27. Balcarres. Colin, Earl of: *Memoirs touching the Revolution in Scotland*, ed. Lord Lindsay, Bannantyne Club, 1841. See: Linklater and Hesketh: *For King and Conscience*, op. cit., p.220.
28. *Orain Iain Luim*, p.192, lines 2460–62.
29. Hopkins: *Glencoe*, op. cit., p.176, note 195. Linklater and Hesketh: *For King and Conscience*, op.cit., p.220.
30. David Graham to Cannon, 19th Sept. 1689. SRO:GD/26/8/41.
31. Andrew Murray Scott: *Bonnie Dundee*, op.cit., p.190.
32. James MacPherson: *Original Papers; containing the Secret History of Great Britain*, London, 1775, vol.1, p.270.
33. *Letters*, p.264–5. I have revised the spelling to avoid the excessively irritating interpolations arising from the abbreviation of some words, e.g. 'which' appears as w[hi]t[c]h.
34. ibid., p.239.
35. Mac Alasdair Ruaidh in: *The MacDonald Collection of Gaelic Poetry*, op.cit., pp.74–81. Mac do dh'Iain Lom in *Patrick Turner's Collection of Gaelic Songs*, op. cit., p.141–3.
36. *Orain Iain Luim*, op.cit., p.188, lines 2404–7.
37. ibid., p.192, lines 2454–6.
38. ibid., p.194, lines 2481–3 and 2487–9.
39. ibid. p.20, lines 190–3 and 184–5.
40. Balhaldy, p.271.
41. ibid., p.270–1.

CHAPTER TWELVE

Saint Bride's

Chaill mi àrmainn mo stuic,
Mo sgiath làidir 's mo phruip,
Iad ri àiteach an t-sluic is feur orr'.
                                        Iain Lom

(I have lost the heroes of my race, my strong shield and supports,
the grave-trench is their habitation and the grass grows over them.)

DUNDEE WAS BURIED on the 28th or 29th, probably the latter[1]
and Pitcur, who died of his wounds on the 29th, was placed beside him
either at the same time or subsequently.

Dundee's body, having rested possibly in the Stewart Room or Earl
John's room, was carried out of the castle and over the Banvie Burn to
the church of St Bride at Old Blair. The burn here runs in a deep ravine
and on the east bank high above it under dark trees there is a narrow track,
level at first but finally rising up over a low mound and leading into the
west end of the church. St Bride's is 18–20 feet wide and perhaps 70–80
feet long with few windows and those small. It is roofless now but its walls
are complete.

The sad procession, with flaming torches lighting the gloom, followed
their dead leader; Dunfermline and those other friends who had followed
him from the beginning, old Lochiel and tall, dark Alasdair from
Glengarry, the youthful island chiefs, the officers of the Irish and James
Philip of Almerieclose who told us so much about him while he was in
Lochaber and before, but sadly was never able to add his account of the
battle and the funeral to those many lines, nearly 4,000 in all, which he
had inscribed in his little book. Perhaps there came others too who had
not been in time for the battle; young Robert Stewart of Appin with the
Tutor of Appin, John Stewart of Ardsheal, Lochiel's son John, the hesi-
tant Cluny MacPherson, Coll of Keppoch and the giant Alasdair
MacAlasdair of Glencoe, soon himself to be a victim of treachery and
oppression. The pipers strode before, filling the dark Banvie Glen with
their sad laments, the mourners crowded into the church behind them
and stood silent while the prayers were said and the coffin lowered into

the vault at the south-east corner of the church.

When the 7th Duke of Atholl opened the vault in 1884 he had the bones of Dundee and Pitcur gathered up and reburied there. It was impossible to determine which were Dundee's which suggests either that the coffins had rotted away or that there were none in the first place; perhaps haste and confusion had made it impossible to obtain any. In 1889, the two hundredth anniversary of Killiecrankie. the Duke attached a plaque to the wall above the vault, remembering Dundee and his gallant attempt to replace his rightful King on the throne of Britain.

Notes
1. *A Military History of Perthshire 1660–1902.* 2 vols. Perth, 1908, ed. The Marchioness of Tullibardine; quoting An Account of the Proceedings of the Meeting of the Estates in Scotland (London 1689–90, no.44,p.106), she says that Dundee was buried on the 29th July.

Postscript

IN IRELAND on the evening of the 28th July, the day after Killiecrankie, the results of Schomberg's efforts began to be apparent and three merchant ships, the *Phoenix*, the *Jerusalem* and the *Mountjoy* (the last made famous in song as the 'dancey ship that broke the boom and saved the Apprentice Boys') accompanied by *H.M.S. Dartmouth* entered the Foyle river. Both the banks as far as the boom were lined with Irish soldiers and the forts along the banks had artillery, but not enough as it turned out, nor were the artillerymen well enough trained to stop the Navy and merchant ships.

The *Mountjoy*, after a period of being grounded in shallow water near one of the banks and thus a prey to Irish soldiers, reached the boom and sailed into it, breaking the iron portion, while sailors with axes broke the wooden part. The ships arrived at the quay at Derry at ten o'clock that night and unloaded their supplies of food. Derry was fed at last.[1]

The siege of Derry was lifted on the 31st July. The event which had been so much desired by Dundee and the King, which would free an Irish army to help the Highland Scots, had come about, but not in the way they wished. It merely marked the beginning of the collapse of James's fortunes in Ireland. In Scotland the death of Dundee had the same effect. Amongst William's supporters fear and alarm spread at the news of Killiecrankie, but when they heard that Dundee was dead their spirits rose and many of them realised that the campaign was already virtually over. Dundee's army, though swollen to 5,000 by new recruits after the successful battle, was broken in spirit by the death of its great leader and by the eventual realisation, after the disasters of Dunkeld and the Haughs of Cromdale, that Cannon, who replaced him, was not the man to lead a Highland army. He was ineffective, uninspiring, too bound to the military disciplines in which he had been trained – disciplines which the greater mind of Dundee had been able to discard. The chiefs drifted away and the Highlands became quiet again – for the time being. As Balhaldy put it:

> But so soon as Dundee's death was generally known, the scene changed, and all those mighty preparations, and that universall spirit of Jacobitism, vanished into nothing.[2]

The Highland bards, back in their mountain and island fastnesses, remembered the battle and the many who had fallen and their kind commander. But they knew that the splendid victory, as great as Inverlochy, was not worth the sacrifice of the one man who might have restored James to his throne and saved the Highlands from the bloody encounter at Culloden, the horror of its immediate aftermath and the destruction of culture and community.

Dr. Archibald Pitcairn wrote a Latin epitaph, '*Ultime Scotorum*', for Dundee. It should be better remembered today when many confuse him with Montrose or forget his Rising altogether, while others remember him only as Bluidy Clavers – that figment of a bigoted and overheated imagination.

The poet Dryden, who did not make any of these mistakes, rendered Pitcairn's Latin into English:

O last and best of Scots, who didst maintain
Thy country's freedom from a foreign reigne,
New people fill the land now thow art gone,
New gods the temples and new kings the throne!
Scotland and thow didst in each other live,
Thow wouldst not her nor could she thee survive.
Farewell, who dyeing didst support the State,
And couldst not fall but with thy country's fate.

Notes
1.   Patrick Macrory: *The Siege of Derry*, op. cit., pp.290–313.
2.   Balhaldy, p.283.

Bibliography

Antrim, Angela, Countess of: *The Antrim MacDonnells*, Belfast (Ulster Television Ltd.), 1977.

Balcarres, Colin, Earl of: *Memoirs touching the Revolution in Scotland*, ed. Lord Lindsay, Edinburgh (Bannantyne Club), 1841.

Balfour Melville, E. (ed.): *Proceedings of the Estates, 1689-90*, Edinburgh (Scottish History Society).

Balhaldy, John Drummond of: *Memoirs of Sir Ewen Cameron of Locheill, Chief of the Clan Cameron, with an introductory account of the history and antiquities of that family and of the neighbouring clans*, Edinburgh (Abbotsford Club), 1842.

Barrington, Michael: *Grahame of Claverhouse, Viscount Dundee*, London (Martin Secker), 1911.

Browne, James: *A History of the Highlands and of the Highland Clans*, 2 vols., London, Edinburgh and Dublin (A. Fullarton & Co.), 1850.

Burt's Letters from the North of Scotland, Edinburgh, (Birlinn), 1998.

Byrne, Kevin: *Colkitto!*, Colonsay (House of Lochar), 1997.

Cameron, Alexander: *The Book of Clanranald*, in: *Reliquiae Celticae, Text, Papers and Studies in Gaelic Literature and Philology*, ed. Alexander Macbain and Rev.John Kennedy, Inverness, 1894, vol.II. Poetry, History, and Philology.

Cameron, Walter: *Clan Cameron and their Chiefs, Presbyerian and Jacobite*, in: *Transactions of the Gaelic Society of Inverness*, vol.XLVII, 1971-72.

Campbell, Lord Archibald: *Highland Dress, Arms and Ornament*, London (Dawsons of Pall Mall), 1969.

Campbell, Duncan: *The Lairds of Glenlyon*, Strathtay (The Clunie Press), 1984.

Campbell, John Lorne (ed. and translated): *Highland Songs of the '45*, Edinburgh (John Grant), 1933.

Campbell Paterson, Raymond: *A Land Afflicted, Scotland in the Covenanter Wars 1638-1690*, Edinburgh (John Donald), 1998.

Celtic Monthly, vol.XIX, 1911.

Chambers, Robert: *History of the Rebellion in Scotland under the Viscount of Dundee and the Earl of Mar in 1689 and 1715*, 3 vols., Edinburgh (Constable), 1829.

Clark, Wallace: *The Lord of the Isles Voyage. Western Ireland to the Scottish*

Hebrides in a 16th century galley, Naas, Co. Kildare (The Leinster Leader Ltd.), 1993.

Cowan, Edward: *Montrose For Covenant and King*, Edinburgh (Canongate), 1995.

Currie, W.M. of Balilone: *With Sword and Harp, Clan Mhurrich (Currie), The Warrior Poets*, Milngavie (Heather Bank Press), 1977.

Dalrymple, Sir John, of Cranstoun: *Memoirs of Great Britain and Ireland from the Dissolution of the last Parliament of Charles II*, 3 vols., 2nd edition, London, 1790.

D'Alton, John: *Illustrations, historical and genealogical, of King James's Irish Army list (1689)*, Dublin, 1861.

Drummond Norie, W: *Loyal Lochaber*, Glasgow, 1898.

Duffy, Maureen: *Henry Purcell*, London (Fourth Estate), 1994.

Dunbar, John Telfer: *History of Highland Dress*, London (Batsford), 1979.

Dwelly, Edward: *The Illustrated Gaelic-English Dictionary*, Glasgow (Gairm), 1988.

Forbes Leith, William: *Memoirs of Scottish Catholics during the Seventeenth and Eighteenth Centuries*, 2 vols., 1909.

Fraser, James: *Chronicles of the Frasers. The Wardlaw Manuscript entitled 'Polichronicon seu policratica temporum, or, the true genealogy of the Frasers' 916-1674*, ed. William Mackay, Edinburgh (Scottish History Society), 1905.

Gibson, John Sibbald: *Lochiel of the '45*, Edinburgh (University Press), 1994.

Gillies, William A: *In Famed Breadalbane*, Strathtay (The Clunie Press), 1987.

Gordon Cumming, Constance: *Memories*, Edinburgh (Blackwood), 1904.

Graham, David, to Cannon, 19th Sept. 1689. SRO: GD/26/8/41.

Grant, I.F.: *The MacLeods*, Edinburgh (Spurbooks), 1981.

Haldane, A.R.B.: *The Drove Roads of Scotland*, Newton Abbot (David & Charles), 1973.

——: *Three Centuries of Scottish Posts. An Historical Survey to 1836*, Edinburgh (University Press), 1971.

Hastings, Max: *Montrose, The King's Champion*, London (Gollancz), 1977.

Haswell, Jock: *James II*, London (History Book Club), 1972.

Hill, James Michael: *Celtic Warfare 1595-1763*, Edinburgh (John Donald), 1986.

Historical Manuscripts Commission, Buccleuch and Queensberry MSS, vol.ii.

Hopkins, Paul: *Glencoe and the End of the Highland War*, Edinburgh (John Donald), 1986.

Howlett, Hamilton: *Highland Constable. The Life and Times of Rob Roy MacGregor*, Edinburgh and London (Blackwood). 1950.

Innes-Smith, Robert: *Glamis Castle Guidebook*, Derby (Pilgrim Press), 1997.

Inventory of Lochiel Charters, SRO:GD1/658.

de Johnstone, Chevalier: *A Memoir of the 'Forty-Five*, London (Folio Society), 1958.

Journey to the Western Isles. Johnson's Scottish Journey. Retraced by Finlay J. MacDonald, London and Sydney (MacDonald & Co.), 1983.

Lang, Andrew. (ed): *The Highlands of Scotland*, Edinburgh, 1898.

Lenihan, Padraig: *Celtic Warfare in the 1640s*, in: *Celtic Dimensions of the British Civil Wars*, ed. John R. Young, Edinburgh (John Donald), 1997.

Lenman, Bruce: *Jacobite Risings in Britain 1689-1746*, London (Methuen), 1984.

Letters of John Graham of Claverhouse, ed. Andrew Murray Scott in: *Miscellany of the Scottish History Society*, vol.11, Edinburgh, 1990.

Linklater, Magnus and Christian Hesketh: *For King and Conscience*, London (Weidenfeld & Nicolson), 1989.

The Lyon in Mourning or a Collection of Speeches, Letters, Journals, etc. related to the affairs of Prince Charles Edward Stuart. By the Rev. Robert Forbes, A.M., Bishop of Ross and Caithness, 1746-75, ed. Henry Paton, 3 vols. Edinburgh (Scottish Academic Press), 1975.

MacAulay, John: *Birlinn. Longships of the Hebrides*, Cambridge and Isle of Harris (The White Horse Press), 1996.

MacCulloch, Donald B.: *Romantic Lochaber Arisaig and Morar*. Edinburgh and London (Chambers), 1971.

The MacDonald Collection of Gaelic Poetry, Inverness, 1911.

MacDonald, Alexander: *Song and Story from Loch Ness-side*, Inverness (printed for the Gaelic Society of Inverness), 1982.

MacDonald, Donald J., of Castleton: *Clan Donald*, Loanhead, Midlothian (MacDonald), 1978.

MacDonald, Norman H.: *The Clan Ranald of Lochaber*, published by the author, (8 Ethel Terrace. Edinburgh EH10 5NB), undated.

——: *The Clan Ranald of Knoydart & Glengarry*, published by the author, (as above) 1979.

MacInnes, Alan. I.: *Clanship, Commerce and the House of Stuart 1603-1788*, East Linton (Tuckwell Press), 1996.

Mackay, Hugh, of Scourie: *Memoirs of the War Carried on in Scotland and Ireland, 1689-91*, Edinburgh, 1833.

Mackay, William: *Urquhart and Glenmoriston. Olden Times in a Highland Parish*, Inverness, 1893.

Mackenzie, A.: *History of the Camerons*, 1884.

MacLean, Calum I.: *The Highlands*, Edinburgh (Mainstream), 1990.

MacLean, Fitzroy: *Highlanders*, London (Adelphi), 1995.

MacLean, John A.: *The Sources, particularly the Celtic Sources, for the History of the Highlands in the 17th Century*, Ph.D. Aberdeen, 1939.

MacLean Sinclair, A.: *The Clan Gillean*, Charlottetown (Hazard and Moore), 1899.

MacLeod, Canon R.C.: *The Island Clans during Six Centuries.*

Macmillan, Somerled: *Bygone Lochaber, Historical and Traditional.* Printed for Private Circulation, 1971.

MacNeil of Barra: *Castle in the Sea,* London and Glasgow (Collins), 1964.

Macpherson, Alan G.: *The Posterity of the Three Brethren. A Short History of The Clan Macpherson,* published by the Clan Macpherson Association, Canadian Branch, 1993.

MacPherson, James: *Original Papers; containing the Secret History of Great Britain,* London, 1775.

MacPherson, William, of Dalchully: *The Chiefs of Clan MacPherson,* Edinburgh (Oliver and Boyd), 1947.

Macrory, Patrick: *The Siege of Derry,* Oxford (University Press), 1988.

Martin Martin: *A description of the Western Islands of Scotland,* Edinburgh (The Mercat Press), 1981.

Matheson, William (ed.): *An Clàrsair Dall. The Songs of Roderick Morrison and his music,* Edinburgh (Scottish Gaelic Texts Society), 1970.

Memoirs of the Lord Viscount Dundee, The Highland Clans and the Massacre of Glenco. etc. by an Officer in the Army, ed. Henry Jenner, London (F.E.Robinson & Co.), 1903.

Miscellany of the Scottish History Society, vol.ix, Edinburgh, 1958.

Moir, D.S.: *Scottish Hill Tracks, Old Highways and Drove Roads, Part 2, Northern Scotland,* Edinburgh. 1975.

Murray, W.H.: *Rob Roy MacGregor his life and times,* Glasgow (Richard Drew Publishing), 1982.

Napier, Mark: *Memorials and Letters illustrative of the Life and Times of John Graham of Claverhouse, Viscount Dundee,* 3 vols., Edinburgh (Thomas G. Stevenson), 1859.

Nicolson, Alexander: *History of Skye. A record of the families, the social conditions and the literature of the island,* ed. Alasdair Maclean, Portree (Maclean Press), 1994.

Ollard, Richard: *The Escape of Charles II after the Battle of Worcester,* London (Constable), 1998.

Ò Baoill, Colm (ed.): *Bàrdachd Shìlis na Ceapaich, c.1660 – c.1729.* Edinburgh (Scottish Gaelic Texts Society), 1972.

——:*Eachann Bachach and other MacLean poets,* Edinburgh (Scottish Gaelic Texts Society), 1979.

——:*Gair nan Clàrsach,* Edinburgh (Birlinn),1994.

Orain Iain Luim. Songs of John MacDonald, Bard of Keppoch, ed. Annie M. Mackenzie, Edinburgh (Scottish Gaelic Texts Society), 1973.

Philip of Almerieclose, James: *The Grameid, an heroic poem descrptive of the Campaign of Viscount Dundee in 1689.* Edited from the Original Manuscript with Translation, Introduction, and Notes by the Rev. Alexander D. Murdoch, F.S.A. Scot., Edinburgh (Scottish Historical Society), 1888.

Pollard, Michael and Tom Ang: *Walking the Scottish Highlands: General Wade's Military Roads*, London (André Deutsch), 1984.

Robertson, James Irvine: *The First Highlander, Major-General David Stewart of Garth CB, 1768-1829*, East Linton (Tuckwell Press), 1998.

Sanderson, William: *A Compleat History of the Life and Reign of King Charles*, 1658.

Scott, Andrew Murray: *Bonnie Dundee*, Edinburgh (John Donald), 1989.

Scott, Sir Walter: *Redgauntlet*, London and Glasgow (Collins Clear-Type Press), undated.

Scottish Historical Review, vol.III. A.H.Millar: translation of Iain Lom's Oran air feachd Righ Seumas.

Sheuglie, *A trew and particular informatie of the death of Grant of Sheuglie and what occasioned the same impartially related.* SRO: GD112/43/17/8.

Simms, J.G.: *Jacobite Ireland 1685-91*, London (Routledge & Kegan Paul), 1969.

The Statistical Account of Scotland 1791-1799, Inverness-shire, Ross and Cromarty, Wakefield (EP Publishing Ltd.), 1981.

Stevenson, David: *Alasdair MacColla and the Highland Problem in the Seventeenth Century*, Edinburgh (John Donald), 1980.

Stewart, Colonel David of Garth: *Sketches of the character, manners, and present state of the Highlanders of Scotland; with details of the military service of the Highland Regiments*, 2 vols. Edinburgh (John Donald), 1977.

Stewart, John of Ardvorlich: *A History of Clan Cameron*, published by the Clan Cameron Association, 1974.

Terry, Charles Sandford: *John Graham of Claverhouse Viscount of Dundee 1648-1689*, London (Constable), 1905.

Tullibardine, The Marchioness of, (ed.): *A Military History of Perthshire 1660-1902*, 2 vols., Perth, 1908.

Turner, Patrick: *Collection of Gaelic Songs*, Edinburgh, 1813.

Walker, Patrick: *Six Saints of the Covenant*, ed. D. Hay Fleming, 2 vols., London, 1901.

Watson, William J.: *The History of the Celtic Place-Names of Scotland*, Dublin (Irish Academic Press), 1986.

Wishart, Rev. George, D.D. (ed.): *The Memoirs of James Marquis of Montrose 1639-1650*, London (Longmans, Green & Co.), 1895.

Wilcock, John: *The Great Marquess. Life and Times of Archibald, 8th Earl and ist (and only) Marquis of Argyll (1607–1661)*, Edinburgh and London (Oliphant Anderson and Ferrier), 1903.

Williams, Ronald: *Montrose. Cavalier in Mourning*, Glasgow (?) (Barrie and Jenkins), undated.

——: *Sons of the Wolf*, Colonsay (House of Lochar), 1998.

Youngson, A.J.: *Beyond the Highland Line. 3 Journals of Travel in Eighteenth Century Scotland. Burt, Pennant, Thornton*, London (Collins), 1974.

Index